6H

A HOUSE IN BOW STREET

CRIME AND THE MAGISTRACY, LONDON 1740–1881

Also by Anthony Babington

NO MEMORIAL
THE POWER TO SILENCE

A HOUSE
IN BOW STREET

Crime and the Magistracy
London 1740-1881

ANTHONY BABINGTON

MACDONALD·LONDON

First published in Great Britain
by Macdonald & Co (Publishers) Ltd
St Giles House, 49-50 Poland Street, London, W.1.

© Anthony Babington, 1969

SBN 356 02849 6

Made and printed in Great Britain by

W. & G. Baird, Ltd., Belfast

To the memory of the late
SIR ROBERT BLUNDELL,
Chief Metropolitan Magistrate, 1960-67,
who wished this book to be written

CONTENTS

LIST OF ILLUSTRATIONS

between pages 144 and 145

A*

In Bow Street is a house
celebrated all over the United Kingdom
and, it may be said, the whole world.

Old and New London
by Edward Walford (published 1813)

CHAPTER ONE

THOMAS DE VEIL'S LONDON

SOME time in 1740 Colonel Thomas De Veil, a justice of the peace for the County of Middlesex and for the City and Liberty of Westminster, decided to move his magistrate's office from Thrift Street, now called Frith Street, in Soho to a house at Bow Street in Covent Garden.

Why De Veil made this move is not known. It might have been due to the expiration of his old lease or possibly the growth in volume of his work as a justice had made it necessary for him to acquire larger premises. Whatever the reason, it is easy to imagine that a man of De Veil's character and temperament must have been drawn almost irresistably to the locality of Covent Garden, which at that time had become the centre of gaiety, vice and bohemianism for the entire metropolis.

The name Covent Garden was a verbal corruption of 'convent garden', for the whole of this area had once belonged to the Abbots of Westminster and had comprised seven acres of pasture land, used partly as a burial ground and partly for the cultivation of fruit and vegetables. During the Reformation the garden was confiscated by Henry VIII and in 1552 it was bestowed by way of a grant on John Russell, Earl of Bedford. At the extreme south of the land the Russell family built their London mansion Bedford House, facing on to the Strand, and the rest of it they hired out in plots for the grazing and the stabling of horses.

In 1630 the 4th Earl of Bedford applied to Charles I for a licence to build houses to the north of the private garden to the back of Bedford House. The King, who was very much opposed to the indiscriminate expansion of London, granted a licence but only, it is believed, on condition that any development of the area must be of such a scale and manner as to provide a distinguished ornament to the capital. The building plans were entrusted to the architect Inigo Jones of whom the Earl of Bedford was the principal patron. Jones had made a special study of Italian style and design and had recently finished the magnificent Whitehall Banqueting House. The result of his work was the famous Covent Garden Piazza, a square, or more precisely a rectangle, with terraced houses on the northern and eastern sides, a small church to the west, and the garden wall of Bedford House to the south. Charles I took a close, personal interest in the new buildings and visited them on several occasions while they were being erected. He must have been well satisfied that his condition had been fulfilled as the Piazza with its tall, Italian-style houses, its arches, arcades and external stuccoes was generally considered to have given London an architectural adornment which was both graceful and impressive.

Before this the rich, aristocratic families had begun to leave their homes in the City and to spread out westwards. Between the Thames and the Strand they built a line of stately mansions—such places as Somerset House, Essex House, York House and the Savoy Palace—each with its gardens stretching down to the river, its shaded terraces and its own set of watersteps. And now the fashionable, new Piazza became the favourite place for the London residences of the nobility and the gentry. Writing in 1829 John Thomas Smith, who had conducted a great deal of research into the subject, said, 'Covent Garden was the first square inhabited by the great; for immediately upon the completion of the houses on the north and east sides of Covent Garden, which were all that were uniformly built after the design of Inigo Jones, they were everyone of them inhabited by persons of the first title and rank, as appears by the parish books of the rates at that time'. The residents, he adds, transformed the locality into 'the most, and indeed the only fashionable part of the town'.

In the vicinity of the Piazza, during the years immediately following its completion, a new residential area came into being and the whole of Covent Garden was transformed from an empty space into a densely populated neighbourhood.

Bow Street, so-called because it was shaped like a bow, is said to have been built in 1637. However, the Bedford Estate Records show that the first building-leases, five in number, were granted for the west side of the street in 1660; four more building-leases were granted for the east side in 1673. From then on there was a steady development on both sides of the street. We have it from John Strype, writing some years later, that the road was 'Open and large, with very good houses, well inhabited, and resorted to by gentry for lodgings, as are most of the other streets in the parish'.

The surviving maps of the seventeenth century Westminster—like Hollar's which was printed in 1658—emphasize the bow-like aspect of Bow Street. It did not, at that time, reach as far north as Long Acre, but swung round in a distinct arc in the region of Hart Street (now Floral Street), while its southern extremity terminated where Tavistock Street is to-day. *Stow's Survey* in 1755 shows little change to the south, although below the intersection of Russell Street the name of the road had then become Charles Street; at the northern tip there had been a considerable alteration, for there Bow Street is shown to enter a rectangular space called Broad Court, from which a small road runs into Long Acre. In the first large-scale Horwood plan of this area, published in 1799, Bow Street is directly joined to Long Acre by an alleyway known as Bow Court. Finally, in *Murray's Handbook for London* in 1851 we find Bow Street as it is now, with its northern end continuing into Long Acre, and its southern end connected directly with the Strand by Wellington Street—the name given to Charles Street after the Napoleonic Wars.

By the beginning of the eighteenth century the character of Covent Garden was undergoing a perceptible change. It was, perhaps, inevitable that the ultra-fashionable Piazza and the locality all about it should attract a swarm of tradesmen, artisans and others who were needed to cater for the requirements of the wealthy. At the same time the narrow passages, the darkened alleys, and the secluded courtyards which separated the streets and the houses drew in a far less respectable segment of the community. Another factor affecting the type of inhabitant settling in the neighbourhood was the continuing tendency of the nobility and the aristocracy to drift westwards as other areas were developed further and further from the walls of the City. Soon after the Restoration the newly-built St. James's Square superseded the Piazza as the centre of fashion, and in the early days of the eighteenth century

Mayfair was further developed with the setting up of the palatial mansions of Cavendish Square, Hanover Square and Grosvenor Square. However, one of the major factors which contributed to the transformation of Covent Garden was that it was becoming the principal artistic and theatrical locality of London.

The years which followed the accession of Charles II in 1660 formed one of the most dynamic periods in the history of the English stage. Although the post-restoration era is usually associated with bawdy comedies, which were, no doubt, a reaction from the narrow and repressive influences of Cromwellian puritanism, it was also a time in which the London theatre was completely revitalised and in which, incidentally, women instead of men appeared for the first time in feminine roles.

The Theatre Royal, Drury Lane, was built in 1663, on a site leased from the Earl of Bedford. The Opera House in the Haymarket was opened in 1704. An old and derelict theatre in Lincoln's Inn Fields was reconstructed in 1714. The Little Theatre, also in the Haymarket, was built in 1720 and the magnificent Covent Garden Theatre in Bow Street was completed in 1732 on the site of the present Royal Opera House. This age saw the advent of a small group of versatile and talented actors and actresses. Men of the calibre of Garrick, Betterton, Quin and Macklin and women like Kitty Clive, Mrs. Pritchard, Peg Woffington and Mrs. Cibber. It was a time of experimentation, both in the manner of acting and the mode of presentation.

Not only the theatre people became the frequenters of Covent Garden. The knowledgeable John Thomas Smith tells us that an 'immense concourse of wits, literary characters, and other men of genius' were accustomed to gather in the numerous coffee-houses, taverns and wine-cellars within its boundaries, and he mentions, amongst others, such names as Dryden, Pope, Hogarth and Dr. Samuel Johnson.

During the reign of Charles II the coffee-house became the centre of London life, most men having their favourite place to which they would go to read the newspapers and to discuss the topics of the day. Johnson had been advised before he came to London that, 'By spending threepence in a coffee-house he might be for some hours every day in good company'. The coffee-houses of Covent Garden were famous. There was Will's at the corner of Russell Street and Bow Street, and also in Russell Street, Button's and Tom's. In the Piazza itself was the Bedford, close to the rear entrance of the Covent Garden Theatre, and Tom King's in front of the Church which Inigo Jones had built on the west side of the square and which in 1645 had been dedicated to St. Paul. After Tom King died his widow, Moll, carried on his coffee-house as an all-night brothel fixing up her customers with prostitutes in exchange for a procuress's fee. Hogarth has depicted Tom King's coffee-house in the early hours of the morning in a way which leave no doubt as to its principal purpose. Around the square there were other places of a similar character, notably the Finish and Mother Douglas's.

The streets of Covent Garden and the Strand became the chosen haunts of the prostitutes. John Gay, author of *The Beggar's Opera* wrote:

> Of Drury's mazy courts and dark abodes,
> The harlots' guileful paths who nightly stand,
> Where Catherine Street descends into the Strand.

And the 22-year-old James Boswell, freshly arrived in London from Edinburgh, prided himself on his continence although he was, 'surrounded with free-hearted ladies of all kinds: from the splendid Madam at fifty guineas a night, down to the civil nymph with white-thread stockings who tramps along the Strand and will resign her engaging person to your honour for a pint of wine and a shilling'.

This was an age of lawlessness and disorder in which the power of the mob and the violence of the criminal were ever paramount. An unpopular policy, a provocative declaration, or merely an unfounded rumour could set in motion the bloodiest of riots to such an extent that Henry Fielding was to describe the mob as 'that large and powerful body which forms the fourth estate of this community'. And yet the very idea of a professional police force would have been anathema to the vast majority of the population, conjuring up as it did the vision of governmental repression and a quite unwarrantable interference with the liberties of the subject. The streets of London were accorded their sole protection by the elderly, decrepit watchmen and the reluctant, unpaid constables, both working under the direction of a magistracy which had grown as inefficient as it was corrupt.

Not only the total inadequacy of policing arrangements but also the lack of any proper system for lighting the streets contributed to the growing ascendancy of the night-time criminal. Outside the limits of the City oil lamps burned intermittently in the principal streets from 6 p.m. to midnight—though only during winter months and not on nights when the moon was full. However, even these lights were of an unsatisfactory nature and frequently went out; even more frequently the street-lighters failed to fulfil their completed rounds in the early part of the evening and some streets were left in total darkness.

At the lowest end of the crime scale were the pickpockets and the shoplifters. Picking pockets was practised on such a scale that a guide-book of the period informed its readers, 'A man who saunters about the capital with pockets on the outside of his coat deserves no pity'. And a foreign visitor to London wrote, 'Pickpockets are legion. With extraordinary dexterity they will steal handkerchiefs, snuff-boxes, watches—in short, anything they can find in your pockets. Their profession is practised in the streets, in churches, at the play, and especially in crowds'. This particular offence was committed by thieves of all ages, particularly by young boys and girls. Richard Oakey, who was hanged in 1723, had become particularly adept in the swift and silent cutting off of ladies' pockets. Working with a gang he used to trip up a woman from behind and even as she fell he would have removed her pocket. Another trick of his was to seize a woman in his arms as a coach sped by and to say to her, 'Take care, Madam, you will be run over'. He would be then away before his surprised or grateful victim noticed her loss.

Some pickpockets went to remarkable lengths in carrying out their thefts. Mary Young, convicted and hanged in 1740, used to operate principally in churches and she had a pair of artificial arms made for herself so that she could sit in a pew with the false hands folded piously on her lap while she used her real hands to steal from those who were seated next to her.

More dangerous and more daring were the street-robbers known as 'footpads'. The alleys, courts and lanes in London were 'like a vast wood of forest', said Henry Fielding, 'in which a thief may harbour with as great security as the wild beasts do in the deserts of Africa or Arabia'. Footpads were on the prowl at all times of the day and night. Fanny Burney regretted the impossibility of taking a walk before breakfast when she was in London 'because of the danger of footpads and robbers', but night-time was even more perilous and the period of dusk was generally known 'the Footpad Hour'.

The ineffectiveness of the police became even more apparent when criminals were operating in gangs. In 1712 a band of thugs known as the Mohocks terrorised the streets of London. A newspaper report at the time spoke of them assembling at a rendezvous, intent upon mischief, and continued, 'their way is to meet people in the streets and stop them and begin to banter them, and if they make any answer, they lay on them with sticks, and toss them from one to the other in a very rude manner. They attacked the watch in Devereux Court and Essex Street and made them scower; they also slit two persons' noses, and cut a woman in the arm with a penknife that she is lam'd. They likewise rolled a woman in a tub down Snow Hill, that was going to market, set women on their heads. misusing them in a barbarous manner'.

Another newspaper complained that pickpockets, street-robbers and highwaymen 'are grown to a great pitch of insolence at this time, robbing in gangs, defying authority, and often rescuing their companions, and carrying them off in triumph'. One night about twenty men armed with pistols and cutlasses stormed the Gatehouse where one of their confederates was detained, wounded the jailor, and released the prisoner. Footpads were as callous as they were daring. They would often hamstring the persons they had robbed by cutting the sinews of their legs in order to prevent their escape. It was small wonder that Smollett felt constrained to write, 'thieves and robbers are now become more desperate and savage than they have ever appeared since mankind was civilised'.

No person was safe and equally no home was secure. Madam Roland, speaking from her personal knowledge, said that when the wealthy left London in the summer they took with them all their articles of value or else sent the lot to their bankers, because 'on their return they expect to find their houses robbed'.

The highwaymen were regarded both by the public and amongst the criminal fraternity as being the princes of the underworld. It is difficult to understand why they had so glamorous a reputation in the eighteenth century and, indeed, why their image has been so romanticised ever since. By and large they were simply robbers on horseback and many of them had deplorable backgrounds. The notorious Dick Turpin who was hanged in 1739 was a farmer's son from Essex. Before becoming a highwayman he led a small gang of housebreakers who habitually indulged in violence, terrorism and rape. He was known to have committed at least two cold-blooded murders and he was probably responsible for a great many more. And yet many highwaymen were proud of their own fame and proud too of their personal code of conduct. Their place in the public's estimation was well-recognized, as for example, their right to travel in the first cart whenever they were among a batch of prisoners making the final journey from Newgate Gaol to the gallows at Tyburn.

The highwayman made travel hazardous and uncomfortable. The Abbé Le Blanc, writing of his experiences in England a few years before the execution of Dick Turpin, said, 'It is usual, in travelling, to put ten or a dozen guineas in a separate pocket, as a tribute to the first that comes to demand them . . . about fifteen years ago, these robbers, with a view to maintaining their rights, fixed up papers at the doors of rich people about London, expressly forbidding all persons, of whatever quality or condition, from going out of town without ten guineas and a watch about them under pain of death'.

The roads just outside London were the favourite hunting-ground of the highwaymen. The inhabitants of a number of suburbs used to organise private forces of vigilantes to patrol the turnpikes until the late evening; and closer to the Metropolis, especially in the area between Kensington and Hyde Park Corner, and in the vicinity of Marylebone Gardens, squads of soldiers sometimes escorted travellers in and out of the town. Even in the heart of London a hold-up was a frequent occurrence. Horace Walpole has told how he was in his dining-room one Sunday evening when he heard a commotion outside. 'A highwayman had attacked a post-chaise in Piccadilly', he wrote; 'the fellow was pursued, rode over the watchman, almost killed him, and escaped'. On another occasion, Horace Walpole himself encountered two highwaymen on a moonlit night in Hyde Park. One of them fired his pistol accidentally, grazing Walpole's face with the shot and stunning him.

Everyone in London had their own theories about the causes of the mounting lawlessness. A lot of people blamed it on the large numbers of disbanded soldiers and sailors roaming the country without work and without subsistence. Others held that it was due to drunkenness and cheap gin. A few— but a very few—saw a possible cause in the harsh administration of the Poor Laws and the way in which the homeless and the destitute were hounded from parish to parish, coupled with the terrible social conditions of the poor. Henry Fielding was told by Saunders Welch, the High Constable of Holborn, of certain houses in Bloomsbury which took in lodgers for twopence a night and crammed beds into every available space. Saunders Welch went on to say that, 'In these beds, several of which were in the same room, men and women, often strangers to each other, lie promiscuously, the price of a double bed being no more than threepence, as an encouragement to them to lie together: that as these places are adapted to whoredom, so they are no less provided for drunkenness, gin being sold in them all for a penny a quartern, so that the smallest sum of money serves for intoxication'. In one such house Saunders Welch counted 58 people, 'the stench of whom was so intolerable, that it compelled him in a very short time to quit the place'. Henry Fielding adds an account of his own experience in Shoreditch where he saw two small houses emptied of nearly 70 men and women, 'amongst whom was one of the prettiest girls I have ever seen, who had been carried off by an Irishman, to consummate her marriage on her wedding night in a room where several others were in bed at the same time'. If any of these miserable creatures fell sick, said Fielding, they were turned out on the streets where, 'unless some parish officer of extraordinary charity relieves them they are sure miserably to perish, with the addition of hunger and cold to their disease'.

Whatever the reasons, the precincts of the capital and its approaches were deteriorating into a state of lawlessness which bordered on anarchy, and the machinery for preserving the peace was becoming increasingly impotent. The ancient system, with its corner stones in the amateur magistrate and the part-time constable, had worked comparatively well throughout the ages in the rural areas of Britain but had proved completely unadaptable to an expanding urban community. At the beginning of the eighteenth century the basic problem remained unsolved—and barely appreciated.

It was in a London such as this that Colonel Thomas De Veil opened his Office at Bow Street.

CHAPTER TWO

KEEPING THE PEACE

WHEN the Bow Street Office was first opened in the early eighteenth century, the methods of maintaining, or trying to maintain a state of law and order in Britain, were the outcome of a gradual, spasmodic, and largely unco-ordinated process of evolvement which had lasted from an age even prior to the Norman Conquest.

The early system had been inexpensive and simple, based as it was on the principles of mutual security and mutual responsibility. The population was divided up into small groups each member of which was automatically liable for the misdeeds of the others. Accordingly, if one person committed an offence, the rest of his group were under an obligation to seize him and to bring him to justice. If they failed to perform this duty they were made to pay a collective fine. Apart from this, every individual was responsible for his own protection and if, for instance, some person had suffered a theft, he was permitted to recover his stolen property by force—if necessary with the help of his friends and neighbours.

In those days, Britain was still emerging from a tribal into a national concept of existence and the whole civic and legal administration was designed on a patriarchal basis. The territorial divisions, which played such an important role in later development, consisted of the township, the smallest unit, which was the common possession of the family group; the hundred, comprising several townships; and the shire, the forerunner of the modern county, made up of a number of hundreds. Both the shire and the hundred possessed their own judicial and administrative authority.

After the Norman Conquest the general notion of the 'Kings Peace' became more pronounced. In return for the allegiance of his subjects the monarch offered to provide his people with a state of peace and security. The principal contact between the king and the people was the sheriff, a royal delegate who gradually became the ruler of the county having authority over its revenue, policing, military force, courts and gaols. Even though he was essentially an administrative officer the sheriff was nevertheless responsible for applying the laws and preserving the peace, and it was he who presided at the county court and the hundred court.

Even before the Conquest the English kings had claimed the prerogative of being the fountain of justice and during the twelfth century they began to send royal commissioners, the early judges of assize, throughout the country to administer the law. From 1176 onwards certain parts of England were visited each year by these itinerant justices who were directed, amongst their other duties, to enquire into all the crimes which had been committed in the localities through which they passed.

At the very end of the twelfth century two new officers of justice were introduced. Firstly the coroner, who was given many duties to perform in connection with the administration of the criminal law. For instance he had to hold suspects in custody, to supervise accusations of felony and to keep a record of the persons who had been outlawed. On the whole, the responsibilities of the coroner overlapped the work of the sheriff, and indeed the principal reason for his creation was that the Crown was becoming increasingly suspicious of the sheriff's growth of power. The second innovation was the conservator of the peace, which office came into being in 1195 when Richard I issued commissions to some of his knights ordering them to preserve the peace in the more unruly areas of the kingdom. Their powers and duties were only loosely defined at the outset but later they were given authority to deal with minor offences.

Meanwhile, in the hundred and the township the policing and criminal justice continued to be conducted on a practical, though a very rough-and-ready basis. The peace officers, the tithing-men, the borsholders, the headboroughs and the chief pledges, were all unpaid and performed their duties in their spare time. The chief instrument for the pursuit of criminals was the ancient system of 'hue and cry'. This was essentially rural in origin and decreed that when the hue and cry had been raised, every man was obliged to lay aside his work and to join in the chase, which continued irrespective of duration and distance until the fugitive had surrendered himself or had been killed. If he happened to be slain by one of his pursuers, it was regarded in law as justifiable homicide.

The English countryside was infested with bands of robbers who raided houses and sometimes plundered whole villages during the night. The towns were in an equally lawless condition and a contemporary account of London in 1150 says, 'It was then a common practice in the city, that a hundred or more in a company, young and old, would make nightly invasions upon the houses of the wealthy, to the intent to rob them; and if they found any man stirring in the night that were not of their crew, they would presently murder him, insomuch that when night was come no man durst adventure to walk in the streets'.

The Statute of Winchester was passed in 1285 in an effort to suppress the growth of crime, both in the towns and in the countryside. The preamble to this Act stated that 'robberies, murders, burnings and thefts, have been more often used than heretofore' and went on to say that it had become necessary 'for to abate the power of felons'. Hundreds were reminded of their ancient responsibility for all robberies committed within their boundaries 'so that the whole Hundred where the robbery shall be done . . . shall be answerable'. The efficiency of hue and cry was to be increased requiring every male citizen between the ages of fifteen and sixty to keep arms according to his rank and station for the purpose of keeping the peace. A highway clause ordered that all roads which led from one market town to another were to be cleared of undergrowth for a distance on both sides so that robbers could not lie in hiding to waylay travellers. For the protection of towns and boroughs, the Statute introduced a compulsory system of watches to be mounted on all gates during the hours of darkness.

In the reign of Edward I (1272–1307) firm measures were taken to preserve law and order in London. The City—which was then the only residential quarter—was divided into twenty-four wards, to each of which were allocated six watchmen under the supervision of an alderman. In addition, there was a roving watch which was provided to assist the stationary watchmen. The City gates were open during the daytime but two officials, 'skillful men and fluent of speech,' were placed on duty at each gate to check on all persons passing through. During the hours of darkness the gates were kept shut and the taverns were closed, and no-one was allowed to walk about the streets carrying arms, 'unless he be a great man, or other lawful person of good repute, or certain messengers, having their warrants to go from one place to another with lanthorn in hand'. Even these precautions were not always effective, for in 1286 Edward I was obliged to deprive the City of its mayor and to place it in the control of a specially appointed warden because of the number of robberies in the streets.

During the fifty-year reign of Edward III, from 1327 to 1377, a number of important developments took place in the procedure for keeping the peace, some of which have had a profound influence on the way of life in this country ever since. The structure of rural society was then progressing from the old semi-tribal pattern to a unified community existence under a strengthening centralised government, and even the ancient family unit, the township, had been replaced by a new territorial division called the ecclesiastical parish. Under these conditions the system of policing by mutual responsibility was becoming more and more unworkable. Soon after he ascended the throne, Edward III instituted a new official, the petty, or parish constable, to replace the ancient peace officers whose usefulness had long been outmoded. The name 'constable' was borrowed from the French. It was applied formerly by two English statutes to minor officials who had performed a limited range of duties. The petty constable, however, was envisaged as the principal custodian of the law in the village, the hundred, the county and the town. He was to be unpaid, except for certain small allowances and expenses; his office was to last for one year and it was to be served in rotation by all the parishioners, rather like the other parish officials such as the churchwarden and the sidesmen. Essentially the constable's duties were to be performed in his spare time, but his importance derived from the fact that he was an Officer of the Crown charged with keeping the King's peace. By the constables' oath of service they swore that they would arrest 'all those who shall make any contest, riot, debate or affray, in breaking the said peace, and shall bring them into the house of comptor of one of the sheriffs'. If any wrongdoers escaped they were to raise hue and cry and 'follow them from street to street, and from Ward to Ward until they be arrested'.

Perhaps even more important historically than the institution of the petty constable was the introduction of the justice of the peace. The power and influence of the sheriffs had long been on the decline. Holders of this office were themselves largely responsible for their gradual eclipse, for time and again during the twelfth and thirteenth centuries, they had abused their power and many of them had been convicted of oppression and extortion and had been dismissed from office. In consequence, the monarchs had started to view their sheriffs with increasing mistrust and had deliberately curtailed their powers. Although they were left with the responsibility for bringing all who were charged with serious crimes before the itinerant judges, their own jurisdiction, after the Magna Carta, had been confined to petty offences. The coroners too were falling into disfavour with the court, owing principally to their virtual freedom from official control. The office of coroner was nominally an independent one. He was elected within the county and continued for life unless, for specified reasons, he was discharged by Royal Writ.

In 1327 Edward III extended the system of conservators of the peace throughout the whole of England by a statute which provided that 'in every shire good and lawful men shall be assigned to keep the peace'. These conservators were originally conceived as executive officers with the duties of suppressing riots and arresting offenders, but within a few years their powers had been enlarged and they were authorised to punish as well as to apprehend. A statute passed in 1344 described the conservators as, 'two or three of the best of reputation in the counties', and authorised them to combine with the itinerant judges in trying cases of felony and trespass but not, it is interesting to note, to form courts of their own. However, the Statute of Labourers in 1349 provided they should form a quarterly court to enforce its terms, which were solely directed to controlling the service and the wages of agricultural workers in the period of serious labour shortage after the Black Death had decimated the available manpower.

The Act which instituted justices of the peace was passed

in 1361 and provided that 'in every county in England shall be assigned for the keeping of the Peace, one Lord, and with him three or four of the most worthy in the county, with some learned in the law'. Their powers and duties were fully enumerated. They would restrain offenders and rioters and 'pursue, arrest, take and chastise them . . . and cause them to be imprisoned and duly punished according to the Law and Customs of the Realm'. They were authorised to 'hear and determine at the King's Suit all Manner of Felonies and Trespasses' committed in their counties, and also to commit prisoners on indictment for trial by the judges on all the more serious charges. By expressly stating that some of the justices should be 'learned in the law', Parliament was clearly setting out the policy that every county commission should contain a proportion of qualified lawyers. However, this requirement was consistently ignored throughout the following centuries.

The historian, G. M. Trevelyan, has written, 'The institution of Justices of the Peace, local gentry appointed by the Crown to govern the neighbourhood in the King's name, was a move away from inherited feudal jurisdictions. But it was also a reversal of the movement towards bureaucratic royal centralization: it recognized and used local connections and influence for the King's purposes, a compromise significant of the future development of English society as distinct from that of other lands.'

In 1362 another statute decreed that the justices of the peace must hold their sessions on four occasions every year. This was the origin of the County Quarter Sessions which have persisted to the present day.

At first no specific conditions were laid down for a person's appointment to the Commission of the Peace, but gradually a series of qualifications were introduced. In 1389 it was ordered that justices must be 'most sufficient knights, esquires and gentlemen of the land'. There was an added requirement in 1414 that they must reside within their counties, and in 1439, that they must have land there to a minimum value of £20 a year. Names were added to the Commission by the king, usually on the advice of the circuit judges, and when he was appointed the new justice was obliged to take an oath of allegiance to the Crown, and following the Reformation, to receive the sacrament according to the usages of the Church of England.

Even after the institution of justices of the peace, sheriffs did not lose all their former powers but they still remained responsible for levying hue and cry, for the pursuit, apprehension and imprisonment of offenders and for the execution of sentences. The responsibilities of the coroner were systematically whittled down to his present-day jurisdiction of inquiring into cases of suspicious death and determining the ownership of treasure-trove.

There can be little doubt that the justices of the peace were considered initially to be enormously successful. For one thing they did not abuse their powers as the sheriffs had done; for another, they had the complete trust and confidence of the Parliament, most of whose members, like themselves, consisted of the landed gentry.

The new peace officers, the petty constables, also worked reasonably well in country districts—provided they were not expected to show too much intelligence or initiative. The office of constable was never shared equally by the residents of each parish, but was performed solely by the small-holders or the minor tradesmen. Methods of selection were obscure and sometimes by tradition the occupation of a certain house, or the fact that a man was living in a certain neighbourhood, automatically made him liable for appointment. Service as a constable might always be avoided by paying a certain sum into parish funds, which regularly exempted the more well-to-do, and in Tudor times the custom of 'constables by proxy' was developed. There were perpetual constables who were paid from year to year by the persons for whom they were nominally acting as deputies. Bacon said of them that they were 'of inferior, yea, of base condition', and Blackstone remarked that, considering their standard, it was just as well that they remained in complete ignorance of the powers entrusted to them by law.

If service as a constable was unpopular in country districts it was even more so in towns, where apart from being unduly burdensome, it often involved a great deal of personal danger. The town constable, like his rural equivalent, had no official uniform and was armed only with a long stave which served both as a weapon and as an emblem of office. For the most part he went about his duties unaccompanied and there was little opportunity of summoning assistance even if he ran into trouble. In addition, all the functions connected with his office had to be carried out in his spare time. Daniel Defoe once described the appointment as being an 'insupportable hardship' and continued, 'it takes up so much of a man's time that his own affairs are frequently totally neglected, too often to his ruin. Yet there is neither profit nor pleasure therein'.

A man required no property or other qualifications to fit him for service as a petty constable, which was hardly surprising since the office was so little sought after. But in spite of its limitations, its inefficiency and all its manifold disadvantages, it was generally considered in Britain that this method of policing was the best which was available in the light of the national independence of character.

It has been said that under the Tudors and the Stewarts the justices of the peace, their numbers always increasing, gradually set themselves up as the rulers of the country. These were the days long before County, Borough and District Councils, when the only form of local government authority was that of justices in Quarter Sessions. Between 1500 and 1600 by various statutes, the justices were given control of nearly every aspect of county life. They regulated wages, prices, profits, employment, marriages, wearing apparel, apprenticeship and housebuilding and they even enforced compulsory church attendance on Sundays. Systematically they were put in charge of the regulations dealing with weights and measures, the maintenance of bridges, the licensing of inns, the upkeep of roads, the administration of the Poor Law and the building and control of local prisons, known as 'Houses of Correction' or 'Bridewells'. They also became completely responsible for the appointment and the supervision of the petty constables.

On the whole they performed these duties with honesty and diligence, so much so that Sir John Smith was to write in 1589 that 'There never was in any commonwealth devised a more wise, a more dulce and gentle, nor a more certain way to rule the people'. Even more authoritative was the opinion of Sir Edward Coke, who became Chief Justice of King's Bench in

1613, that, 'The whole Christian world hath not the like office as Justice of the Peace if duly executed'.

During the eighteenth century the autocratic administration of the justices was extended still further and they were given virtual control over the maintenance of public buildings, the direction of local finance and the appointment of most of the regional officers. The justices retained the great majority of their administrative responsibilities until County Councils were created in 1888. All this, of course, was additional to the peace-keeping duties for which they were originally intended.

There was no fixed number of justices of the peace during the seventeenth and eighteenth centuries. Records show that in the year 1650 there were about 2,500 people in the Commission, and in 1700 this figure had been increased to 3,000. Just because a man was appointed to the Commission it did not necessarily follow that he performed any magisterial duties and, in fact, it has been estimated that during the period from 1650 to 1700 there were probably only about 700–800 justices who habitually devoted themselves to their work.

The distribution of magistrates was never organised on a systematic basis, though in theory every district was supposed to have its quota who lived in the locality. With the expansion of London and the growing custom for county gentlemen to possess a town residence in addition to their country seat, there were many rural areas which were denuded of their squirearchy for long periods of the year. Consequently it became extremely difficult to fill the Commission out of those who remained, the smaller landowners, the farmers, the yeomen and the traders. For one thing, the work of a justice was considered to be essentially an occupation for the aristocracy; for another, the office was not widely coveted among the middle classes for, as Edmund Bohun wrote in 1693, a man who was offered an appointment to the Commission often felt that it would 'occasion him much loss of time, some expense, and many enemies, and, after all, will afford him little or nothing towards bearing these inconveniences'.

If the growth of residential London was causing difficulties for the peace-keeping system in the country it was providing far greater problems within its own boundaries. The new streets and the new squares had no feudal tradition, nor had the Metropolitan parishes the slightest vestige of the manorial heritage upon which the magisterial scheme had always been based. Further, the duties of a London justice, if conscientiously performed, would have been an almost full-time occupation instead of a pleasant and indolent pastime which could be co-ordinated so easily with the life of a country squire.

In fact, the system was never adapted to meet the needs of an urban society and, as will be seen, it was debased and corrupted by a body of magistrates who cared for nothing outside their personal gain. By the time the Bow Street Office was opened in 1740 the justice of the peace in London was amongst the most despised and detested members of the community.

CHAPTER THREE

THE DECLINE OF THE SYSTEM

A number of authors who have written about the early days of the Bow Street office have fallen into the error of assuming that it formed a properly constituted criminal court. It was, in fact, Colonel Thomas De Veil's own private residence, from the ground floor of which he carried on his magisterial duties. At that time justices of the peace had no courts for their day-to-day judicial work and, indeed, even Quarter Sessions were usually held in the Shire Hall or else in a hired room at the principal inn of a county town.

Quarter Sessions were undoubtedly the main events in the justices' calendar. It was there that they exerted the principal part of their judicial as well as their administrative powers, in a dual capacity, the two components of which were never very clearly segregated. In some counties, Quarter Sessions were attended by the majority of the eligible justices and were opened with a great deal of pomp and pageantry. First of all there was a formal procession through the town, followed by the reading of the Commission and the Royal Proclamation by the clerk of the peace. Then the swearing in of the jurors and the Chairman's carefully-prepared 'Charge to the Grand Jury', an exposition which would be discussed and remembered for many months afterwards. In other counties the opening could pass off almost unnoticed. Richard Burn commented in 1776, 'I have known many a Quarter Session where not above two or three justices attended—many adjournments of a Session which were never attended at all'.

The criminal jurisdiction of the justices at Quarter Sessions was exceedingly wide, extending to all crimes except treason, which was only triable at Assizes. The normal size of a Bench was three or four magistrates, but by custom, if a case was expected to entail any legal difficulties, arrangements were usually made for a visiting judge to become a member of the court. There would always be a jury, for at common law, trial by jury was essential in every instance where the accused disputed his guilt.

During the sixteenth and seventeenth centuries courts of Quarter Sessions habitually imposed sentence of death. During the eighteenth century, however, a general practice seems to have arisen whereby all capital charges were committeed to Assizes to be dealt with by a High Court Judge. Nevertheless, it was only in 1842 that Quarter Sessions were deprived of their long-disused right to try cases of murder.

Sitting with his colleagues at Quarter Sessions formed only a small part of the judicial work of the conscientious justice, and he discharged many other duties from his own home. It was there that he granted warrants and summonses, made orders and took recognizances. There also he dealt with petty offences and conducted preliminary enquiries into more serious crimes which had been committed in his locality.

The jurisdiction of magistrates to try cases on their own without a jury was derived from a long succession of statutes which authorised, sometimes one justice, sometimes two, to decide the issue of guilt or innocence in a summary manner and after recording a conviction, to punish by fining, whipping, placing in the stocks, or committing to a 'house of correction' or a county gaol. Down through the ages parliament created more and more of these summary offences but omitted to protect the accused by laying down any set rules of procedure for the trial. Consequently, the hearing always took place in private at a magistrate's house and often what occurred was a travesty of justice from which the convicted person, be he a thief, vagrant, poacher or brawler, had little or no chance of appealing either against his conviction or against his sentence.

The magistrate, whilst in office, was continually on duty. If, in passing, he overheard a person swearing a profane oath or came across someone on the roadway the worse for drink he could, on the spot, impose a fine or order a period in the stocks or in prison. Officially he was supposed to report every conviction he had made and every sentence he had passed at the next Quarter Sessions, but this was rarely done and the justice was not obliged to maintain a record-book or any sort of register.

During the seventeenth century the justices in most counties began to meet periodically in local groups, the precursors of still existing Petty Sessional Divisions. These sittings were mainly devoted to administrative and licensing work but were used for the trial of offenders as well. Again, no definite procedure was laid down; the sessions were not announced in advance and took place in private at the house of one of the justices or at a village tavern; and the accused had no absolute right to be represented by an attorney. Various statutes endowed these Petty Sessional Courts, as they were called later on, with wide powers of punishment. Under an Act in the reign of Charles II, three magistrates sitting together could sentence a prisoner to seven years transportation for burning a hay-rick.

The magistrate also combined the roles of policeman and public prosecutor. From the sixteenth century onwards he was responsible for holding preliminary enquiries into all the crimes committed in his neighbourhood. The suspects and the witnesses would be brought to his home by the village constables for him to conduct his examinations. He was bound by no rules as this part of his work was not considered a judicial proceeding. He could question a person for as long as he wished and then renew the inquest at a later stage. Whilst he was making up his mind he had full power to release the suspect or commit him to prison. The witnesses would be examined individually and in private, and eventually if the magistrate decided to commit the case for trial at Assizes or Quarter Sessions, the defendant might appear there before the jury without the smallest notion of the nature of the evidence which was going to be produced against him.

It was customary when a crime had been committed to report it as soon as possible to the nearest magistrate rather than to a local constable. John Evelyn has told how in the summer of 1652 he was knocked off his horse, tied up and robbed on a road near Tonbridge. Eventually he managed to free himself and to recover his horse. 'I now rode to Colonel Blount,' he says, 'a great justiciary of the times, who sent out the hue and cry immediately.' Both in town and country the justice's house was regarded as the focal point of law and order.

B

Sometimes a magistrate had to assume the role of detective and, supported by his constables, to go out and collect evidence at the scene of a crime. Later he would take over his second function and, at his home, would become the investigating justice. If he decided to commit a suspect for trial he might then become the chief witness for the prosecution giving evidence about his on-the-spot enquiries and his subsequent examinations.

Before considering the deterioration of the justices during the seventeenth century, it should be observed that although in general they were supposed to perform their duties unpaid, there was a provision for eight of them in each county being able to claim a remuneration of 4/- per day for attendance at Quarter Sessions. They received no allowances to cover the employment of any salaried officials in respect of the work they performed at their own homes, but it became customary for most magistrates to have a clerk who was usually some person already on their staff, for instance, an assistant in the management of their estates. There was also a system by which fees were payable by everyone who appeared before a justice on either a criminal or an administrative matter, and in the course of time these fees were used to an increasing extent to pay the salary of the clerk. Owing to the growth in complexity of the law, the next step was for many magistrates to avail themselves of local attorneys to act as their clerks in exchange for all the fees that were received.

It is a matter of some doubt whether justices' fees, or any part of them, were intended to be retained for their own benefit. The terms of their oath were somewhat vague on this point. 'You should take nothing for your office of Justice of the Peace to be done, but of the King, and fees accustomed, and costs limited by statute.' Almost certainly in the period prior to the seventeenth century the magistrates kept nothing for themselves. It is interesting to note, however, that judges were also paid fees by all those appearing before them and were accustomed to keep a large portion of this money as a supplement to their official salaries. The great legal historian, W. S. Holdsworth, has pointed out that some measure of what a judge's fees were worth to him can be assessed from the fact that when the payment of fees was abolished in 1826 the judges' salaries were immediately increased from £2,400 to £5,500 a year.

The first public allegation of wholesale corruption on the part of the magistrates was made by a Member of Parliament in a violent attack on them in the House of Commons in 1601. He alleged that many were known as 'basket justices' because they carried a basket for the reception of gifts from those who came before them in the course of their duty. Although the Member watered down his accusations at a later stage, the term 'basket justices' persisted and in 1693 Bohun wrote of some magistrates, 'who for half a dozen chickens would dispense with a whole dozen of the penal statutes'.

The principal responsibility for the degeneration of the magisterial bench during the seventeenth century lay at the feet of the Government who deliberately removed from the Commission a number of justices who were thought to oppose their policies, and then filled the vacancies with their own supporters. This innovation of attempting to substitute political nominees—mostly men of humble station—for the local squirearchy proved disastrous. Apart from any more serious consequences it caused a total cleavage in the Commission between the country gentlemen, who despised their recent associates socially and distrusted their motives and their methods on an ethical level, and the small traders or shopkeepers who considered that their aristocratic colleagues were idle, pleasure-loving and autocratic.

There can be little doubt that this new type of magistrate, known as 'The Justice of Mean Degree', frequently used his authority for the ends of private gain. Apart from the acceptance of bribes there were ample opportunities of misappropriating the sums of money which were paid out in fines. It soon became apparent that the delicate structures on which had been based the maintenance of local administration and the application of the criminal law were being placed in grave jeopardy. At the close of the seventeenth century the House of Commons moved an address to the King declaring that, 'it would much conduce to the service of His Majesty, and the good of this kingdom, that gentlemen of quality should be restored and put in the Commissions and Lieutenancy, and that men of small estates be neither continued nor put into the said Commissions'.

Whereas the magisterial system in country districts was only tinged with corruption, in heavily populated urban areas it became totally debased. In the Metropolis and in the neighbouring areas of Middlesex and Surrey it was well-nigh impossible to find a suitable type of justice because, as explained by a writer of the time, 'In places inhabited by the scum and dregs of the people and the most profligate class of life, gentlemen of any great figure and fortune will not take such drudgery upon them'. The result was that the authorities had no alternative but to fill the Commission with tradesmen and small-time professionals, whom Smollett has described as 'needy, mean, ignorant and rapacious'. He goes on to say that they 'often acted from the most scandalous principles of selfish avarice'. These people were known as 'Trading Justices' because many of them quite openly earned an income from their fees and from other illicit devices which they employed when exercising their authority as magistrates.

The greatest source of revenue to the trading justices was the granting of bail, for which a small fee was paid by the prisoner. Townsend, the Bow Street Runner, told a Parliamentary Committee at a later date, 'The plan used to be to issue warrants and take up all the poor devils in the streets, and then there was the bailing them, 2/4, which the magistrate had; and taking up a hundred girls, that would make, at 2/4, £11-13-4. They sent none to gaol, for bailing them was so much better'.

Another of their methods was to force the brothel-keepers and the prostitutes in their localities to make regular payments of protection money as a safeguard against arrest and punishment. Sometimes they had a financial interest in the actual brothels and one magistrate at Wapping was known to let out a part of his private house to a prostitute. The trading justices also used to employ their own touts to persuade people to take out warrants and summonses, on which fees were payable, and they were usually open to bribery, provided an adequate sum of money was offered to them.

It was generally recognised that the Middlesex and the Westminster magistrates were amongst the most disreputable of all. Edmund Burke once said in a House of Commons' speech, 'The justices of Middlesex were generally the scum of the earth—carpenters, brickmakers and shoemakers; some of whom were notoriously men of such infamous characters that they were unworthy of any employ whatever, and others so ignorant that they could scarcely write their own names'. In his novel *Amelia*, Henry Fielding has depicted a typical Westminster magistrate who, 'if he was ignorant of the laws of England was yet well versed in the laws of nature'. He made his own interest the guiding principle of his decisions and he was, 'never indifferent in a cause, but when he could get nothing on either side'.

Not only was London plagued by corrupt magistrates but it was also subject to the most inefficient policing arrangements imaginable. The Metropolis was divided up into parishes, each of which was entirely responsible for its own protection—indeed, twelve of them chose to dispense with police altogether. The City and Liberty of Westminster, in which Bow Street was situated, usually had eighty constables, mostly tradesmen of the district who served for a year and went on duty every fifteenth night armed with staves and lanterns. It was always permissible for a constable to hire a substitute. In fact there were about ten men in Westminster who did duty regularly as substitutes for payments of between £8 and £20 a year and they doubtless found this employment acceptable as the majority of them were either very elderly, or were the inmates of workhouses.

As an additional precaution the streets of the Metropolis were supposed to be protected by the watchmen, known as 'Charlies', since it was Charles I who had introduced their more extensive use in 1640. Again they were appointed within the parish and the scales of payment and hours of duty varied from place to place. In a well-known passage in *Amelia*, Fielding has criticized London watchmen in general and said of them that their duty, 'being to guard our streets at night from thieves and robbers, an office which at least requires strength of body, are chosen out of those poor, old, decrepit people who are from their want of bodily strength incapable of getting a livelihood by work. These men, armed with a pole which some of them are scarce able to lift, are to secure the persons and houses of His Majesty's subjects from the attacks of gangs of young, bold, stout, desperate, well-armed villains. If the poor old fellows should run away from such enemies, no-one I think can wonder, unless it be that they were able to make their escape.'

Probably the only efficient watchmen in London, apart from the City which employed a better type of man, were the Chelsea Pensioners who fulfilled the duty in the parishes of St. James's and Marylebone.

Westminster had around 300 Charlies spread over its nine parishes. They were so poorly paid that they had to be re-cruited amongst the sick, the elderly and the destitute. Their duties were to man the watch-houses, usually insecure hovels in which prisoners were confined until a constable came to remove them to the Roundhouse, or to take them to appear before a local magistrate. The watchmen were equipped with a staff, a lantern and a rattle, and had short beats to patrol on which they periodically called out the time of the night or the morning, sometimes adding the comforting reassurance that all was well. However, nobody placed very much reliance on them as peace-officers, and the Abbé Le Blanc writing of highway robbers said, 'In bad times when there is little or nothing to be got on the roads, these fellows assemble in gangs to raise contributions even in London itself; and watch-men seldom trouble themselves to interfere in their vocation'.

As has been noticed in an earlier chapter, London's con-stables and watchmen were helpless against the organised terrorisation of the Mohocks in 1712—a time when Thomas De Veil was twenty-eight, and seventeen years before he first became a magistrate. A report at the height of the Mohock depredations said, 'The Watch in most of the out-parts of the town stand in awe of them, because they always come in a body, and are too strong for them, and when any watchman presumes to demand where they are going, they generally misuse them'.

Eventually, Queen Anne felt obliged to issue a Royal Pro-clamation promising a substantial reward for anyone bring-ing a Mohock to justice. The Proclamation spoke of the 'great and unusual riots and barbarities which had lately been com-mitted in the night-time, in the open streets, in several parts of the Cities of London and Westminster, and parts adjacent'. The Mohocks were particularly censured because they had 'the boldness to insult constables and watchmen'.

With peace officers of such appallingly low quality it is a matter of great wonder that criminals were ever arrested at all. However, the Government tried to compensate for the inadequacy of the system by relying increasingly on an admixture of bribery, pardons and rewards.

The first step to be taken in point of time was the introduction of the Tyburn Ticket in 1669. This was a reward which was given to anyone who prosecuted a felon and secured a conviction. At that time all prosecutions were undertaken by private individuals at their own expense and it was thought necessary that members of the public should be spurred on to greater efforts. A Tyburn Ticket was granted by a judge or a magistrate and afforded the recipient a lifelong exemption from liability to serve in any kind of parish office including, of course, the office of petty constable. The ticket could be transferred once with all its rights. It was this which made it such a valuable acquisition, as many people, particularly in the wealthier parishes, were willing to pay a good price in order to avoid a turn of service as a constable. In the seventeenth and eighteenth centuries a Tyburn Ticket was usually worth about £20, though a House of Lords Committee reported in 1817 that transfer fees of as high as £200 and £300 had not been unknown. The system was finally abolished in 1826.

In 1692 a further effort was made to halt the growth of crime by the offer of financial awards for those who had taken part in a successful prosecution, and free pardons to accomplices who turned 'King's Evidence'. These prosecution payments were known as 'Blood Money' and were made in addition to the granting of Tyburn Tickets. On a conviction for a serious felony the sum of £40 was divided amongst the prosecutor and his key witnesses, and smaller amounts were payable on convictions for lesser offences. From time to time when lawlessness was getting completely out-of-hand, as for instance when the Mohocks were terrorising the Metropolis in 1712, the Government would offer supplementary rewards by Royal Proclamation. One such proclamation issued in

1728, promised a payment of £100 to every person who instigated a successful prosecution for felony.

Private individuals, too, habitually offered bribes on their own account. Without an effective police force the best course for the victim of a theft or a robbery, was often to advertise a substantial reward for anyone who could help him to recover his property, with an express or an implied provision that no questions would be asked.

One disquieting consequence of all this was the emergence of the amateur 'thief-takers' who were to play such a sinister role in the years that followed. They were men, for the most part, with unsavoury backgrounds who made a discreditable living by prosecuting and giving evidence at criminal trials, and also, by working hand-in-glove with thieves and receivers to negotiate the return of stolen property.

Another class of people who thrived under these circumstances were the part-time informers who brought infringements of the law to the notice of the authorities in return for payment. One of Fielding's characters in *Amelia* remarks, 'Informers are odious, there's no doubt of that, and no-one would care to be an informer if he could help it, because of the ill-usage they always receive from the mob'. The unpopularity of informers with the public was very real, for a report in the *Covent Garden Journal* speaks of them being 'punished by buffeting, kicking, stoning, ducking, be-mudding, etc., in short, by all those means of putting (sometimes quite, sometimes almost) to death, which are called by that general phrase of mobbing'.

CHAPTER FOUR

JUSTICE DE VEIL

THOMAS DE VEIL was born in 1684 at a house near St. Paul's Churchyard in the City of London. His father, the Rev. Dr. Hans De Veil, was an impecunious Huguenot minister from Lorraine who had settled in England some time previously and had been for many years employed as the library-keeper at Lambeth Palace.

For the details of Thomas De Veil's life we must rely very largely on an anonymous book of memoirs which was published in 1748, barely two years after his death. The purpose of this biography was clearly stated on the second page: 'We have the memoirs of many able statesmen, great captains, gallant seamen, and indeed, of all the professions', wrote the unknown author, 'but the memoirs of a magistrate, the life of a justice of the peace, has scarce hitherto appeared, and yet it will be found that this, like all other characters, requires particular talents, and the qualities which render a man capable of shining therein are not so common or so trivial as many people think'.

Indeed, there was nothing in the least commonplace or trivial in the personality and the exploits of the founder of the Bow Street office as revealed through the pages of these memoirs.

Thomas De Veil underwent a very strict upbringing, particular emphasis being placed by both his parents on his manners and his education. From the start he showed a great propensity for learning, and no doubt he received considerable encouragement and assistance from his father who was a scholar of some repute. Dr. Hans De Veil had made a special study of Hebrew and rabbinical literature and was the author of two learned books, one a treatise on ancient sacrifices and the other a commentary on the minor prophets. But young Thomas was not destined for an academic career and when he was sixteen the family's straitened circumstances made it necessary for him to abandon his studies and to learn a trade.

Accordingly he was apprenticed to a mercer in Queen's Street, Cheapside, very close to his own home at St. Paul's.

Everything went extremely well for a year. The mercer was delighted with his well-behaved and industrious apprentice and Thomas was as happy as he was interested in his work. Then suddely the mercer's business failed and he was forced to close it down without having sufficient funds to repay even a proportion of Thomas's apprenticeship fee. Dr. Hans De Veil had by now spent all the money he could afford on his son's career, so from the tender age of seventeen, Thomas was obliged to make his own way in the world.

Throughout his life Thomas De Veil always met the varying changes in his fortunes with philosophical acceptance. Undeterred by his early mischance he decided to become a professional soldier and he enlisted as a private in the infantry. In the eighteenth century, commissions in the armed forces were generally obtained by purchase, though a few were sometimes granted through the ranks on the field of battle, so it must have required a considerable amount of spirit for a youth with De Veil's background to embark deliberately on a life which, apart altogether from its manifold dangers, held out a prospect of years of brutalized discipline, subservience and privation. Very little is known about De Veil's military career, but it was during his years as a soldier that he shaped his personality and formulated his approach to the subsequent adventures of his life. It appears that he took part in William III's campaign in Flanders and he was later posted to Toby Caulfield's regiment in Portugal, though still as a gentleman-ranker.

Summarizing De Veil's subsequent successes the memoirs reflect that he 'passed thro' many scenes of life, and raised himself by his personal merit, from carrying a brown musket, to make a very considerable figure in the world'. The author attributes this achievement to De Veil's ability to make the right sort of friends, to his courage and his indefatigable diligence, and also to his cultivation of what is called 'a certain boldness in address'.

We know that during his travels as a soldier De Veil exhibited a remarkable aptitude for learning foreign languages, and it might well have been in the capacity of an interpreter that he first came into contact with Viscount Galway, the commander of the British expeditionary force in Portugal. At first, the memoirs tell us, Galway was prompted by a desire to help a gentleman in distress, but as his knowledge of De Veil increased, 'he began to have a much great respect for him and employed him as a kind of secretary'. In 1702, when De Veil was twenty, he was granted a commission as an ensign in the Dragoons, and two years later at Lisbon he was promoted to the rank of captain.

After the Peace of Utrecht in 1713, De Veil's regiment was disbanded and he himself was returned to England on half-pay. By that time he was married, and 'having a family, and a love for company, and a taste for pleasure, he found it impossible to maintain the former, and gratify the latter' on the small income he was receiving. Apart from his other commitments he had managed to accumulate considerable debts, so he retired for a while to a country village to live cheaply and to straighten out his financial affairs.

Captain De Veil's ambition and his appetite for comfortable living had been whetted by his years as an army officer. Having cleared his debts he came up to London intent 'to push his way in the world', and he opened a private office in Scotland Yard at which he offered his services in drafting petitions to the War Office and the Treasury on behalf of disbanded officers and other persons who were seeking grants, privileges and favours. He was extremely skilful at this work, and as his reputation grew, it became more and more profitable.

However, it was obvious that De Veil's particular talents fitted him for a superior occupation to that of a professional tout, and several of the influential friends from his army days suggested to him that they might assist him to become a justice of the peace for Westminster and Middlesex, with a view to improving both his status and his prospects.

Geographically the City and Liberty of Westminster was a part of the County of Middlesex, but in 1618 it had been granted a separate Commission of the Peace, it is believed in order that the Government might exercise a more direct control over the magistrates in the locality surrounding the Houses of Parliament. Since the jurisdiction of a magistrate was limited to the area of his commission it was, in fact, highly unsatisfactory if his powers were confined to a district so small as the City and Liberty of Westminster. For instance, if a Westminster justice granted a warrant, and before it could be executed the fugitive escaped into the County of Middlesex, then the warrant was completely ineffectual until it had been endorsed by a Middlesex justice. So, for the sake of administrative convenience a number of magistrates in the Westminster Commission were usually appointed to the Middlesex Commission as well.

De Veil was probably delighted at the opportunity of becoming a justice, but nevertheless he delayed his decision because, 'He had a high opinion of the office of magistrate and he thought that there were many things with which a man ought to be thoroughly acquainted' before he accepted such an appointment. Apart from other considerations one forms the impression that De Veil was one of those people who do not like to undertake a task unless they are satisfied that they will do it really well. Therefore, he began to study the nature of the office and the powers of a justice of the peace and it was not until he thought he had acquired sufficient knowledge of the subject that he informed his friends that he was ready to proceed. He became a magistrate for Middlesex and for Westminster in 1729, when he was forty-five, and set up his first office at a house in Leicester Fields. In the course of time he was also appointed a justice for the counties of Essex, Surrey and Hertfordshire, and for the Tower of London.

A contemporary portrait of De Veil, sketched towards the end of his life, shows him as having cold, calculating eyes and an excessively sensual mouth. Indeed, we know that his overriding weakness was his sexual laxity. Although he was married four times and had no less than twenty-five legitimate children, the memoirs tell us that, 'His greatest foible was a most irregular passion for the fair sex, which as he freely indulged, he made it often the subject of his discourse'. We are also told that, 'as he was not very nice in his morals, so was no hypocrite in his discourse; he had his failings, he knew them, and made no secret of them'.

Another of De Veil's faults was his extravagance: 'He

loved money, and affected magnificence; he was a man of pleasure and never wanted resources, for what it constantly requires unbounded expense'. Yet there was a thrifty side to his nature as well. He gave his advice and his time freely to his friends, but always insisted on being repaid for his smallest expenses because, as he explained with his customary candour, it was much better to charge for such things than to forbear to do these services on account of their cost.

Leicester Fields, where De Veil opened his office, was the site of the present Leicester Square, but it was then a rough, sparsely-populated heath—a favourite resort of the footpads and the robber-gangs. The new justice was active, courageous and thorough. He quickly made a mark by the steadfast performance of his duties, and he was soon regarded as one of the most effective magistrates in London.

Although De Veil has been almost universally branded as a 'trading justice', the evidence in support of this charge is somewhat inconclusive. The author of the memoirs, who is by no means restrained in exposing De Veil's failings, never openly accuses him of corruption, but seems to draw a definite distinction between De Veil's methods and those of his more disreputable colleagues. Trading justices, says the anonymous writer, were 'low, needy and mercenary' people, despised by their superiors and hated and dreaded by the common people. But De Veil, 'though he did much of their kind of business, did it in another manner, so that though his office was very profitable, yet it was not liable to any scandal; on the contrary, he was not only exact in what he did himself, but (as they came his way) rectified other peoples' mistakes, and was a great check upon such as had nothing but interest in view . . .'

In his early days as a magistrate De Veil ran into trouble from a trading justice, referred to in the memoirs as 'Mr. W.' Apparently Mr. W. had committed some irregularity for which De Veil reported him to the Lord Chancellor's secretary. The corrupt justice thereupon went to an upstairs room at a Coffee-house in Leicester Fields and sent a message to De Veil asking to see him there immediately. De Veil complied with this summons and no sooner had he entered the room then Mr. W., sword in hand, grossly insulted him and challenged him to fight. De Veil refused and Mr. W. struck

at him with his sword, causing him a serious injury. Fortunately the noise of the altercation attracted the attention of
people downstairs and they rushed in and disarmed Mr. W.
before he could inflict further harm on his helpless adversary.
De Veil seems to have acted with the greatest propriety
throughout; the memoirs tell us that he was both calm and
discreet, and 'told his brother justice that disputes between
magistrates were regulated by the law and not by the sword'.
De Veil also invited Mr. W. to submit their point of difference
to a superior court and after that, if he still felt aggrieved,
De Veil assured him he could have 'the kind of satisfaction
he should then think fit to require'.

In a report on this affair the *Gentleman's Magazine* disclosed that Mr. W. was, in fact, a justice called Webster and
that he stabbed De Veil 'in the belly about five inches deep'.
However, De Veil appears to have staged a quick recovery and
to have suffered no lasting after-effects. The Treasury accounts
for the year 1734 show that he received a grant of £250, made
as a result of his prayer for compensation for having been
stabbed through the body and constantly molested by bad
characters owing to his magisterial activities. The stabbing
might have referred to the Mr. W. incident, for the memoirs
speak of no other occasion around that period when De Veil
suffered any injury.

In 1735 De Veil took on, single-handed, one of the largest
and the most desperate robber gangs which had ever operated in London. The identities of the criminals were well
known, but they were in league with a bunch of disreputable
solicitors who managed invariably to keep them out of
trouble. Showing his usual fearlessness De Veil began quite
openly to collect evidence against these people and he was
making such good progress that they grew alarmed and decided to kill him. 'With this in view, they posted themselves
for several nights, in a convenient place in Leicester Fields,
in the hopes of meeting him either as he went out, or returned
to his own house.' However, before they could achieve their
purpose one of the members of the gang lost his nerve and
called on De Veil offering to turn king's evidence against his
confederates. As a result, the whole gang was broken up and

six men, including a solicitor, were tried and convicted at the Old Bailey.

As a consequence of this and other exploits, De Veil's stature increased immeasurably and he came to be considered, 'as a person very capable of doing great service in his station, and of becoming such a magistrate as in all times is much wanted, but was never more so than at that juncture, when a great spirit of corruption reigned'.

Early in 1736 De Veil left Leicester Fields and opened a new office in Thrift Street, Soho. In that same year the Government introduced their detested Gin Act, and in the Metropolis, De Veil proved himself to be one of the few magistrates with sufficient courage to endeavour to enforce its provisions.

Towards the end of the seventeenth century, when Britain had been running into increasing difficulties with her balance of trade, an attempt was made by the Government to improve the position by encouraging the production of cheap spirits— notably gin—which could be made from home-grown corn. An additional reason for this policy may have been, as Daniel Defoe once suggested, that it was 'good for landed interests and England had a parliament of landowners'. At any rate, whereas the inns and taverns, which mostly sold ale, were licensed and strictly controlled by the justices, the sale of gin was completely unsupervised. In 1725 it was estimated that there were about 6,000 shops and houses in London, excluding the City, where gin could be bought at most hours of the day and night, and it was even being peddled in the streets from stalls and barrows.

The social consequences of the surfeit of cheap gin were appalling. Amongst the poorer classes, men, women and children were only too ready to avail themselves of such a convenient form of escapism from their terrible living conditions and became, in the alluring words of a spirit-shop advertisement, 'drunk for 1d and dead drunk for 2d'. Inevitably gin drinking took its toll in human lives, and in the early part of the eighteenth century the number of deaths in London increased to over double the total number of births.

In 1729 the Government introduced its first Gin Act in an attempt to price gin beyond the reach of the poor. This statute imposed a duty on all cheap spirits and also required spirit-retailers to purchase an inexpensive licence. However, it was never seriously enforced and was totally repealed in 1733 at the instigation of the wheat-growers who complained that they were being seriously affected by declining sales.

The orgy of gin drinking continued unabated and in 1736 the Government, in a mood of sheer desperation, hurried through another statute, the provisions of which were far more drastic than those which had been so recently repealed. The Gin Act of 1736 made it compulsory for every retailer of spirits to purchase a licence costing £50 and imposed a substantial spirit duty. A section of the Act also authorised rewards for informers. These measures were met with open defiance by the people of London and, in fact, only two of the £50 licences were ever taken out.

De Veil incurred the fury of the mob through his endeavours to enforce the new statute. In January, 1738, two informers took refuge at his house in Thrift Street and a large crowd assembled outside demanding that the men should be handed over to them. When De Veil refused, the mob became menacing and threatened to pull down his house. Eventually he was obliged to read a proclamation under the Riot Act and to send for the assistance of the military. After the soldiers arrived De Veil arrested a man called Roger Allen, who had been the leader of the riot, and promptly committed him to Newgate Gaol to await trial.

At first the Government declined to prosecute Allen, for fear of provoking further disorders, but De Veil 'took up the matter so warmly, and insisted so much upon the continued danger he was in if some stop was not put to such kind of tumults, that a prosecution was ordered.'

In May, 1738, Roger Allen was tried in the Court of King's Bench at Westminster. On his behalf it was pleaded that he was insane, and the jury, well-knowing the falsity of this defence, seized on the opportunity of acquitting him. After the verdict Allen received a tremendous ovation from the vast crowd outside the court. In Old Palace Yard he paused to make a short speech. 'Gentlemen,' he said, 'I thank you kindly for this honour, but the great liberty of mobbing a justice now and then, and my own life had certainly been lost, if I had not had the wit to prove myself a fool.'

Another unpopular statute which De Veil had to enforce from his Thrift Street office was the politically inspired Licensing Act of 1737, which gave the Lord Chamberlain a power of censorship over the English Theatre.

But in spite of the opprobrium De Veil was encountering by conscientously performing his duties, the memoirs tell us that he was now 'in the height of his glory.' His ambition was undiminished. 'He wanted credit and power . . . and was never happier than when surrounded by a number of people, whom he could influence by his nod.' He also wanted wealth, 'that he might live in his own way, which was magnificent enough, and gratify his propensity to pleasures, which were very expensive'.

In 1740, at the age of fifty-six, De Veil transferred his home and his office from Soho to a larger house in Bow Street.

CHAPTER FIVE

DE VEIL AT BOW STREET

THE house which achieved such fame as the Bow Street Office stood on the west side of the road. Like most of the property in that locality it was owned by the Duke of Bedford, and from the records, the building lease seems to have been granted in 1703. It was, in fact, the fifth house to the north from the corner of Russell Street, although when streets were numbered towards the close of the eighteenth century it was given the number 4 because the corner house, as is shown by the 1799 Horwood map, was actually facing into Russell Street.

According to the collecting books of the Poor Rate for the parish of St. Paul's, Covent Garden, De Veil moved into the house some time between the 15th May, 1739, and Christmas Day, 1740. It was then rated at a value of £70, which was the fourth highest rating allocated among the forty or so properties on both sides of Bow Street. The former tenant for some years had been a man called John Parker, and it is interesting to see in the Bedford Estate Records that someone of exactly the same name, perhaps a forebear, had been granted a large piece of farmland between Hart Street and Long Acre on the 13th June, 1635.

De Veil took out a new lease from the Duke of Bedford on the 4th September, 1745, for 21 years at a rental of £10 per annum. The counterpart of this document is still with the Bedford Estate Records. It appears that when he first moved into the house De Veil was the sub-tenant or the assignee of a Mary Wright, and although there is no record of the inside accommodation, it is known that he established his office on the ground floor, whilst he used the upstairs rooms as his living quarters.

From the still-existing sketches of the interior of the Bow Street Office, all drawn some years later when John Fielding was the presiding justice, it can be seen that the lay-out was not dissimilar from that of a great many Petty Sessional

Courts in Britain today. The magistrate sat on a dais at one end of the room, with his clerk at a desk immediately below him. There was no dock, but the prisoner stood at a bar facing the clerk and the bench. There were rows of seats on either side, and also a raised gallery for spectators. It would accord with our knowledge of De Veil's character to assume that he was responsible for these arrangements, and this view is corroborated by a passage in the memoirs which states that, 'he sat by the judge at the Old Bailey and sat like a judge in his own office'.

It is not known whether De Veil allowed the general public to watch him conducting his magisterial business at Bow Street. It is likely that they were permitted to attend on certain occasions, as he received, and doubtless enjoyed, a great deal of publicity in his work at the office. 'No sooner had he performed one remarkable exploit in his judicial capacity, and the world had come to examine and reflect upon it', according to the memoirs, 'but another fell in his way, of as great a consequence to his reputation'.

Even had he no other claim to renown, De Veil deserves to be remembered for being, in all probability, the first magistrate in England who transformed his office into a court of law. This innovation was all the more remarkable when it is remembered that at the beginning of the eighteenth century the Westminster Quarter Sessions were still taking place in a small, nondescript tavern by the side of Westminster Hall; and even the justices of Middlesex regarded it as a mark of peculiar distinction that they were able to hold the sessions, perhaps the most important in the whole country, at their own courthouse, Hicks Hall in Clerkenwell.

When De Veil moved to Bow Street he was still calling himself by his army rank of captain. In February, 1744, he was appointed as colonel of the Red Regiment of the Westminster Militia, a reserve force which was only mobilised in times of national emergency. He always remained very proud of his military status. As a magistrate he would also be known as 'Justice' De Veil, and would have been entitled to append the title of 'Esquire' after his name.

The ambitious De Veil was not satisfied with being acclaimed as one of the most efficient magistrates in London.

'The post he aimed at', according to the memoirs, 'was the confidence of the court and the ministry in his office as justice.' It seems that since the time of Elizabeth I there had usually been some London magistrate who had enjoyed the especial trust of the government in power, and who had received secret allowances for the performance of confidential assignments. Beatrice and Sidney Webb have suggested that there was even an unofficial appointment known as the 'Court Justice', and that the magistrate selected for this honour was charged with the maintenance of order in London and the management of spies and secret agents, and had a general responsibility for counter-espionage.

Certainly if the office of court justice ever existed, De Veil was clearly a most suitable candidate for the post on account of his courage, his prudence and his reliability. It is known now—a fact which the author of the memoirs did not mention —that in February, 1738, De Veil was appointed Inspector-General of Exports and Imports at a salary of £500 for himself with an additional £280 a year for his clerk or substitute. This position was largely a sinecure, though it did entail certain minimal responsibilities in connection with the prosecution of frauds on the revenue; it might have been awarded to De Veil as a concealed payment for his more clandestine activities. His immediate predecessor was Horace Walpole, son of Robert Walpole, the First Lord of The Treasury; Horace had resigned on his elevation to the even more profitable office of Usher of the Exchequer. Other gratuities paid to De Veil out of public funds have come to light since the memoirs were written. For instance, in 1740 he received a grant of £100 from the Treasury for his great diligence as a justice, and he often received sums of money to cover his expenses in the performance of his duties.

In addition to his initiative in setting up his own court, De Veil was probably the first magistrate to make an extensive use of the provisions of the Riot Act for breaking up disturbances in public places. This statute, which was enacted in 1715, had made it a capital offence for a crowd of twelve or more persons to continue together for more than an hour after a magistrate had read out a proclamation ordering them to disperse. The principal object of the Riot Act was to legalize the use of force by the military after the statutory interval of an hour had elapsed; however, there was a great deal of misunderstanding about its general effect, and it was widely believed that until a riot had persisted for at least an hour the troops were not allowed to intervene.

It has already been recounted how De Veil tried to read a proclamation to the demonstrators outside his Thrift Street office in January, 1738. The *Newgate Calendar* recalls an earlier incident when he made use of the Riot Act during a disturbance at the Drury Lane Theatre on the opening night of Henry Fielding's play *Eurydice* in February, 1737. On that occasion the footmen and servants in the gallery made it impossible for the performance to continue. 'Colonel De Veil, then an active magistrate for Westminster', says the account, 'also happened to be present and in vain attempted to read a proclamation against such an outrage, but though they obstructed him in his duty, he caused the ringleaders to be secured, and the next day committed three of them to Newgate.'

In October, 1738, a year after the government had imposed a censorship on the stage, they decided to bring over a company of French players for a short season at the Little Theatre in the Haymarket. It was generally expected that there would be trouble from a hostile audience, still fervently resentful of the restrictive new law, and the indefatigable De Veil was requested to attend the first performance. As soon as the curtain went up there was a pandemonium of hisses and catcalls and the actors were driven into the wings by a cascade of oranges. De Veil mounted the stage and reprimanded the crowd for their 'beargarden behaviour'. At this they started to rip up the benches and forms, and in the general commotion De Veil stood his ground and read a proclamation under the Riot Act. A number of arrests were made by the constables and the troops standing by outside the theatre, but once again the Government was too timid to allow any prosecution to take place. So the matter was let drop, 'and the Colonel was obliged to employ his pen to defend himself against torrents of abuse'.

Whilst he was at Bow Street De Veil built up an enormous reputation for himself both as a detective and as an inquisitor.

His methods of investigating crimes were obvious enough, but at a time when the science of detection was non-existent they must have seemed to be quite unique. The author of the memoirs comments: 'There was no quality by which De Veil was more distinguished than his sagacity, except his diligence. If he was once furnished with a few hints, he knew how to form them into a clue ... when once he had hold of this clue, he never parted with it till he brought the whole discovery to the view of the public.' On one occasion, after a burglary at an eating-house in Chancery Lane, De Veil was interrogating a suspect at his office with little or no evidence to assist him. After a while he suddenly asked the man for the loan of a knife. The suspect produced a pocket knife which, on examination, was found to have a broken end. De Veil sent round a constable to the eating house with instructions to probe the lock. Sure enough the missing tip of the knife was still embedded there, and when it was shown to the suspect he broke down and confessed.

De Veil's prowess grew to such proportions that he was often consulted regarding unsolved crimes outside his own jurisdiction. In 1740 a solicitor was shot dead at his home in Suffolk in circumstances which provided no clue to the identity of the killer. The local magistrates asked De Veil for assistance and his enquiries led to the eventual conviction of the solicitor's own son at Bury St. Edmunds Assizes.

However, De Veil's forte was undoubtedly his skill as an inquisitor. According to the memoirs, 'His natural sagacity, assisted by his experience enabled him to make the most surprising discoveries; he knew so well how to throw those he examined into confusion, and was so able to catch up on their unguarded expressions to piece together broken hints, and sometimes by feigning to know all, put these wretches upon detecting themselves, by justifying against what he knew to be false, that he was very rarely deceived'.

In the absence of a detective force the successful investigation of a crime was frequently dependent on a magistrate's ability to wring a confession from the suspect. In the summer of 1741 a particularly revolting murder occurred when the Principal of Clements Inn was knifed to death by a servant. The servant stuffed the corpse down the outside closet and made it known that his master had suddenly left London. The dead man's brother, being suspicious about his disappearance, asked De Veil to investigate the matter and had the servant taken to the Bow Street Office for interrogation. 'The Colonel being used to such people, examined him so closely, that he soon fell into confusion, and then became sullen, and would answer no questions when asked him.' De Veil committed him to the Gatehouse and suggested that a search should be carried out at Clements Inn. This was done and the corpse was discovered. The servant was hanged a few months later.

Gradually, De Veil took the measure of the London underworld; 'Indeed there was hardly ever a magistrate so dreadful in this respect to these sort of people', wrote his anonymous biographer, 'for the very name of him was sufficient to frighten them, and they fancied his intelligence to be so good, that they were never safe from him.'

In the spring of 1744 at the height of the Jacobite scare, the Government placed De Veil in charge of the rounding up of suspected sympathisers in London. The Bow Street Office became the headquarters for the organisation of special street patrols, surprise raids and searches for hidden arms. A year later De Veil was ordered to seize the Jacobite Lord Dillon, and he led a force of troops and constables to the country seat of the peer in Hertfordshire to carry out the arrest. His claim for the expenses of this operation, totalling £8 9s. 6d., are preserved in the British Museum; one rather surprising item reads: — 'To guard of 80 men, wet through on Tuesday morning in their march from Barnet to Lord Dillon's house . . . £1 1s. 1d.'

It would have been easy for De Veil to abuse the wide authority he was allowed to exercise, but apparently he seldom did so. 'He knew that all the power he had was derived from the law,' the memoirs state, 'and therefore never forgot that they were circumscribed and bounded by the law.' The record books show that between 1733 and 1746 he attended with the utmost regularity at both the Middlesex and the Westminster Quarter Sessions, although he was not elected chairman of either. Nevertheless, according to the memoirs, great respect was always accorded him by the other justices, who regarded him as 'the oracle in the vestry'.

Amongst his brother magistrates De Veil's position must have been unique. In theory he was their equal; in practice his influence and his power were unprecedented. Plainly they accepted his leadership, for in the spring of 1744 he was to the forefront in presenting to George II a declaration of affection and loyalty from the justices of the county of Middlesex; as a result of this De Veil himself, together with two of his colleagues, received the honour of knighthoods. On September 12th of the following year the Middlesex justices' order book shows an entry to the effect that Thomas Lane, Esq., the Chairman of the Court, Sir Thomas De Veil and five other magistrates, met together 'at the house of the said Thomas De Veil in Bow Street' to prepare a further address of loyalty to the king on the occasion of the rebellion in Scotland.

During his years at the Bow Street office De Veil assembled a collection of notes for intending justices, with the principal object of warning them against the devices of unscrupulous attornies. Throughout the eighteenth century the magistrates of London were being constantly harassed by what were known as 'Old Bailey Solicitors', or 'Newgate Solicitors'. These people, who knew every trick of the trade, were always quick to take advantage of the average justice's abysmal ignorance of criminal law and procedure. As the magisterial system made no provision for a qualified clerk, most justices, when conducting their day-to-day judicial business, were completely bereft of any form of professional assistance whatever and were liable, in consequence, to have actions brought against them personally whenever they erred in law.

Soon after his death, De Veil's notes were published under the title, *Observations on the Practice of a Justice of the Peace*. At the outset of the text he administered the warning, 'Justices must be very cautious that they act in all penal statutes according to the letter of the law of that statute'. But the real purpose of the notes, as stated in the preface, was to protect new magistrates from the 'multitude of solicitors and other bad men' who were so prevalent.

In the latter part of his life De Veil became increasingly autocratic and short-tempered with those who appeared before him. He also gave way more frequently to his innate vanity. The memoirs make it clear that, even in his middle age, he was as sexually promiscuous as ever, and that he retained the odious habit of boasting about his amatory adventures. 'He would tell many pleasant stories of a certain gentleman of his own age and calling who had a private closet for the examination of such of the fair sex as were endowed with qualities capable of exciting a certain sort of attention and regard.' De Veil admitted that he sometimes experienced a little difficulty in persuading women to enter this closet, but he claimed that for the most part he was able to fulfil his purpose; his usual compliment on emerging was, 'You see, madam, that I am capable of being particularly diligent and expeditious in doing a lady's business'. In all its history this must have been the only time when the Bow Street Office was put to such a use.

De Veil had a number of mistresses, though they used to cost him very little as the majority of his liaisons were formed with women who were already being kept by another lover. Some of them lived outside London, in the surrounding districts which he was accustomed to visit; so that he was never 'at a loss for a soft companion when in the humour'.

De Veil's obituary notice in the *Gentleman's Magazine* remarked dryly that, 'He served himself by means of his office with a variety of women'. His biographer elaborates on this statement by explaining that whenever a lady of easy virtue appeared before him in the course of his duties, he used to enquire 'if she had a back door to her lodging where a chair might stop without suspicion? At what season her friend was out-of-town or engaged?'

But in spite of his sexual laxity De Veil continued to the end of his life to fulfil his magisterial responsibilities with zeal and energy. He was often placed in situations of extreme danger; never more so, perhaps, than during the footmen's riot about a month before he obtained his knighthood. A full account of this episode was published in *The Daily Advertiser* on 12th March, 1744. Two days previously the footmen of London in a spirit of patriotic fervour, had arranged a meeting at a hall in Panton Street in order to protest against the employment of French footmen by the British aristocracy. The Government feared a major disturbance and ordered De Veil to prevent the meeting from taking place. De Veil ordered the proprietor of the hall to keep all the doors locked, and as an additional precaution, made him deposit the keys at the Bow Street Office.

About half-past six in the evening a large crowd assembled in Bow Street threatening that unless De Veil handed over the keys they would sack his house and put him to death. Several of the ringleaders forced their way inside and confronted the magistrate in his study. There they renewed their demand, but De Veil replied by covering them with a pistol, placing them under arrest, and ordering the servants to bolt the front door.

By this time the mob was increasing both in numbers and in frenzy, and there is little doubt that they were reinforced by a well-known gang of troublemakers. The windows of the office were smashed with stones and hatchets and the front door was broken down. De Veil took up a position at the foot of the stairs, armed with a blunderbuss and six pistols, 'being resolved to die there, and defend to the last moment his poor, terrified family'. The servants had vanished leaving their master to face alone the infuriated hordes which were swarming into the house.

Such was De Veil's intrepidity that no-one dared to attack him and the mob kept their distance, contenting themselves with rescuing their previously arrested companions and wrecking all the property upon which they could lay their hands.

Eventually a posse of troops succeeded in clearing Bow Street and rescuing the besieged inhabitants at the office. De Veil's house, said the newspaper report, resembled a ship after an engagement. He was later awarded £400 compensation for the damage out of the Royal Bounty; but he complained this amount was inadequate and in a petition to the Government, he alleged that the affair had hastened the death of his wife.

A satirical poem which enjoyed a wide circulation shortly after the footmen's riot paid tribute to the courage of De Veil, who 'cool and dauntless saw the Bow Street fray, and taught rebellious lacqueys to obey'.

On the 6th October, 1746, at five o'clock in the evening, Sir Thomas De Veil was at his office examining a prisoner when he suddenly felt very ill. 'A jelly was immediately brought him, which he was accustomed to take when he was at any time faint; he swallowed it, then rose up and went and looked in the glass, stroked his face and then sat down again.' A short while later his condition deteriorated and he lost his speech.

De Veil was an epileptic and it was probably thought at first that this was another of his periodic fits. A surgeon was called who bled and blistered him and ordered him to be put to bed. 'He lay without expressing any sense till the next morning about five o'clock when he expired in the sixty-third year of his age.'

Sir Thomas De Veil was a widower at the time of his death. He was buried at Denham in Buckinghamshire though his connection with that particular locality is unknown.

In any study of the life of De Veil the question must be asked as to whether he really deserved the reputation of a depraved trading justice with which he has been universally stigmatized by posterity. The author of the memoirs, who discusses his character with uninhibited candour, emphasizes his ambition, his extravagance, his promiscuity and his love of pleasure, but never accuses him unequivocally of corruption as a magistrate. In fact, we are told that he kept 'very correct accounts of whatever passed before him' and that 'he was very cautious in all his proceedings'.

There is only one passage in the memoirs which might be interpreted as an insinuation that De Veil sometimes accepted bribes. The author says that many gamblers appeared at Bow Street and they seldom came empty-handed. In spite of this they were 'most unwelcome because no indulgence could be granted, but at the expense of his worship's private reputation, as well as the security of the public'. So far, of course, this is in De Veil's favour. However, these words are followed by the vaguely suggestive sentence, 'And yet they could not be denied . . . ways and means therefore must be used'.

Even if he did accept the occasional bribe from a well-to-do gambler there is strong evidence in support of the contention that De Veil made strenuous efforts to improve the reputation of the Middlesex and the Westminster justices. In his notes for intending magistrates he warned them against the taking of fees or perquisites to which they were not strictly entitled by their oaths of office, in order, as he says, 'to uphold the dignity of that honourable station'.

Moreover, the Middlesex justices' order books for the period show that the magistrates, amongst whom De Veil was one of the leading figures, were becoming increasingly critical of the corrupt behaviour of certain of their colleagues. In 1738 justice Thomas Cotton was accused of taking illegal fees, and in April, 1746, justice Thomas Jones was asked to explain to his fellow magistrates two very dubious incidents with which he had been involved in the course of his official duties. The order book for 1746 also refers to a complaint against a justice Broadhead for extorting money under the cover of his office. He was seen by a group of senior magistrates who attempted unsuccessfully to discuss the matter with him in private, and then reported him to the Lord Chancellor, expressing the opinion that such behaviour was 'illegal, oppressive, and tends to render the Commission despicable'.

In the light of our present knowledge it would seem that Sir Thomas De Veil, the first magistrate at the Bow Street Office, was not entirely deserving of the disrepute which always adhered to his name.

CHAPTER SIX

HENRY FIELDING

WITH the death of Sir Thomas De Veil the Bow Street Office might well have come to an end, for it was not the practice for successive magistrates to occupy the same house. However, De Veil had gone to the expense of converting his office into a private courtroom and this, in all probability, was the principal reason for its continuance in use.

In the past there have been two alternative theories regarding the tenancy of De Veil's house immediately after his death. One group of writers have suggested that another magistrate, Justice Poulson, lived there for the intervening two years before the arrival of Henry Fielding at the end of 1748. Others have contended that De Veil died in October, 1748, not October, 1746, as stated in the memoirs, and that Fielding succeeded him almost at once.

The rating ledgers for the parish of St. Pauls, Covent Garden, prove both these assumptions to be incorrect. The name of Sir Thomas De Veil appears for the last time in their records for the year 1746. In 1747 the occupant of his house is shown as 'Thos. Burdus Esq', and in 1748 it is marked 'No Rates Paid', presumably since there was no tenant for most of the year.

Thomas Burdus was, in fact, a very active justice in the Middlesex and the Westminster Commissions, and he appears to have been the Chairman of the Westminster bench in 1747, the year when he lived in Bow Street, as his name appears at the head of the list of justices in the sessions books for that year. He came from Durham, a county in which he possessed a considerable amount of property, including a number of coal mines.

John Poulson had been an active magistrate for Middlesex and Westminster for a long period. The St. Pauls rating ledgers show that in 1748 he occupied a house with a rateable value of £25 on the east side of Bow Street. Since De Veil's old house, on the opposite side of the road, was unoccupied at that time it is quite possible that Poulson made use of the office there for his official work. Justice Poulson died in December, 1748, a matter of days after De Veil's house was taken over by Henry Fielding.

It is ironical that Henry Fielding, who set a standard of fairness and probity which so profoundly influenced the development of the magisterial system in Britain, should have only become a justice in the autumn of his life, when the flame of his ambition had been quenched, and he was dispirited, broken in health, and resigned to failure in his creative as well as his professional career.

Certainly, Fielding must have had a most endearing character, for we have sufficient opinions from those who knew him personally to gauge the great warmth of their affection for him. As a companion he was generous, gay and amusing. Lord Lyttelton, his lifelong friend, said Fielding had 'more wit than any man I ever knew', and another contemporary wrote that he had been 'for the most part, overflowing with wit, mirth and good-humour'. As he matured his exuberance was tempered by a solemnity of purpose, his levity, by an obsessional antagonism to arrogance, graft and hypocrisy. Throughout, he remained compassionate, observant and receptive. In one of his novels he makes someone remark, 'I am a man myself, and my heart is interested in whatever can befall the rest of mankind'. This was, perhaps, his own guiding philosophy.

Henry Fielding was born in Somerset in 1707. His father, the Hon. Edmund Fielding, a nephew of the Earl of Denbigh, was an impecunious army officer who rapidly squandered the residue of his family fortune, partly on the gambling tables, and partly by his thriftless manner of life. His mother, the daughter of Sir Henry Gould, a well-known judge of the King's Bench, died when Henry was only eleven, leaving her six young children in the care of her improvident husband.

Two years after the death of his wife, Edmund Fielding decided to marry the widow of an Italian immigrant who already had a family of her own. His second marriage gave rise to a family quarrel which resulted in Henry being removed from the care of his father and being appointed a Ward of Court. Sir Henry Gould had died a few years earlier, and

Lady Gould, a forthright and dominating woman, immediately commenced a chancery suit against her son-in-law both to obtain the guardianship of her six grandchildren, and to deprive him of the estate at East Stour in Dorset which the judge had deliberately settled on Mrs. Fielding as a security against her husband's irresponsibility. After a long legal wrangle, judgment was given in favour of Lady Gould; she was granted the custody of the six children, and a trust was set up to administer the income of the East Stour estate on their behalf.

Edmund Fielding, who played no further part in Henry's upbringing, had six sons by his second wife and married twice more after her death. He lived until 1741 by which time he had risen to the rank of Lieutenant-General.

Having succeeded in her action, Lady Gould bought a large house in Salisbury, which was then called New Sarum, to provide her grandchildren with a country home. Henry was sent as a boarder to Eton at the age of twelve; amongst his school-fellows were George Lyttelton, later Lord Lyttelton, who in the course of time was to become his principal patron, and also the future statesman, William Pitt.

It is believed that Fielding left Eton during the summer of 1724, when he was barely seventeen. Although his portrait was never painted during his life, he is known to have been outstandingly goodlooking in his younger days. According to his first biographer, Arthur Murphy, a personal acquaintance, he was over six feet tall, well-built, and possessed of a 'remarkably robust' constitution. Even at the age of seventeen he was headstrong and chose to go out into the world rather than become an undergraduate at a university. Perhaps he shared the sentiments he voiced through a character in his novel, *Joseph Andrews:* 'Being a forward youth, I was extremely impatient to be in the world, for which I thought my parts, knowledge, and manhood thoroughly qualified me.'

In 1725 Henry Fielding commenced his erratic, turbulent, adult life when he went on a visit to Lyme Regis, accompanied by a personal valet. While there he attempted unsuccessfully to abduct a beautiful, teenage heiress with whom he had fallen passionately in love, and as a result, both he and his valet were taken before a local justice and were bound over to be of good behaviour and keep the peace.

Very little is known of Fielding during the years 1726 and 1727, but it is thought that about the end of that period he came to London, where his cousin Lady Mary Wortley Montagu had become a dominant figure in the select circles of intellectual society. In January 1728 he published his first poem, and the following month, under the patronage of Lady Mary, his first play *Love in Several Masques,* was produced at the Drury Lane Theatre with the glamorous actress Anne Oldfield in the leading part. The play ran for four nights, by no means an entirely unsatisfactory achievement for an aspiring young playwright in an age when a run of a month was considered a major success. At any rate the twenty-year-old Fielding was probably not discouraged for, according to Arthur Murphy, 'Disagreeable impressions never continued long upon his mind; his imagination was fond of seizing every gay prospect, and in his worst adversities, filled him with sanguine hopes of a better situation'.

In March, 1728, Fielding enrolled as a student in the faculty of literature at Leyden University in Holland, which at that time was enjoying a notable reputation in the academic world. He broke off his studies at Leyden prematurely in the summer of 1729 because an allowance of £200 a year, promised to him by his father, had failed to materialise, and his own paltry income from his share of the East Stour estate was proving insufficient to maintain him. And so, at the age of twenty-two, he was obliged to earn his own living; as he put it himself, he had no choice but to become, 'a hackney-writer or a hackney-coachman'.

Fielding settled in London towards the end of 1729 with the intention of becoming a professional dramatist. During the next five years he had twelve plays produced, some of which were quite successful and must have made him a not inconsiderable amount of money. However, one of his friends has said that, 'if ever he possessed a score of pounds, nothing could keep him from lavishing it idly, or make him think on the morrow'. As a result he was usually impecunious and he was often living on the verge of destitution.

Lady Mary Wortley Montagu continued to interest herself in her cousin's literary career, but she found it a cause for regret that his plays so frequently suffered from the economic pressure under which they were written. He was forced by necessity, she says, 'to publish without correction, and throw many productions into the world which he would rather have thrown into the fire'. Arthur Murphy confirms Lady Mary's opinion in this respect and reveals that when Fielding had contracted to write a play he would stay out late at a tavern and then work through the night in order to deliver his completed script in the morning.

Henry Fielding's plays were mostly social satires, and as such they bore a contemporary stamp which has precluded their survival beyond his own times. Although very few of the pernicious customs, the absurdities, and the pretensions of the life around him evaded the witty and probing shafts of his pen, it is particularly interesting, in view of his subsequent appointment, to notice his ridicule of magistrates and the law.

Justice Squeezum, in *The Coffee-House Politician,* is portrayed as a London 'trading justice' of the most depraved type. He takes protection-money from the proprietors of brothels and gambling-houses, arrests persons whom he knows to be innocent for the sake of their bail-release fees, and does not control his lecherous instincts when he is interviewing young women in the course of his magisterial duties. In fact, Squeezum is on the bench solely for the illicit profits and the sensual pleasures which arise from his office. In other plays Fielding derides the magistrates in general for their venality and their ignorance.

Lawyers also came in for their share of ridicule in his plays. 'Twelve lawyers make not one honest man', remarks a man in *Don Quixote;* and Fielding attacked repeatedly the extortionate charges made by some solicitors when winding up a testamentary estate.

With regard to the law itself, Fielding criticized the delays, the costs, and the inequalities. 'Golden sands too often clog the wheels of justice and obstruct her course', he makes one of his characters say; 'the very riches which were the greatest

c

evidence of villainy, have too often declared the guilty innocent'.

Those first six years in London, coming at a most formative stage in his development, must have taught Fielding a great deal about human nature. He was introduced to two very different strata of society; on the one hand, the rich, cosseted set amongst whom Lady Mary was an idol; on the other, the mercurial, twilight world of the struggling authors and actors. He moved in turn among the drawing-rooms of the great, and the taverns and coffee-houses of Covent Garden.

Between the theatrical seasons Fielding used to pay regular visits to his grandmother, Lady Gould, in Salisbury. After she died in the summer of 1733 her house was kept on as a home for his sisters. It was while he was staying there that he met his future wife, the beautiful Charlotte Craddock, who was the elder of two sisters, then living with their widowed mother in the neighbourhood. Henry and Charlotte were married at a small village church just outside Bath in November, 1734. It was a virtual elopement, very much against the wishes of Mrs. Craddock, but she soon forgave the couple and when she died a few months later she left Charlotte about £1,500.

Shortly after his marriage Henry Fielding returned to London to resume his career as a playwright. He stayed with his wife at lodgings just south of the Strand, and during their short time there he put on two new plays at Drury Lane. However, on the death of his mother-in-law in February 1735 he and Charlotte returned to the West Country where they remained on a protracted holiday at East Stour for the remainder of the year. Early in 1736 they came back once more to London, and for the next eighteen months Fielding's plays were devoted mainly to political satire, aimed against Sir Robert Walpole's Ministry.

Sir Robert had held his seat in Parliament since 1701, and since 1721 he served continuously as First Lord of the Treasury, in those days the equivalent of the office of Prime Minister. Although he was unquestionably an outstanding debater and a brilliant parliamentarian, his methods of administration were generally acknowledged as being as unscrupulous as they were corrupt.

Walpole had been returned to power once again at the general election in 1734, and his grip on the country seemed almost unshakeable. But during 1735 the opposition benches were strengthened by the acquisition of two exceptionally gifted young men, Fielding's old school-fellows William Pitt and George Lyttelton, both of whom, still in their late twenties, were destined to play important parts in Walpole's eventual downfall.

Fielding had gone into theatrical partnership with an American, James Ralph. Together they formed their own company of comedians and took over the Little Theatre in the Haymarket as a permanent home for their productions.

It was not merely the friendship of Pitt and Lyttelton which prompted Fielding to lend his talents as a satirical dramatist in the campaign against the Ministry. He was spurred on by his aversion to parliamentary corruption, by the means of which, he said, 'the meanest, lowliest, dirtiest fellow will be able to root out the liberties of the bravest people'.

During the period from 1735 to 1737 Fielding became pre-occupied with what he perceived to be the total distintegra-tion of the nation's moral outlook under the debased leader-ship of Sir Robert Walpole. In a succession of satirical comedies he ranged his attacks far and wide, condemning in turn drinking, gambling, luxury, ostentation, humbug, social inequality, and above all, the unjust application of the law. He returned constantly to his criticisms of the cupidity of solicitors, especially when they were employed in winding up the estates of the deceased. 'Two men, it seems, have lately been at law', says one of his characters, 'for an estate which both of them have lost, and their attorneys now divide between them.'

Fielding was one of the first writers to ridicule the system by which debtors, unable to meet their liabilities, might be thrown into prison, and then, 'with both power and will their debts to pay', they were sometimes kept in captivity for the rest of their lives. Most of his disapproval was not of the laws themselves, but of the administration of the legal system. The law, he said, was founded on reason, but now it was in the process of shaking off its founder.

The first of the plays staged by Fielding and Ralph at the Little Theatre was *Pasquin,* which proved so popular it was kept on for a run of over sixty nights. Fielding followed this success with a series of other satires in a similar vein until the summer of 1737. Colley Cibber, the manager of Drury Lane at this time, paid tribute to Fielding's work by saying, 'Religion, laws, government, priests, judges and ministers, were laid flat at the feet of this Herculean satirist'. Not the least remarkable aspect of Fielding's writing during those two years, was that he, a reputed libertine, should have developed such rigid, puritanical tendency in his viewpoint.

At length Sir Robert Walpole could tolerate this raillery no longer. In May, 1737, he rushed a Bill through Parliament making it necessary that every play which was produced for 'hire, gain or reward' should have been previously granted a licence by the Lord Chamberlain. This requirement, which remained in force until 1968, had the effect of terminating Henry Fielding's career as a dramatist; it also resulted in the immediate closure of all the London theatres except Covent Garden and Drury Lane.

During 1737 the family estate at East Stour was sold, the purchase money being divided equally between Henry Fielding, his brother, and his four sisters. Each of them received a rather meagre sum of about £260. By this time Fielding had two daughters of his own and it was essential for him to find a new form of livelihood. Despite his age, for he was then thirty, he decided to enter a profession to which he had been immensely attracted all his life. Leaving his wife and his infant family at Salisbury, he enrolled at the Middle Temple as a student of the Inns-of-Court.

Even Fielding's biographer, Arthur Murphy, who always emphasized the hedonistic side of his nature, agreed that he devoted himself to his legal studies with remarkable intensity, only breaking out occasionally to savour 'the wild enjoyments of the town'. As a result, he completed in less than three years a syllabus which usually necessitated six or seven, and he was called to the Bar in June, 1740. His feat was even more notable in view of the fact that during his final year as a student he had entered into the field of political journalism, and had become the editor of a thrice-weekly opposition newspaper called *The Champion*.

With his personality, ability, and his erudition, Fielding might well have been destined for the High Court bench, but at this stage he began to suffer from the repeated and increasingly severe attacks of gout which eventually transformed him into a helpless cripple. He practised at the Bar, both in London and on the Western Circuit, for about three years, all the time fighting a losing battle against his growing physical infirmity. Eventually he acknowledged the futility of the struggle and he abandoned for ever his aspirations in the law.

On February 2nd, 1742, after nearly twenty-one years in office, Sir Robert Walpole was overthrown, and the political faction to which Fielding had given such steadfast support finally came into power.

A few weeks later Fielding published his first novel, *Joseph Andrews*. Although it was generally well-received, it did not bring him much financial benefit, as he had sold the manuscript outright for the sum of £183 11s. od. But poverty and his own infirmity were not Fielding's only worries at this time. His favourite daughter, Charlotte, died at the age of five, and his wife's health was steadily deteriorating. David Garrick tried to help by reviving one of Fielding's old plays at Drury Lane with a brilliant cast headed by himself, Mrs. Pritchard, Macklin, and Peg Woffington. As so often happens with revivals it proved to be far too dated and was a complete failure.

Fielding's next serious prose publication was his *Miscellanies*, which he brought out in three volumes in April, 1743. Again the work was acclaimed in the literary world, but that year and the next were a period of privation and sorrow for him, culminating with the death of his wife during the autumn of 1744. Later on Lady Mary Wortley Montagu wrote of the relationship between Henry and Charlotte: 'He loved her passionately and she returned his affection; yet they had no happy life for they were almost always miserably poor, and seldom in a state of quiet and safety'.

After the death of his wife, Fielding moved into a house in Boswell Court, on the site of the present Law Courts, to the north of Fleet Street. His sister, Sarah, herself a novelist of some distinction, came to live with him there and other members of the household included his seven-year-old daughter, Harriet, and his late wife's personal servant, Mary Daniel. According to Arthur Murphy, Fielding was so much affected by his bereavement that for a time his friends were afraid he might lose his reason.

Before the end of 1744, George Lyttelton and the Duke of Bedford, both of whom were not only Fielding's friends but were also his admirers and political associates, entered a coalition Ministry under the leadership of Henry Pelham. The following year when Charles Stewart, the Young Pretender, invaded England across the Scottish border, Fielding started up a weekly periodical called *The True Patriot,* designed, as the name implied, to rally support for the nation, the government, and the House of Hanover. After the defeat of Charles Stewart at the Battle of Culloden, the need for patriotic fervour was somewhat abated and the final issue of the periodical appeared in June, 1746.

In addition to his spirited editorship of *The True Patriot,* Fielding was rendering additional assistance to the Government by publishing various tracts and pamphlets in defence of their policies. It might have been expected, especially in view of his straitened circumstances, that he would have been rewarded with some worthwhile appointment in recognition of his labours, but this was not to be. However, some small attempt was made to recompense him by making him a magistrate, for his name appears in a Commission of the Peace for the County of Middlesex, dated 20th June, 1747. How this came about is not known; indeed, it is a fact which has not been noticed by any of Henry Fielding's biographers to date. It is certain that he did not take up his duties as a justice at that time, because he neither swore the oaths of office, nor did he register the necessary property qualification for Middlesex.

The years 1746 and 1747 were largely devoted by Fielding to the writing of his immortal novel, *Tom Jones.* In dedicating the book to George Lyttelton he wrote: 'I partly owe to you my existence during the great part of the time in which I have been employed in composing it'. Perhaps Lyttelton's financial support at this period was not wholly motivated by an admiration for Fielding's literary abilities, but was also attributable to his valuable work as a propagandist for the new Ministry.

In November, 1747, amidst the derision of his critics and his political opponents, Fielding was married to Charlotte's maid, Mary Daniel. At the time he was forty and she twenty-six. A bare three months after the wedding, Fielding's second wife gave birth to a son—a happening which must have caused great delight to his many detractors.

Mary Daniel was no beauty. According to Lady Louise Stuart, Lady Mary Wortley Montagu's grand-daughter, 'The maid had few personal charms, but was an excellent creature, devotedly attached to her mistress and almost broken-hearted for her loss'. She goes on to describe how Henry Fielding and Mary were drawn together by Charlotte's death: 'In the process of time he began to think he could not give his children a tenderer mother, or secure for himself a more faithful housekeeper and nurse'. By a commendable act of friendship and loyalty, the rising politician, George Lyttelton, attended the marriage and gave Mary Daniel away.

Understandably enough, the Fieldings did not continue to live at Boswell Court, but moved to a secluded house in Twickenham. Here, for most of the year 1748, Henry was editing another pro-government paper called the *Jacobite's Journal*, the last edition of which appeared on 8th November, 1748. By then Henry Fielding had embarked upon the final phase of his career, as he had already assumed the office of an active magistrate for the City and Liberty of Westminster.

CHAPTER SEVEN

HENRY FIELDING AT BOW STREET

EARLY in 1748 Henry Fielding passed the bitter comment, 'a heavier load of scandal hath been cast upon me, than I believe ever fell to the share of any single man'.

It was, indeed, an age in which scurrility and vituperation were the accepted currency of public life; when no mercy was asked, and no quarter given between protagonists for differing causes. And Fielding had made a multitude of enemies in his literary and political activities. The notion of Henry Fielding, the idealistic reformer, the impassioned declaimer against corruption, now debasing himself to become a trading justice, was far too good an opportunity for his adversaries to miss.

The journal, *Old England*, mocked his new appointment with a lampoon:

> Now in the ancient shop at Bow,
> (He advertises it for show),
> He signs the missive warrant.
> The midnight whore and thief to catch,
> He sends the constable and watch,
> Expert upon that errand.
> From hence he comfortably draws
> Subsistence out of every cause
> For dinner and a bottle.

Even Lady Mary Wortley Montagu, a faithful ally in the past, wrote in disgust about 'the highest of his preferment being raking in the lowest sinks of vice and misery'. And she added, 'I should think it a nobler and less nauseous employment to be one of the staff officers that conduct nocturnal weddings'.

It is certain that in making Fielding a justice of the peace for Westminster, his friends in the government imagined they were ensuring him a reasonable income for the rest of his life—a significant reflection on the appallingly low reputation of the London magistrates at the time. Even the Duke of Bedford, who had just become Secretary of State for the Home Department, the equivalent of our present Home Secretary, shared in this belief; for some years later Fielding revealed that the Duke had stated on several occasions, 'that he could not indeed say that acting as a principal justice of the peace in Westminster was on all accounts very desirable, but all the world knew it was a very lucrative office'.

A great deal of obscurity still surrounds Henry Fielding's decision to become an active magistrate. In her factual biography, published in 1910, Miss G. M. Godden asserted that his official appointment to the Westminster Commission took place on 30th July, 1748. Unfortunately, Miss Godden did not identify the document from which she derived this knowledge, and it has never come to light in any subsequent research. In the absence of direct information it would seem a reasonable assumption that Fielding made up his mind to adopt a magisterial career during the summer of 1748. He was then an acting, or nominal, justice for Middlesex, but would have been unable to sit at the County Sessions as he had not yet registered the essential property qualification of a freehold, or a leasehold, to the value of £100 a year. However, no property qualification was required by the justices for Westminster, and as the formalities were only minimal, Fielding could be sworn in without much delay. A number of the Westminster Commissions for the relevant period are now missing so it is impossible to verify the date of his appointment from this source.

We know that, initially, Henry Fielding did not propose to take over the Bow Street Office, for on the 25th October, 1748, his sister Ursula wrote to a friend saying that he intended 'to administer justice' from the house at which he was then living in Brownlow Street, near Drury Lane. He did not remain there very long as the *General Advertiser,* reporting one of his cases on the 2nd December, 1748, described him as 'Justice Fielding of Meard's Court, St. Anne's'—which was a tiny cul-de-sac in Soho. Finally, we have the much quoted paragraph in the *St. James's Evening Post* of 8–10th December, denoting his arrival at the Bow Street Office:

Yesterday John Salter was committed to the Gatehouse by Henry Fielding, Esq., of Bow Street, Covent Garden, formerly Sir Thomas De Veil's, for feloniously taking out of a bureau in the house of the Rev. Mr. Dalton, a quantity of money found upon him.

It is apparent from the records of the Westminster justices that throughout the month of November in that year Fielding has been extremely busy, taking recognizances and committing prisoners for trial. Having shown from the outset how seriously he was taking his new responsibilities, it was not altogether surprising that he should have decided to move into the empty Bow Street Office early in December.

In spite of the fact that the basest motives had been attributed to him in becoming a magistrate, Fielding himself regarded his appointment as something of a challenge—perhaps the greatest and the final challenge of his whole life. He was finished as a playwright, he had failed as a barrister; his only novel had been cordially, but unenthusiastically received; he was burdened with poverty and ill health. Above all, his reputation was tarnished, his principles defiled, and his conceptions had been twisted beyond recognition. And yet, he set out on his ultimate mission in a spirit of virtual dedication. He was fully aware of the magnitude of his task—he once likened it to the cleansing of the Augean Stables by Hercules—for by this time the venality of the magistrates and the inefficiency of the constables all over the Metropolis had reached their lowest ebb.

Some idea of Fielding's physical condition when he moved to Bow Street, and also of the malice of his critics, is provided by a letter from a young poet, Edward More, to a friend. More, to whom, incidentally, Fielding had been of considerable assistance, wrote: 'Fielding continues to be visited for his sins so as to be wheeled about from room to room . . . his disorder is the gout and intemperance the cause'.

By sheer good fortune Henry Fielding was brought into contact at that time with two honourable men, Joshua Brogden and Saunders Welch, both of whom shared his views and were ready to join to the utmost in his endeavours. Brogden, who became his clerk at the Bow Street Office, had been a magistrate's clerk before. It had been generally assumed that he was at Bow Street with Sir Thomas De Veil, on the strength of a footnote in Fielding's introduction to his book of reminiscences, *Journal of a Voyage to Lisbon,* which was written some years later. His reference had also provided the principal authority for the accepted theory of De Veil's corruption. What Fielding said was this: 'A predecessor of mine used to boast that he made one thousand pounds a year in his office; but how he did this (if indeed he did it) is to me a secret. His clerk, now mine, told me I had more business than he had ever known there; I am sure I had as much as any man could do'. When Fielding spoke about 'a predecessor', it is not clear whether he means a predecessor at Bow Street, which might narrow the possibilities to De Veil, Purdus and Poulson, or a predecessor as Chairman of the Westminster Sessions, which could be anyone of a number of people, but not De Veil, as he never presided over the Westminster Bench.

A lot more will be said about Saunders Welch in due course, and it is sufficient for the moment to notice that he had occupied the position of High Constable of Holborn for about a year when Fielding came to Bow Street. The office of High Constable was a part-time function which usually lasted for a duration of between one and three years. As a rule, it was performed by a successful tradesman—Saunders Welch was a grocer—and carried no official remuneration apart from a limited scale of allowances, although there were, of course, ample opportunities for illicit profit. Considering the period in which he lived, Saunders Welch was a high constable of quite exceptional honesty and skill. In fact, after working with him for six or seven months, Henry Fielding said he was 'one of the best officers who was ever concerned in the execution of justice, and to whose care, integrity, and bravery the public hath, to my knowledge, the highest obligations'.

At the end of 1748 and the beginning of 1749 Henry Fielding must have wondered where to begin his forlorn crusade against the forces of the underworld. First of all, he had to ensure his own financial security, and declining to boost his income by the unscrupulous devices of the trading justice, he persuaded the government to pay him a regular salary out of public service money. The amount he was given is unknown, but it was probably just sufficient to provide him with a bare subsistence. In addition, he received a meagre income from his magistrate's fees, though he said later that he had reduced this sum from an annual total of £700 'of the dirtiest money on earth', to little more than £300, most of which was used up in the payment of his clerk.

When the Fieldings took up residence at Bow Street their family consisted of two children, Harriet, the surviving child of Henry's first marriage, and their son William who was then barely ten months old. Mrs. Fielding had her second baby soon afterwards, a daughter who only lived another year.

In a letter written by Horace Walpole we are left an account—albeit distorted by irony and prejudice—of Henry Fielding's domestic life at this time. Two of Walpole's rich young friends, Rigby and Bathurst, had taken one of the latter's servants round to Bow Street in the evening to charge him with attempted murder. Upon arriving at the office, they asked for Fielding, but, says Walpole, 'He sent them word he was at supper, that they must come the next morning. They did not understand that freedom, and ran up, where they found him banqueting with a blind man, a whore, and three Irishmen on some cold mutton and a bone of ham, both on one dish—and the dirtiest cloth.' The blind man was Henry's half-brother, John, and the 'whore' was his wife. The three Irishmen might well have been actors as Bow Street was in the heart of the theatrical locality.

London magistrates, like those in the country, dealt with any work which originated in the vicinity of their houses. Owing to the geographical position of the Bow Street office, a number of cases came there from the area of Holborn, which was within the jurisdiction of the County of Middlesex, and others from Covent Garden and the Strand, which were in the jurisdiction of the City and Liberty of Westminster. It was, therefore, desirable for the presiding magistrate at Bow Street to be a justice for both Middlesex and for Westminster.

Henry Fielding took his oaths for the Westminster Commission on the 25th October, 1748. During the next few months he was also permitted to officiate as an acting magistrate for Middlesex, by virtue of his appointment in June 1747. Even so, this was hardly a satisfactory state of affairs, and on the 13th December, 1748, he wrote to the Duke of Bedford:

My Lord,

Such is my Dependance on the Goodness of your Grace, that before my Gout will permit me to pay my Duty to you personally, and to acknowledge your last kind Favour to me, I have the presumption to solicit your Grace again. The Business of a Justice of the Peace for Westminster is very inconsiderable with the Addition of that of the county of Middlesex. And without this Addition I cannot completely serve the Government in that office. But this unfortunately requires a Qualification which I want ...

Fielding continued by asking the Duke to grant him leases of houses, adding up to an annual value of £100, from the Bedford estates. The Duke complied with this request, and on the 11th January, 1749, Fielding was enabled to take the necessary property oath for the Middlesex Commission. Thereafter, he swore the sacramental oath on the 26th March, and the oath of abjuration on the 5th April. He had then completed all the formalities for becoming a full Middlesex justice.

Amongst the records of the Westminster Quarter Sessions there is an entry for the adjourned session commencing on the 17th May, 1749, which reads: 'Mr. Fielding was elected Chairman of this present session and to continue until the 2nd day of the next'. Although there is no note of his subsequent re-election, his name continued to head the list of justices until he ceased to attend, so it may be assumed that he stayed on as Chairman throughout the whole of the time he was an active member of the Westminster Commission.

In an instance of journalistic carelessness the *General Advertiser*, around that time, announced that, 'Counsellor Fielding, one of His Majesty's Justices of the Peace, was chosen Chairman of Sessions at Hicks Hall for the County of Middlesex'. However, the Middlesex records show that justice Thomas Lane was continuously Chairman of Sessions from 1738 until 1752, and that Henry Fielding, in fact, never held this appointment at all.

It has been suggested that Sir Thomas De Veil and his successors at Bow Street were styled unofficially as the 'Principal

Magistrate for Westminster'. There seems to be no basis whatsoever for this theory. Admittedly, Henry Fielding did refer
to himself by such a title, but he was almost certainly alluding
to his position as Chairman of Westminster Sessions. In 1761,
seven years after Henry's death, John Fielding described his
half-brother as having been for some time 'principal acting
Magistrate for the County of Middlesex and City and Liberty
of Westminster'. At one stage there might well have been a
strong rumour that Henry was going to be elected Chairman
of Middlesex, as well as of Westminster Sessions, but never-
the less, John's inaccuracy is a little surprising.

Before Henry Fielding arrived at Bow Street there could
have been very few, if any, full and authentic reports of the
proceedings which took place at a magistrate's house or in his
office, for such matters were regarded as private hearings.
However, from the outset, Fielding arranged for the details of
his cases, written by his clerk, Joshua Brogden, to be published regularly in certain newspapers. His object was not self-
publicity, but rather to inform as wide an audience as possible
of the types of offence then prevalent, the steps he was taking
to overcome them, and to give an occasional dissertation on
the requirements of the criminal law.

A typical example appeared in the *St. James's Evening Post*
in the middle of December, 1748. It was an account of a committal by Fielding on the previous day of a man called Jones,
who had attacked and wounded a young woman with a cutlass.
The report ended:

It is hoped that all Persons who have lately been robb'd or
attack'd in the Street by Men in Sailor's Jackets, in which Dress
the said ones appeared, will give themselves the trouble of resort-
ing to the Prison in order to view him. It may perhaps be of some
advantage to the Publick to inform them (especially at this time)
that for such Persons to go about armed with any Weapon whatever, is a very high Offence, and expressly forbidden by several old
Statutes still in force, on Pain of Imprisonment and Forfeiture
of their Arms.

This was one of the earliest of Fielding's celebrated 'ad-
monitions' to the public which were to play such a large part
in his campaign against crime during the next few years.

A months after his election as Chairman of Westminster

Sessions, Henry Fielding was called upon to deliver a Charge to the Grand Jury of Westminster. This event took place on the 29th June, 1749, and it must have been a significant occasion for him as it was the first time since becoming a magistrate that he had been given the opportunity of making an official pronouncement. Fielding's fellow justices were so impressed by his Charge that they passed a resolution asking him to have it printed and published, 'for the better information of the inhabitants and public officers of this City and Liberty in the performance of their respective duties'. The *Monthly Review* commented: 'This ingenious author and worthy magistrate, in this little piece, with that judgment and knowledge of the world, and of our excellent laws (which the publick, indeed, could not but expect from him) pointed out the reigning vices and corruptions of our times [and] the legal and proper methods of curbing and punishing them . . . .'

Henry Fielding's Charge, copies of which have survived to this day, is a lucid essay in faultless prose, abounding with legal learning, intellectual brilliance and human understanding. He dealt at some length with the history and importance of the Grand Jury system. Then he explained the nature of the offences which would come before the jurors. Finally, he outlined the patterns of licentious behaviour which were at that time pervading the Metropolis.

Perhaps when he spoke about the pernicious effects of libel, Fielding was moved by the recollections of his personal experiences:

If praise and honour, and reputation, be so highly esteemed by the greatest and best of men, that they are often the only rewards which they propose to themselves from their noblest actions; if there be nothing too difficult, too dangerous or too disagreeable for men to encounter, in order to acquire and preserve these rewards; what a degree of wickedness and barbarity must it be, unjustly and wantonly to strip men of of that on which they place so high a value?

Early in 1749 Henry Fielding published his great novel *Tom Jones*. It has been estimated that some ten thousand copies were sold in the first year, although the book was not particularly well received in literary circles, and was bitterly attacked by Fielding's more vociferous critics for what they alleged to be its general tone of immorality.

The hours worked by Henry Fielding in the performance of his magisterial duties were prodigious. He remained on duty nearly every evening, and sometimes stayed up for the whole night conducting examinations and enquiries. In addition, when his health permitted, he used to lead personally the raids carried out by his constables on the gaming houses in the vicinity of Bow Street. A few years later, in paying a tribute to Joshua Brogden, Fielding said that his clerk had sat for 'almost sixteen hours in the twenty-four in the most unwholesome, as well as nauseous air in the universe, and which in his case corrupted a good constitution without contaminating his morals'.

If Fielding had ever doubted that the peace-keeping arrangements in London were hopelessly inefficient, he was given a very good example of their complete inadequacy a few days after he had delivered his first Charge to the Grand Jury. On the evening of Saturday, 1st July, 1749, some sailors alleged that they had been robbed of some money at a brothel in the Strand. They gathered together a crowd of supporters and started a demonstration outside the house in question. The crowd rapidly increased in number and became more violent in temper; no doubt it was joined, in due course, by the usual contingent of trouble-markers who scented an opportunity for excitement and violence.

Two beadles—virtually the non-commissioned officers of the watchmen—came on the scene and endeavoured to disperse the mob. They succeeded in arresting one of the ringleaders, but he was forcibly rescued from their custody, and realizing the hopelessless of the situation they deemed it prudent to withdraw. Subsequently a small body of constables appeared. By this time the crowds were attacking the house; the windows were all smashed, the prostitutes stripped of their clothing, and the furniture was heaped up to be burnt in a huge street bonfire. When the flames from the blaze were threatening the neighbouring buildings on both sides of the road, an effort was made to call the parish engines, but without success.

Seeing that the situation was beyond their control the

constables hurried away to find a magistrate who could summon the assistance of the military. Henry Fielding, however, had gone to the country for the weekend and no other justice could be discovered. The officer in command of the troops at Somerset House in the Strand was informed of the position and he decided, on his own authority, to send out a detachment consisting of a corporal and twelve men. The force, together with the constables, succeeded in clearing the brothel, but was unable to make any impression on the large crowd assembled outside. Eventually they were reinforced by a much stronger contingent of soldiers, and after a great deal of fighting the rioters were finally dispersed at about three o'clock the following morning.

On the Sunday evening the demonstration was resumed. The mob stormed the night-prison and the watch-house, and rescued all the prisoners who had been arrested on the previous night. In the Strand two more brothels were attacked and partly demolished and, as before, the furniture from them was burned in the street.

Towards midnight the riot had reached extremely dangerous proportions. The mood of the crowd was becoming uglier, fires were raging perilously close to the houses, and the constables and watchmen had abandoned any attempt to maintain order. At this juncture the High Constable of Holborn, the redoubtable Saunders Welch, was returning through the Strand after dining with a friend in the City. He took stock of the situation and, as he said afterwards in his sworn information at Bow Street, 'despairing of being able to quell the mob on his own authority, and well knowing the impossibility of procuring any magistrate at that time who would act, (he) applied to the tilt-yard for a military force, which with much difficulty he obtained, having no order for a justice of the peace for the same'.

Saunders Welch returned to the Strand accompanied by an officer and forty soldiers. At Welch's suggestion they marched up the street with drums beating, and this had the desired effect of dispersing the rioters.

The following morning Henry Fielding returned to London and set about the task of examining the prisoners who had been arrested during the weekend. Before the culprits were brought to the office under an armed guard, a massive crowd assembled in Bow Street with the professed purpose of staging their rescue. Fielding addressed the mob from a window of his house, exhorting them to 'depart to their own habitations', and Saunders Welch went out into the Street and made a similar plea from there—but all to no effect. Fielding, therefore, sent word to the Secretary at War requesting a detachment of soldiers to guard his house, and the speedy arrival of the troops might well have accounted for the fact that no serious attempt was made to release the prisoners.

Amongst the persons committed by Fielding as a result of the Strand riots was a youth named Bosavern Penlez, the son of a clergyman, who had been arrested by the watch in possession of a quantity of linen, later identified as having been stolen from one of the demolished brothels. Penlez was convicted at the Old Bailey in August, 1749, for an offence under the Riot Act, and he was hanged at Tyburn two months later. It was doubtful if the charge was a good one as there was no evidence that proclamation under the Riot Act had ever been read. Nevertheless, the Grand Jury had also found a case against Penlez on a capital charge of burglary, but this indictment, supported by far stronger evidence, was never proceeded with at the Old Bailey, by the direction of the trial judge, Chief Justice Wills.

There was a national outcry at the execution of Penlez who, it was alleged, somewhat illogically, was being hanged simply on account of his very laudable detestation of brothels. Equally illogically, Fielding became the scapegoat for public fury on the ground that he should never have committed Penlez for trial in the first place.

Bosavern Penlez was given a hero's burial at the Church of St. Clement Danes in the Strand, and the tirades against Fielding continued for many weeks afterwards, one newspaper going so far as to suggest that, as well as being directly responsible for the young man's death, the magistrate was plainly in secret partnership with the keepers of the three brothels which had been destroyed.

Henry Fielding was so shocked and angered by all this general vituperation, that he published a pamphlet setting out the true facts of the case and justifying his own part in it.

Perhaps he had not yet learned that ignorant abuse, emotional venom, and calculated distortion, will always be the occupational hazards of a magisterial career.

CHAPTER EIGHT

THE WAR AGAINST CRIME

In and around London, towards the close of the 1740's, the highwayman, the footpad, and the house-breaker were consolidating their scarcely-challenged supremacy over the weak and ineffectual parish peace-officers. Horace Walpole was not exaggerating when he wrote in a letter to an absent friend, 'you will hear little news from England, but of robberies; the numbers of disbanded soldiers and sailors have all taken to the road, or rather the street; people are almost afraid of stirring after it is dark'.

Even when criminals had been captured there was an insufficiency of gaols to accommodate them and very often, owing to the shortage of fetters, the prisoners had to be chained together permanently in small groups.

The Government's reaction to the situation was pusillanimous in the extreme. The only method of combating the crime-wave, in their opinion, was to encourage members of robber-gangs to turn King's Evidence, so they offered a special reward of £100, together with a free pardon, to any accomplice in a murder or a robbery who would give information about it, provided that he had not been personally responsible for a killing.

Many of the most thoughtful and the most discerning writers in that age regarded the drift into moral degeneracy with unmitigated gloom. John Brown, in his exposition on *Manners and Principles,* conformed to this view; 'By a gradual and unperceivable decline,' he said, 'we seem to be gliding down from ruin to ruin'.

It would be difficult to assess how much Henry Fielding was infected by the contemporary mood. Certainly his most recent biographer, Mr. F. H. Dudden, considers that around this time he passed through a period of deep melancholy. 'His recent experiences at Bow Street, and his recent researches into the causes of crime', says Mr. Dudden, 'had inspired him with a depressing conviction of an almost universal wrongness of things. His old cheerfulness had well-nigh vanished.' On the other hand, Arthur Murphy, who was probably a visitor to Bow Street, speaks about Fielding's continued hospitality and generosity to his old friends, in a passage which conveys the impression that the ebullient good-humour of his earlier years had not completely deserted him even then.

Henry Fielding was possessed of certain qualities which would have enabled him to become an outstanding magistrate in his own, or in any subsequent generation. He had a fearless independence of spirit, a complete inpartiality of approach, a breadth of human understanding, and an infinite knowledge of law and procedure. He felt very little emotional affinity with his own social class. In 1743 he wrote that, 'the splendid palaces of the great, are often no other than Newgate with the mask on'; and added, 'a composition of cruelty, lust, avarice, rapine, insolence, hypocrisy, fraud and treachery, glossed over with wealth and title have been treated with respect and veneration, while in Newgate they have been condemned to the gallows'.

At a time when the authorities were bereft of any purposeful ideas for the prevention of crime, Fielding propounded an overall scheme which, even if his reasoning was faulty in some respects, provided London with a realistic basis both for its policing and its magistracy.

One of the first problems was to obtain some help in the administration of the Bow Street Office, as there was obviously far too much work to be handled by one justice. On the 21st July, 1749, Fielding wrote to Lord Hardwicke, the Lord Chancellor, enclosing a copy of his Charge to the Grand Jury, and also a vanished document which he described as, 'my Draught of a Bill for the better preventing street Robberies etc., which your Lordship was so kind as to say you would peruse'. He continued:

Your Lordship will have the goodness to pardon my repeating a desire that the name of Joshua Brogden may be inserted in the next Commission of the Peace for Middlesex and Westminster, for whose integrity and Ability in the Execution of his office I will engage my credit with your Lordship, an engagement which appears to me to be of the most sacred nature.

For some reason Henry Fielding never succeeded in getting his clerk appointed a magistrate. However, his wish for an assistant was soon granted, as the records show that his blind half-brother, John, became a justice for Middlesex on the 29th June, 1750, although he did not take his property oath until the following January. In 1751 John also became a justice for Westminster.

A fact which has attracted surprisingly little attention from legal historians is that under Henry Fielding the Bow Street Office, whilst remaining a private room in a magistrate's ordinary residence, was conducted on the lines of a superior court, in an atmosphere of judicial dignity and according to the strictest principles of legal propriety. The office continued to be maintained solely out of the fees which were recoverable by law and by custom from arrested persons, prisoners and applicants for process.

Fielding believed that the public should be entitled to attend at his office, not only when he was performing his judicial functions such as trying cases or taking depositions, but also when he was engaged on his police duties, carrying out the examinations of suspects and witnesses. He never sat for any regular court-hours, but considered himself as being permanently on duty, except on the rare occasions when he was resting in the country.

The Bow Street Office dealt with a great variety of cases. During the first few months of 1749 Fielding committed to the New Prison men and women charged with such crimes as burglary, assault, riot, coining, brothel-keeping and smuggling. He also had to try a host of minor offenders like drunkards, gamblers, prostitutes, vagrants and beggars.

The justice administered by Henry Fielding was a sagacious blending of sternness, understanding and compassion. He respected the life and the property of the law-abiding citizen, and he knew how easily the delicate structure of society could be imperilled by the forces of disorder; therefore, he wasted little sympathy on the robber, the armed thug, the vandal or the rioter. On the other hand, he felt the deepest pity for the neglected victims of an economic system founded upon inhumanity and self-interest.

The vast number of Fielding's cases which were reported in

the newspapers make it possible to form a fairly accurate assessment of his judicial methods. At a time when the law made little or no distinction between the punishment of adults and juveniles, he always showed an especial consideration for the young; for instance, when he tried a boy of twelve on a charge of theft:

The parents of the child (both of whom had an extreme good character) appeared; and the mother fell into agonies scarce to be conceived. In compassion to her, and to the tender years of the child, the Justice, instead of sending him to prison, which would have probably ended with the death of the mother, and in the destruction of the son, recommended to his father to give him an immediate private correction with a birchen rod.

Fielding also sympathised with the wretchedness of the poor. Once he tried three paupers for begging but, 'they appeared to be in so dreadful a condition with sickness as well as with poverty that the Justice . . . dismissed them'. And when a diseased woman was brought before him, charged with stealing some blankets, he bound her over to be of good behaviour and recommended her to a hospital.

The essential kindliness of his character was apparent in every aspect of his work, even in his activities as a criminal investigator. One day a girl came to his office in tears, complaining that she had been robbed of all her money as she had queued for a ticket outside the Covent Garden Theatre. Fielding comforted her and arranged for her to be given a free pass at the next performance.

It would be incorrect to claim that Henry Fielding advocated a more tolerant or a more lenient penal system. The theory of corrective punishment was not propounded until 1764, when the Italian writer Cesare Beccaria wrote his remarkable treatise on the subject. All the same, Fielding habitually made use of the 'bind over' as a penalty for juveniles and for first offenders. Further, he favoured the imposition of less severe punishments for small thefts; 'in which case,' he said, 'the prisoners will be kept apart from the felons and not sent to Newgate as they are now. By this slight alteration of the law, I am convinced the lives of many hundreds of His Majesty's subjects will be saved, and the first theft will often prove the last which, at present, I am afraid, is very rarely the case'.

Fielding often voiced his doubts on the efficacy of the methods then in use for the punishment of minor offenders. In particular, he criticized the sentencing of convicted vagrants to the Bridewells, the houses of detention which existed all over the country for the confinement of the wantonly idle. 'What good consequence can there arise', he asked, 'from sending idle and disorderly persons to a place where they are neither corrected or employed, and where with the conversation of many as bad, and sometimes worse than themselves, they are sure to be improved in the knowledge, and confirmed in the practice of iniquity?'

Again, it seemed to him that it was generally useless to send prostitutes to prison where, at the finish of their sentences, they would be faced with two alternatives; the first, to return to prostitution and to be imprisoned repeatedly until they eventually succumbed to veneral disease; and the second, to become beggars and to swell, 'the prodigious numbers that throng the streets already'.

Before criticizing Fielding for not suggesting any constructive alternative methods of punishment for these sort of offences, it is as well to reflect that even today, over two hundred years later, we have not yet discovered an entirely satisfactory solution to these problems.

An essential factor in Henry Fielding's scheme for the fight against crime was that the Bow Street office should become the nerve-centre for the policing of the whole of Westminster and Middlesex. With no centralised police force, and no effective liaison between the peace officers of the various parishes, it was extremely difficult to achive even a limited co-ordination of effort. To overcome this obstacle Fielding decided to make a direct appeal to the public. On the 20th February, 1749, the following paragraph appeared in the *General Advertiser*:

NOTICE AND REQUEST TO PUBLIC

All persons who shall for the future suffer by robbers, burglars, etc., are desired immediately to bring or send the best description they can of such robbers etc., with the time, place, and circumstances of the fact to Henry Fielding Esq. at his house in Bow Street, or to John Fielding Esq. at his house in the Strand.

Similar notices were published regularly in the newspapers and the Fieldings began to compile a register in which they recorded the details of all the house-breakings and robberies of which they were notified, together with lists of stolen articles, names of suspects, and particulars of the arrests and trials of the culprits.

Henry Fielding was insistent that every law-abiding citizen must co-operate with him in his struggle with the underworld. Sometimes he announced in the Press that he would be examining prisoners in his office at a certain time, and he would invite anyone who had recently suffered at the hands of robbers to attend there for the purpose of making identifications.

As regards his arrangements for policing the Metropolis, Fielding's plan was extremely modest—indeed, it had to be, since he had no regular funds with which to employ a professional, or even a semi-professional force. At that time, Westminster was divided into nine parishes, and had a total of 80 constables and about 300 watchmen in all. It was plain from the outset that this orthodox body of peace-officers would never be capable of enforcing Fielding's aggressive tactics, so he recruited a special group of six volunteer 'thief-takers', all ex-constables who had completed their tours of service, and he formed them into a mobile squad under the command of his able lieutenant, Saunders Welch. These men held themselves in readiness to turn out at a moment's notice, and were the precursors of the force known later as the Bow Street Officers, or the Bow Street Runners, which in the course of time, was to win for itself a world-wide reputation.

After Henry Fielding's death, his half-brother, John, wrote about the formation of the thief-takers. He explained that they had all offered their services after finishing their year of duty as parish constables, because they were 'actuated by a truly public spirit against thieves, and being encouraged by (Henry Fielding) continued their diligence and were always ready, on being summoned, to go in pursuit of villains'. According to John, these men were paid for 'extraordinary and dangerous enterprises', but certainly no such payments have ever come to light in any government accounts for that period. Presumably the thief-takers accumulated a considerable sum of reward-money for successful prosecutions, and for the rest they were bound together, John said, 'by the connections of good fellowship, friendship, and the bonds of society'.

It was, indeed, an extraordinarily amateurish way of policing one of the most important localities in the world. The theory was simple. After a robbery or a house-breaking, a message would be rushed to Bow Street, and the thief-takers, or as many of them as were available, would set out in immediate pursuit. Strangely enough the system worked remarkably well. This was due partly to the fact that the London criminal had never before been confronted by any organised opposition, and also to the ever-increasing knowledge and proficiency of the thief-takers.

Fielding's ideas for the effective control of the criminal went much further than the purposeful reorganisation of the Bow Street office. On the 9th October, 1750, the *General Advertiser* reported:

We hear that an eminent magistrate is now employed in preparing a pamphlet for the press, in which the several causes that have conspired to render robberies so frequent of late, will be laid open; the defects of our laws inquired into, and methods proposed which may discourage, and in a great measure prevent this growing evil in the future.

In January, 1751, Henry Fielding published his *Enquiry into the Causes of the Late Increase of Robbers,* a treatise designed, so he said, 'to rouse the civil power from its present lethargic state'. In the introduction he bluntly stated that, 'The streets of this town and the roads leading to it will shortly be impossible without the utmost hazard'. Even if the robbers were arrested, he went on, they could rarely be brought to justice. They might be rescued by their own gang; the prosecutor might be bribed or intimidated not to proceed; or else, one of the Newgate solicitors might rig up an effective defence for them and procure a number of perjured witnesses to support it.

The first cause of crime, according to Fielding, was idleness and the expensive diversions of the lower classes of society. He attacked in particular the freedom from any sort of control enjoyed by places of public entertainment. Largely as a result of his criticisms, an Act was passed in 1751, bringing the music and dancing halls in London and Westminster under the supervision of the justices of the peace.

Next, Fielding turned to drunkenness; 'this odious vice', he called it; 'indeed, the parent of all others'. He elaborated on the appalling consequences of the continued vogue of spirit-drinking, and suggested higher taxes on gin, and a much firmer control over the places where it was sold. Many of the provisions of the Gin Acts of 1751 and 1753 were based on his proposals. It was the latter of these two statutes which introduced our present system whereby the magistrates deal with the granting or refusing of licences, and are entrusted with a general surveillance of all licensed premises.

In the initial sections of his *Enquiry,* Fielding also criticized the craze for gaming and lotteries, and the application of the Poor Law. He then turned to the defects in the criminal law and criminal procedure. A month after the publication of his work, a Parliamentary Committee was set up under Sir Richard Lloyd, 'to revise and consider the laws in being, which relate to felonies and other offences against the peace'. The Lloyd Committee, of which Pitt and Lyttelton were both members, was strongly influenced by Henry Fielding's views and made a number of recommendations which accorded closely with his suggestions. As a result, several statutes were enacted during the next few years which profoundly affected the future development of the British criminal law.

Writing from his experience at the Bow Street office, Fielding said, 'Now the one great encouragement to theft of all kinds is the ease and safety with which stolen goods may be disposed of'. In the first place, the owner of stolen property frequently inserted an advertisement in the papers, telling the thief that if he returned it he would be handsomely rewarded and no questions would be asked. However, if the loser 'should prove either too honest or too obstinate, to take this method of recovering his goods, the thief is under no difficulty in turning them into money', on account of the great number of pawnbrokers who were only too ready to deal in stolen goods. Fielding suggested that it should be made an offence to compound a theft by means of a public advertisement in a newspaper, and also that the activities of pawnbrokers should be closely regulated by the justices.

At that time the receiving of stolen property was not a specific offence, and a receiver could only be charged as an 'accessory after the fact' to the original theft. This entailed a procedural difficulty, because an accessory could not be tried until the principal offender had been convicted. It followed, in fact, that if the thief managed to escape, or if he was acquitted, the receiver could never be charged at all.

Fielding proposed that the receiving of stolen property should be made an offence in itself, but this did not come about until many years later. However, by an enactment in 1752, any person advertising a reward for the return of lost or stolen goods was made liable to a fine of £50. The Lloyd Committee also inspired a Bill in 1752 which would have made it necessary for pawnbrokers to obtain a justices' licence. This Bill was passed by the House of Commons, but it was held up and eventually shelved by the House of Lords.

In a section of the Enquiry dealing with the apprehension of criminals, Fielding reprimanded the public for failing to give more help to their peace-officers. If a rogue was in trouble in certain areas, twenty or thirty armed villains were ready to come to his assistance, but the constable and the watchman could rely on no support whatever. 'Officers of justice have owned to me,' he said, 'that they have passed by (well-known robbers) with warrants in their pockets against them, without daring to apprehend them.'

It is worth noticing that Fielding never envisaged, or at any rate never mentioned, the possibility of forming a uniformed, professional police force to solve this problem. Instead, he urged that the peace-officers should acquire more knowledge of their powers, and that the private citizens should be more aware of their own duty to aid in the maintenance of public order. Unfortunately, people were not encouraged to arrest felons by the hope of praise; rather were they discouraged by the fear of shame. 'This person of the informer is in fact more odious than that of the felon himself', he commented. 'And the thief catcher is in danger of worse treatment from the populace than the thief.' In praising the resolution of his amateur thief-catchers, he said, 'if to do good to society be laudable, so is the office of thief-catcher; and if to do this good at the extreme hazard of your life be honourable, then is the office honourable'.

Fielding condemned the system by which criminal prosecutions had to be brought by, and in the name of, a private individual, for this resulted in a large number of known offenders never being charged at all. The victim of a crime might be deterred from charging the culprit by threats or intimidation; he might be too indolent to embark on legal proceedings; he might be tender-hearted and, in an era when every felony was nominally a capital offence, averse to taking away the life of a fellow-being; above all, he might be unable or unwilling to bear the costs involved in a prosecution. On this last point Fielding said that rather than bearing the expenses of attending a trial, very often at a great distance from his home, and paying the costs of his witnesses, 'a poor person plundered by a thief usually conceals the felony and accepts his loss'. The answer to this, Fielding suggested, was that the county or the nation should pay the expenses of all prosecutions. This proposal was adopted in part by the Lloyd Committee, and an Act of 1752 gave a court discretion to allow the costs of a poor prosecutor in every conviction for felony. In 1754 another Act empowered a similar award to cover the expenses of witnesses. Many years later Fielding's ideas were implemented more fully and our present procedure was introduced, whereby the great majority of criminal prosecutions are financed out of public or county funds and are presented in the name of the Crown.

When a thief was arrested and brought to trial, Fielding said, he 'still hath sufficient hopes of escaping, either from the caution of the prosecution's evidence, or from the hardiness of his own'. It was particularly difficult to convict street robbers, for usually the prosecution case depended on the testimony of an accomplice, and this by itself was very often insufficient to establish guilt. 'Street robberies,' Fielding wrote, 'are generally committed in the dark, the persons on whom they are committed are often in chairs and coaches, and if on foot, the attack is usually begun by knocking the party down, and for the time being depriving him of his senses.' Even the less barbarous thieves generally took the precaution of 'flapping the party's hat over his face' to avoid identification. Unless the culprits were caught in the act, which was unusual, they were generally acquitted by a jury.

To remedy these latent weaknesses in criminal procedure Fielding suggested two drastic remedies. Firstly, that evidence of the prisoner's bad character should be admissible against him, in spite of the fact that he had not himself adduced evidence of his own good character. And secondly, that once the prosecution had established a *prima facie* case on the uncorroborated evidence of an accomplice, the prisoner should then be required to establish his innocence, 'by proving an alibi, or by some other circumstances; or to produce some reputable person to his character'. The British legal procedure has, in fact, never made the defendant's bad character admissable in evidence, except in very special circumstances; neither has it departed from the general principle that the burden of proof should always be borne by the prosecution. However, Fielding's view that there was a need for a whittling down of the manifold advantages enjoyed by the defence at a British criminal trial has been repeated from time to time by prominent lawyers right up to the present day.

Although he considered that far too many pardons were granted to convicted robbers under the Royal Prerogative, Fielding was intensely critical of the frequency of executions, and of the method in which the hangings were carried out. Fundamentally, a public execution was supposed to produce an atmosphere of terror and shame amongst the onlookers, but 'experience hath shown us that the event is directly contrary to this intention'. The triumphal procession from Newgate to Tyburn; the huge crowds; the condemned prisoner's final speech from the scaffold; the veneration, the excitement, the acclaim—all these tended to turn a day of infamy into a day of glory.

He suggested that executions should be conducted with much greater solemnity and should be witnessed by as few spectators as possible. Further, they should take place very soon after the crime itself, 'when public memory and resentment are at their height'. At the end of a trial, he said, the court should adjourn for four days, and then the prisoner should be brought back, sentenced to death, and executed forthwith just outside the court, 'in the sight and presence of the judges'.

The Lloyd Committee supported Fielding's contention that there were too many executions. His proposal for the speedier carrying out of the death sentence was put into effect in 1752 in respect of executions for murder, by an act which provided that, unless the judge knew of reasonable cause for delay, the condemned murderer was to be hanged two days after the passing of sentence.

Two other suggestions of Fielding's resulted in immediate legislation. The first was that magistrates should have greater powers for suppressing gaming-houses and brothels; the second, that they should be able to arrest beggars and vagrants on suspicion, in order that enquiries could be made concerning their circumstances.

The Enquiry was received with interest and with praise; even Horace Walpole, no friend to Henry Fielding, described it as 'an admirable treatise'. The *Monthly Review* in January, 1751, paid this glowing tribute:

The public hath been hitherto not a little obliged to Mr. Fielding for the entertainment his gayer performances have afforded it; but now this gentleman hath a different claim to our thanks, for services of a more substantial nature. If he has been heretofore admired for his wit and humour, he now merits equal applause as a good magistrate, a useful and active member and a true friend to his country. As few writers have shown so just and extensive a knowledge of mankind in general, so none ever had better opportunities for being perfectly acquainted with that class which is the main subject of this performance.

CHAPTER NINE

THE LAST PHASE

IN spite of his continued ability to undertake a prodigious amount of work, Henry Fielding's health was deteriorating rapidly. On the 28th December, 1749, the *General Advertiser* anonunced: 'Justice Fielding has no mortification in his foot as has been reported: that gentleman has indeed been dangerously ill with a fever, and a fit of the gout . . . and is now so well recovered as to be able to execute his office as usual'. The paper also disclosed that Fielding was undergoing treatment from a Dr. Thomson, who was, in fact, a well-known quack.

The truth of the matter was that Fielding was striving desperately to arrest his progressive decline, and he was trying out one remedy after another. Sometimes he achieved a short-term alleviation of his suffering and then he was restored, as he said, to 'that cheerfulness which has always been natural to me'; but invariably the 'cures' brought him no lasting relief, and usually he was thrown back into the depths of despair.

His physical appearance must have borne the marks of his frequent bouts of illness, for a clergyman who met him at a dinner party in the early part of 1751 referred to him cruelly in a letter as, 'a poor, emaciated, wornout rake'.

Like many middle-aged men in failing health, Henry Fielding was perpetually worried about the future of his wife and children after he was dead. His meagre income was barely sufficient to meet the day-to-day expenses of their home, and even the money he earned from his writing was quickly expended on the urgent necessities of living. Yet he steadfastly refused to derive any dubious financial benefits from his position as a magistrate. In the last year of his life, recollecting the poverty of his final winter at Bow Street, he described 'the gloomy aspect' of his private affairs and truthfully added, 'for I had not plundered the public or the poor of those sums which men, who are always ready to plunder both as much as they can, have been pleased to suspect me of taking'.

In spite of his constant anxiety about sickness and money, Fielding never deviated from his ultimate object of establishing the Bow Street Office both as a well-conducted court of justice and as an efficient police-centre for Westminster and the surrounding districts.

After his half-brother John had settled in as his assistant at the end of 1751, Henry had more opportunity to concentrate his attention on the suppression of the housebreaker and the highway-robber. But even with two active magistrates at Bow Street, the pressure was in no way abated, and on occasions Henry Fielding was known to have spent between fifteen and twenty hours continuously investigating a single case. The newspaper reports of the period bear witness to the fact that the Office was seldom idle. *The Gentleman's Magazine* in February, 1751, announced that on the previous evening, 'Justice Fielding having received information of a rendezvous of gamesters in the Strand, procured a party of guards, who seized forty-five at the tables, which they broke to pieces, and carried the gamesters before the justice, who committed thirty-nine to the Gatehouse and admitted six to bail'. In a subsequent edition of the same paper it was disclosed that at four o'clock one morning Henry Fielding had led a raid on premises where a masquerade was in progress, in a search for some highwaymen. Henry 'obliged the company to unmask and give an account of themselves', but all to no avail for the report continued, 'It is supposed that these fellows had notice of his coming before he could get upstairs and so made off in the crowd, for none of them were taken'.

The duties of a London magistrate in the eighteenth century were by no means free from danger. In such a lawless age an act of vengeance could be perpetrated comparatively simply in the dark and unprotected streets, and even during interrogations or committal proceedings the suspect and the prisoner often reacted with violence.

The *General Advertiser* in January, 1753, recounted an incident which had occurred at Bow Street when Henry Fielding was examining two men charged with the theft of five silk handkerchiefs. 'They behaved in a very impudent and saucey manner', the paper stated, 'and one of them said he wished he had a pistol about him to blow the Justice's brains out'. Eventually the situation became so disorderly that a party of soldiers was summoned to remove the prisoners to Newgate.

Henry Fielding never tired of urging his view that the manifold defects in the law, combined with the difficulties in bringing a successful prosecution, were enabling far too many guilty criminals to avoid conviction. Sometimes he used to invite influential people to visit the Bow Street Office to witness for themselves the inadequacies of the system. In February, 1753. *The Covent Garden Journal* reported that a number of Members of Parliament had watched Fielding examing suspects at his office, and had reported that they were 'sensible of the necessity of a law to detain all such suspicious vagabonds till they can be advertised and seen by persons lately robbed'. However, Parliament was not to enact any statute on these lines for many years to come. It is likely that Fielding was voicing a personal sentiment in his novel *Amelia* when he made a magistrate declare, 'And to speak my opinion plainly, such are the laws, and such the method of proceeding, that one would almost think that our laws were rather made for the protection of rogues than for the punishment of them'.

The public soon became accustomed to Fielding's incessant appeals for information regarding the commission of crimes. Every week *The Covent Garden Journal* published a notice:

All persons who shall for the future suffer by Robbers, Burglars etc. are desired immediately to bring or send the best Description they can of such Robbers etc. with the Time and Place, and the circumstances of the Fact to Henry Fielding Esq. at his house in Bow Street.

In addition to all his other activities Fielding was still finding time to write, and he published *Amelia* in December, 1751, for the copyright of which he received the sum of £1,000 from Andrew Millar, the printer. The advent of another novel by Henry Fielding evoked a great deal of interest in literary circles, but on the whole the work was badly reviewed, one of the few favourable comments coming from his stern critic, Dr. Samuel Johnson, who said that he had read it through without pausing from beginning to end; later on Dr. Johnson described *Amelia* as being 'the most pleasing of all the romances'. The character of *Amelia* in the story was generally recognized to be drawn from the memory of Fielding's beloved first wife. Lady Mary Wortley Montagu also believed that in creating the other principal figure in the book, Captain Booth, Henry had given his readers 'a true picture of himself'.

At the time *Amelia* was published Henry Fielding was on the point of embarking on the last of his journalistic ventures, *The Covent Garden Journal.* Many of his friends sought to dissuade him from editing a new paper as they considered that it would not be in keeping with the reputation for impartiality and detachment he was achieving as a magistrate. But Fielding was convinced that this periodical would provide him with a perfect medium for the advancement of his ideas on legal and social reform.

The first number of *The Covent Garden Journal* appeared on the 4th January, 1752. In setting out its editorial policy, Fielding announced that although the paper was to be non-political, it would discuss the matters of public importance which were largely ignored by the rest of the Press. At the start it was a bi-weekly, being published on Tuesdays and Saturdays, but after about six months it was restricted to one issue a week. Very little information has ever emerged concerning either the financial supporters, or the members of the staff of *The Covent Garden Journal.* It appears to have been produced by Henry Fielding and a small group of assistants, one of whom was Joshua Brogden, the Bow Street clerk, and another, it has been suggested, might have been Henry Fielding's first biographer, Arthur Murphy.

A regular feature in the journal, under the heading 'Covent Garden', was an account of some of the cases which had come before Fielding in his office. These were not reported for their sensational appeal, or even for their intrinsic news value, but rather in an effort to instruct the public in the initial phases of criminal procedure, and often, to show how the defects in the law, and the inefficiency of the policing system, enabled so many guilty prisoners to slip through the net.

The Covent Garden Journal also carried the news of the day, articles, satires, readers' letters and advertisements. The last edition appeared on the 25th November, 1752, when Fielding announced that he had 'neither the inclination nor the leisure' to continue with it. In his final Editorial he urged his subscribers to start taking the *Public Advertiser*, the name which was to be adopted by the old *General Advertiser*. Henceforth all the Bow Street announcements would appear in this paper, and Mr. Brogden, 'with the consent of Justice Fielding', would contribute the criminal news.

In the early part of 1753, Henry Fielding became personally and emotionally involved in a case which will remain for all time one of the greatest mysteries of legal history. The story commenced on January 1st when an eighteen-year-old girl, Elizabeth Canning, from the City of London, spent the day with her aunt and uncle in Middlesex. In the evening they escorted their niece as far as Moorfields where they left her to walk home by herself. Miss Canning then disappeared and was not seen again until twenty-eight days later, when she turned up one night at the house of some friends in London; she was in a pitiful condition, weak, pale and emaciated, and wearing scarcely any clothing.

As soon as she had sufficiently recovered, Elizabeth told her story. Shortly after her aunt and uncle had left her on New Years Day, she said, two unknown men had attacked and robbed her. She had been dragged to a house where an old gypsy woman and two girls had tried to persuade her to stay with them and become a prostitute. When she had refused they had stripped her half naked, forced her up some stairs, and locked her in an empty hayloft; she had been warned that if she uttered a sound there her throat would be cut. Miss Canning told how she had stayed in the loft for a whole month, seeing no-one, and subsisting on a mince pie she happened to be carrying in a pocket, and a few pieces of mouldy bread which she had found on the floor, together with a jug of water. Eventually, half-starved and desperate, she had forced her way out and escaped. She could provide no clue as to the whereabouts of the house in which she had been held captive, except that on one occasion, through a crevice in the hayloft wall, she had seen the Hertford stage-coach passing by along the road.

Friends and neighbours of the Canning family, appalled by Elizabeth's ordeal, raised a fund to prosecute her captors. They drove her in a coach along the Hertford road to see if she could identify the house, and she selected one at Enfield-Wash which was, in fact, a brothel run by a woman known as Mother Wells. Inside the house Miss Canning was able to identify the old gypsy, who turned out to be a widow named Mary Squires, and a prostitute who bore the somewhat inappropriate name of Virtue Hall.

Elizabeth Canning's supporters carried all the occupants of the house before a local magistrate who conducted an enquiry as a result of which the two older women were committed to prison, Mother Wells for keeping a disorderly house, and Mary Squires for stealing part of Miss Canning's clothing. Why the justice did not deal with the far more serious matter of the unlawful confinement has never been disclosed.

Miss Canning returned home, 'where she continued to languish in a very deplorable condition'. Her friends, feeling aggrieved by the course of events, consulted Mr. Salt, a solicitor, to see if they might bring further charges against her captors. Mr. Salt advised that the case should be referred to Henry Fielding for 'counsel's opinion'.

At this juncture it is as well to recollect that very few persons outside the Government were aware that Fielding was being paid for his magisterial services. Officially he still ranked as a part-time, lay justice, and he was quite free to earn his own fees as a practising barrister.

Henry Fielding has written in considerable detail the story of his involvement in the Elizabeth Canning affair. On Friday the 6th of February, he said, as he was preparing to go into the country for the weekend, Mr. Salt called round to Bow Street with a set of instructions for counsel's advice. Fielding sent a message through his clerk that he would take the papers away with him, but Mr. Salt insisted on seeing him personally and asked him to read the instructions there and then, as it was a matter of the utmost importance. Fielding reluctantly complied with this request, and Mr. Salt then asked him to interrogate Elizabeth Canning himself, and also

added that, 'it was the very particular desire of several gentlemen of that end of the town that Virtue Hall might be
examined (by him) relating to her knowledge of this affair'.

Fielding's account continued: 'This business I at first declined, partly, as it was a transaction which had happened at
a distant part of the County (of Middlesex), as it had been
examined already by a gentleman, with whom I have the
pleasure of some acquaintance, and of whose worth and integrity I have, with all, I believe, who know him, a very high
opinion; but principally, indeed, for that I had been almost
fatigued to death, with several tedious examinations at that
time, and had intended to refresh myself with a day or two's
interval in the country, where I had not been, unless on a
Sunday, for a long time'.

In the end Henry Fielding gave way to Mr. Salt's entreaties
and postponed his departure from London. Next day he
examined Elizabeth Canning and was deeply moved by her
story for, as he wrote, 'there is something within myself which
rouses me to the protection of injured innocence'. It was in
this impassioned state of mind that he rashly confused his
professional with his magisterial duties by issuing warrants
for the arrest of all the residents at Mother Wells' establishment. In the course of his subsequent examinations of the
prisoners, Virtue Hall, the prostitute, confessed to the absolute truth of Elizabeth Canning's statements.

At the Old Bailey in February, 1753, Mary Squires was
convicted of the robbery of Miss Canning's clothes and sentenced to death, in spite of the fact that she produced a number of witnesses to testify that she had been in Dorset at the
time of Miss Canning's abduction. Mother Wells was convicted as an accessory after the fact to the robbery, and she
was sentenced to be burned in the hand and imprisoned in
Newgate for six months. The first part of the sentence was
carried out immediately and an onlooker described how a
crowd of enraged spectators 'shouted with delight at the smell
of the burning flesh'.

After the trial was finished the case remained a focus of
public attention. Two opposing factions were formed; some
holding that the convictions had been proper, and others,
that Elizabeth Canning and Virtue Hall had committed per-

jury and that Miss Canning, in reality, had staged her own disappearance in order to spend a month with a lover, to procure an abortion, or to be treated for syphilis. As the argument raged, newspapers, periodicals and pamphlets came out in support of both sides.

The Lord Mayor of London, Sir Crisp Gascoyne, who had attended the trial, had been extremely disquieted by the verdict. Not only did he find it difficult to believe Elizabeth Canning's evidence, but also there were several discrepancies between her initial description of the place of her captivity, and what was later discovered from an inspection of Mother Wells' house. Sir Crisp carried out a private interrogation of Virtue Hall during which she told him that her statement to Henry Fielding and her evidence at the Old Bailey had both been false. He therefore obtained a respite of sentence for Mother Wells and Mary Squires, and pressed for the whole matter to be re-opened.

As a result of the Lord Mayor's intervention, and a subsequent enquiry by the Law Officers, Mother Wells and Mary Squires were pardoned, while Elizabeth Canning was indicted for perjury. In due course Miss Canning appeared at the Old Bailey, where she was convicted and sentenced to one month's imprisonment in Newgate, followed by seven years transportation. Fielding continued to believe in her innocence, convinced that she had been starved by the two older women to compel her to become a prostitute. Naturally enough, Fielding himself was assailed for his own part in the affair and it was alleged that he deliberately extorted false information from Virtue Hall. He answered these accusations in a pamphlet, *A Clear State of the Case of Elizabeth Canning*, from which I have taken my previous quotations.

To the end of her life Elizabeth Canning maintained that her story had been perfectly true. Whilst serving her sentence in New England she married a well-to-do farmer of good family by whom she had five children. She only once returned to England, on a short visit some years later, and she died in America in 1773, at the age of thirty-eight.

Henry Fielding's last winter at Bow Street coincided with a serious outbreak of criminal violence in London. A short while later John Fielding wrote: 'About the latter end of the year 1753 a most notorious gang of street-robbers, in number about fourteen, who divided themselves into parties, committed such daring robberies, and at the same time such barbarities, by cutting and wounding those they robbed, in every part of this Metropolis, as to spread a general alarm through the town, and deterred his Majesty's subjects from passing and repassing on their occasions after night'. King George II, in his speech from the throne in November of that year, remarked, 'It is with the utmost regret I observe that the horrid crimes of robbery and murder are, of late, rather increased than diminished'. The Government was at a complete loss how to deal with the situation. In desperation they turned to Henry Fielding.

Fielding, who was by then a very sick man, was on the point of journeying to Bath as a last chance of restoring his health. When he received a summons from the Duke of Newcastle, the Secretary of State of the Home Department, he was, to use his own words, 'almost fatigued to death with several long examinations, relating to five different murders, all committed within the space of a week, by different gangs of street-robbers'. However, the following morning he called on the Duke at Newcastle House in Lincoln's Inn Fields. He was treated with extreme discourtesy. After he had been kept waiting in an unheated ante-room for a considerable time, someone came and told him that the Secretary of State was too busy to see him, but wanted him to prepare forthwith 'the best plan which could be invented for putting an immediate end to those murders and robberies which were every day committed in the streets'.

With his usual devotion to public duty, Fielding overlooked the incivility of his reception at Newcastle House and postponed his trip to Bath until the new task was completed. 'Though this visit cost me a severe cold', he wrote, 'I, notwithstanding, set myself down to work; and in about four days sent the duke as regular a plan as I could form, with all the reasons and arguments I could bring to support it, drawn on several sheets of paper'. His proposals were laid before the Privy Council without delay and were received with warm approval.

Although the actual text of Fielding's plan has not survived the main components are well-known. Henry Fielding himself has written, 'The principal and most material (of the proposals) was the immediately depositing of six hundred pounds in my hands; at which small charge I undertook to demolish the then reigning gangs, and to put the civil policy into such order, that no such gangs should ever be able, for the future, to form themselves into bodies, or at least to remain any time formidable to the public'.

Fielding did not require this sum for the purpose of paying his constables; in fact he never seems to have envisaged a professional police force, but rather he preferred to rely on a small band of dedicated, unsalaried thief-takers. He had made it clear that he had never approved of blood-money payments to those who brought about a successful prosecution; for these rewards, he said, 'instead of curing the evil, had actually increased it; had multiplied the number of robberies; had propogated the worst and wickedest of perjuries'. Therefore, he had prevented the Government from reviving the proclamation offering £100 for the apprehension of a felon, which had been costing the country several thousand pounds a year. Instead, he suggested a much more modest outlay on his new plan.

The proposals which Fielding put forward were simple in the extreme. He wanted a magistrate to be constantly on duty at the Bow Street Office, and the public were to be encouraged by frequent advertisements in the papers to supply the Office there with immediate particulars of all crimes. The thief-takers, 'all men of known and approved fidelity and intrepidity', would be kept at instant readiness to set out in pursuit of criminals. Pawnbrokers, innkeepers, and managers of stables would be kept notified, again by notices in the Press, of the details of all robberies. He needed the £600 for the hire of horses, the employment of messengers, the cost of advertisements, and the bribes he would have to offer to informers.

In October, 1753, the Privy Council authorised a grant of £200 to be made to Fielding as a first instalment of the sum he had requested. A few weeks later an informer was bribed to disclose the hideout of the robber-gang to the Bow Street

Office. The thief-takers attacked and after a ferocious battle in which both sides suffered fatal casualties, seven robbers were captured and the rest were dispersed. Consequently, said Fielding, 'instead of reading of murders and street-robberies in the news almost every morning, there was in the remaining part of the month of November, and in all December, not only no such thing as a murder, but not even a street-robbery committed'.

By this time Henry Fielding's strength had been 'reduced to the last extremity', and he was even too weak to make his proposed journey to Bath. He handed over the Bow Street Office to his half-brother and went to live at Fordhook, his farm in Ealing, which he had acquired a year previously. In addition to his gout he was now afflicted with jaundice and dropsy. Although he recovered sufficiently to resume his magisterial duties for about a fortnight in the latter half of February, 1754, and again for a very brief spell the following April, it seemed that no remedy could arrest his decline. Writing about that winter he has said, 'so ghastly was my countenance, that timorous women with child . . . abstained from my house, for fear of the ill consequence of looking at me'.

On the 30th March, 1754, the *Evening Advertiser* paid one of the very few public tributes ever received by Henry Fielding in his lifetime for his tremendous achievements in the suppression of violent crime. After expressing regret at Fielding's continued illness, and appreciation of his successful methods, the paper continued:

The whole plan, we are assured, is communicated to Justice John Fielding and Mr. Welch, who are determined to bring it to that perfection of which it is capable; so that, if the public do not, by the most gross supiness, continue the evil, street-robberies will soon be unknown in this town.

In the spring of 1754, Henry Fielding was warned by his doctors that his only chance of survival lay in his moving immediately to a warmer climate. He has written of his decision to travel to Portugal and of his subsequent journey there, in the most moving of all his works, *The Journal of a Voyage to Lisbon*. He left Fordhook on June 26th. 'On this day', he said, 'the most melancholy sun I had ever beheld arose'; for he was aware that he was about to see his beloved young family for the last time. He then set off with his wife and his second daughter, Harriet, to board *The Queen of Portugal* at Rotherhithe. At the docks, Saunders Welch had to carry him on to the ship because he had lost the use of his legs. They passed between rows of laughing, jibing sailors and watermen; 'a lively picture', remarked Fielding, 'of that cruelty and inhumanity in the nature of men, which I have often contemplated with concern'.

Their party reached Lisbon six weeks after leaving Ford-hook. In the warmer climate Henry's health improved a little, but both he and his wife suffered an agony of homesickness for their family and their friends. Among the surviving pages of his letters to John, written from the ship and from Portugal, there is no enquiry—indeed, no reference whatsoever—to the work at the Bow Street Office.

Henry Fielding died on 8th October, 1754. He was buried in the graveyard of the British factory in Lisbon. His fellow-countrymen had so little realization of their indebtedness to him that his grave was allowed to become overgrown and neglected. It was only in 1830 that the site of his final resting place was bought for the nation and a memorial was erected there to his memory.

CHAPTER TEN

JOHN FIELDING AND SAUNDERS WELCH

THE death of Henry Fielding passed almost unnoticed in England, except amongst the small circle of his own acquaintances. Even Lady Mary Wortley Montagu, a staunch admirer and a close associate in his younger days, commented unemotionally in a letter to her daughter, 'I am sorry for H. Fielding's death, not only as I shall read no more of his writings, but I believe he lost more than others, as no man enjoyed life more than he did'.

By then Fielding's reputation was at a very low ebb. For years he had suffered from the venom of his political adversaries and the spitefulness of his literary rivals; his personal life, his books, and his magistracy, had all been continuously besmirched, and the campaign of vilification had influenced a number of people who should have been better informed. Boswell once more remarked that Dr. Johnson had 'an unreasonable prejudice against Fielding', to whom he alluded variously as 'a blockhead' and 'a barren rascal'; perhaps this dislike was partly occasioned, as Dr. Burney suggested, by the profligacy of so many of the male characters in Fielding's novels. It is scarcely credible that rumours of Fielding's venality persisted well into the nineteenth century. Sir Walter Scott, writing in 1820, described him as having held, 'the then disreputable office of Justice of Peace for Westminster and Middlesex, of which he was at liberty to make the best he could by the worst means he chose'.

Probably John Fielding was too much of a realist to suppose, when he took over his half-brother's duties at Bow Street, that he was treading a path which would lead him to honour and acclaim. John, a son of the Hon. Edmund Fielding's second wife, had been born in Westminster in the winter of 1721, at a time when Henry, aged fourteen, was just completing his second year at Eton.

Very little is known about John Fielding's early life. He

was brought up, partly in Westminster and partly in Dorset, and it is likely that the atmosphere of his childhood homes was never particularly stable or happy as, after his mother's death when he was only six, his erratic father lost no time in marrying a third wife; and further, none of his five brothers appear to have survived their youth. There is evidence that John entered the Navy, but the loss of his sight would inevitably have terminated his sea-going career.

John wrote of his blindness in the preface to a collection of essays which he published some years later. 'An accident, which everyone but myself deemed a misfortune', he said, 'forced me into retirement at the age of nineteen . . . The rational delights of reflection, contemplation, and conversation soon made me insensible of any loss I had suffered from the want of sight.' Notwithstanding his courageous and philosophical acceptance of his infliction, John Fielding was affected for the rest of his life by the over-sensitiveness which is so often a characteristic of the severely disabled.

In February, 1749, when he had been blind for nearly ten years, John became the resident manager of a firm called the Universal Register Office, which he and Henry Fielding set up at premises in the Strand. Henry was a partner in name only, as at that time he was just settling in as a magistrate at Bow Street. The Universal Register Office began as an employment agency, but gradually extended the scope of its activities to include house and insurance agency, money-lending, the exchange of currency, buying and selling and a host of other activities.

John and Henry Fielding had always been very devoted to each other and now that their homes were separated by such a short distance they undoubtedly met very frequently. One can imagine how John became infected by his half-brother's passionate interest in the suppression of crime, culminating in the suggestion that he himself should become the assistant magistrate at Bow Street. But the Universal Register Office still occupied a great deal of John's time—it was usually open from nine o'clock in the morning until seven o'clock in the evening—and although he was appointed to the Middlesex Commission on the 29th June, 1750, he did not take the property qualification oath until the 15th January, 1754. He joined the Westminster Commission in 1751, but the Sessions' records indicate that he remained inactive until after the summer of 1753.

In November, 1751, John was married to Elizabeth Whittingham of Lichfield in Staffordshire. They had no children, but his bride's adopted niece, Mary Ann, came to live with them and was always treated as their own daughter. A miniature by Nathaniel Hone, painted in 1757, depicts a group consisting of John and his wife with a pretty, vivacious-looking girl, who might be about eleven or twelve years old. When Mary Ann Whittingham was in her late 'teens she consolidated her connection with her uncle's family by marrying Henry Fielding's youngest son, Allen.

It is a matter of regret that no contemporaries of the Fieldings have left a description of the two half-brothers together, illustrating the warmth of their relationship. There are several letters from Henry to John, still in existence, which were written during the last tragic months, both from the ship which carried him on his final journey and from his temporary home in Portugal. These letters commence, 'Dear Jack' and end, 'Your affec' Brother, H. Fielding'.

The fact that John Fielding had moved into his half-brother's house in Bow Street was noted in a paragraph in the *Public Advertiser* on the 13th June, 1754, about the time when Henry was arranging his passage to Lisbon. De Veil's lease had then a further twelve years to run, but without awaiting the formal date of expiry, John was to take out a new twenty-one-year lease on the 11th June, 1763, again at a rental of £10 a year.

After Henry Fielding's death, his widow and daughter returned to England and John immediately assumed responsibility, not only for them, but also for the rest of his late half-brother's family. It was he who organized the sale of Henry's valuable collection of books, and who planned and supervised the education of his sons. In 1755 *The Journal Of a Voyage to Lisbon*, edited by John Fielding, was published for the benefit of Henry's widow and children.

Despite all John's efforts it was plain that his own small income was being stretched to its utmost limits. In 1756 he wrote to Lord Barrington, the Secretary of State for War, suggesting that Mary Fielding should receive a pension from the Government. 'When my brother died', he said, 'he left little more than would answer his just debts, and left a widow and four children, one of which is since dead. This family I have taken to myself and hope from my own labours so long as I live to support them handsomely'. John went on to state that he had told his sister-in-law, 'so long as I have one shilling in the world they shall have the same share of it as if she was my own wife, they my own family'. His proposal was rejected by the Government and he had to continue supporting Henry's family as best he could from his limited resources. In another letter written to the Duke of Newcastle a year later he disclosed, 'I allow my late brother's widow and children one hundred pounds a year out of my salary payable quarterly'. In addition, he used to give money to Henry's surviving sister who had retired to Bath.

As it emerges from his letters and essays, John Fielding's character was predictable and uninvolved; indeed, on many occasions his vanity and self-satisfaction were carried to the point of naïvety; for example when he wrote to Grenville in 1763, 'I know no man's public or private character that will bear a stricter scrutiny than my own, which is my glory and my happiness, and few men have been more industrious to render services to his country nor many more successful'. On the other hand, he was a man of immense integrity, with a kindly disposition which was too often concealed beneath a certain pomposity of manner.

John never allowed his blindness to ruin, or even to circumscribe his life. For him, the darkened world of his maturity always retained its simple fascinations. Thomas Whitehead, a former footman to the Duke of Kingston, published a book of reminiscences in 1792 in which he provided a brief, but revealing glimpse of John Fielding in moments of relaxation. Sir John, as he had then become, was a distant kinsman of the Duke and used to visit him at his various country residences. One summer, Whitehead recounted, Sir John and Lady Fielding spent a week as guests of the Duke at Pierrepoint Lodge. 'As it was very warm weather, Sir John had an inclination to bathe, there being a fine trout river at the south end of the lodge . . . I offered my assistance with

his man to attend him . . . Another time, Sir John was invited
to Thoresby where he was much delighted with the amusements it afforded: he was particularly pleased with the yacht
in the large patch of water; climbing up the railing, quite to
the yard-arm, and feeling out every part of the vessel; thus
amusing himself on board for an hour at a time or more. In
the evening he was placed by the side of a brook, with rod
and line: I have seen him catch perch of a pound weight as
fast as his servant could bait his hook.'

Considering the age in which he lived, John Fielding's
views on punishment were enlightened and progressive. For
at that time the concept of a sentence directed at redemption'
and reform, of a penal system imbued with humanity, of the
retention of an ultimate human dignity, even by the outcast
and criminal, were still unborn. Nearly every offence carried
the penalties of hanging, flogging, transportation or the pillory; and these were administered regardless of circumstances,
regardless of age, and regardless of sex. John took the view
that public hanging should only be used as a punishment for
the worst type of crime. 'Surely', he wrote, 'when it is necessary to make public examples by executions, wisdom, policy
and humanity dictate that the most abandoned, dangerous
and incorrigible offenders should be pointed out for this
melancholy purpose.'

John Fielding had an especial interest in the helpless and
the young. He considered that sending boys to prison was
'much more likely to corrupt than reform their ways'. He was
convinced from his experiences at Bow Street of the desperate
need of some welfare scheme for 'the vast number of wretched
boys, ragged as colts, abandoned, strangers to bed, who lay
under bulks, and in ruinous empty houses in Westminster
and its environs', to prevent them from degenerating into
footpads and pickpockets. His suggestion was that these
juvenile vagrants might be given the opportunity of a career
at sea, either in the navy or the Merchant Service.

In 1756 John had the opportunity to put his ideas into
practice when Lord Paulet, the captain of H.M.S. *Barfleur,*
appealed to him for assistance in finding thirty boys to be
engaged as officers' servants in the ship. John found the necessary number of volunteers from the homeless urchins in

Westminster, and the venture proved so successful it was decided to set up a permanent system of recruitment. For this purpose the public were invited to donate to a charitable fund which was operated from the Bedford Coffee House in Covent Garden, with John Fielding and Saunders Welch as joint administrator-trustees. After two years the project was merged with Jonas Hanway's Marine Society, which had been founded for an identical purpose, and John was placed on the committee of the unified project.

John was also appalled by the social evils of prostitution. In 1758 he published a pamphlet stating that most of the prostitutes in London brothels were less than eighteen years of age, and many were only twelve. Very often, he said, destitute parents turned out their children into the streets, and the boys had no option but to become pickpockets, the girls, to become harlots. He went on to suggest the establishment of a special institution comprising two separate sections: the first, called a 'Preservatory', for girls aged between twelve and fifteen, would train the inmates as domestic servants and then send them out to selected families, who would then assume responsibility for their welfare; the second, called a 'Reformatory', for confirmed prostitutes, would be equipped with living rooms, a chapel, a school, and a laundry, and would be run on a completely self-supporting basis.

A short while later two institutions on the lines John Fielding had proposed were, in fact, set up in London, and he became a governor of each. The Female Orphan Asylum at Lambeth was the Preservatory where abandoned girls received training as domestic servants; the Magdalen Hospital in Goodman's Fields, Whitechapel, the Reformatory, was a home for inveterate prostitutes.

When Henry Fielding decided to retire from the Bow Street Office it had been his wish that he might be succeeded by his half-brother, and that Saunders Welch should replace him as the assistant magistrate. There was something in the character of Saunders Welch which awakened the deepest affection of most of the men who knew him. Henry Fielding, writing in the last year of his life, said he never thought or spoke of Welch, 'but with love and esteem'; and he was described by Dr. Johnson as 'one of my best and dearest friends'. Welch was self-taught and self-made. He was born at Aylesbury in 1711 of pauper parents, and he was educated at the school of the local workhouse. Naturally, under these circumstances, the record of his early life is cursory and inexact. However, it is known that for some reason he came to London where he was apprenticed to a well-known trunk-maker in St. Paul's churchyard, and later he became a prosperous grocer with a shop in Museum Street, Holborn.

Saunders Welch lived in an age when social distinctions outside the higher circles of the aristocracy were not nearly so sharply defined as they later became, and he gained an easy and uncritical acceptance amongst the writers, the artists, and the intellectuals of Covent Garden. There was nothing ambitious, servile or calculating about his nature; indeed, all the descriptions we have of him portray a man of independent spirit, courage and simplicity. Perhaps the truest pictures of his character were drawn by Laetitia Hawkins, who was writing from personal recollection, and John Thomas Smith, whose information was gathered first-hand after Welch's death, from the undimmed memories of his small band of ageing acquaintances.

Miss Hawkins, with her customary prim pedanticism, describes Saunders Welch as being 'in person, mind and manners most perfectly a gentleman'. Intellectually, she says, his tastes led him to literature of rather a grave cast. 'He had a love for the arts and the professors of them, and for foreigners and persons of diffuse knowledge, which procured for him a very enviable situation in society . . . he was not only the associate of men of genius, but in some instances their patron.' Apparently he could also be creative in his own right, as Miss Hawkins discloses that he occasionally contributed light essays to the literary periodicals of the day.

In appearance, says Mr. Smith, Saunders Welch was a tall man, 'and when in the prime of life, robust and cheerful. But although his benevolence was unbounded in times of distress, yet whenever necessity urged him to firmness, he was bold and resolute.' Miss Hawkins, for her part, confirms Welch's happy disposition, yet she could not recall that she had ever seen him laugh, and in his more serious moments he had 'much to tell of men whose follies he viewed with mild regret'.

The first indication that Saunders Welch was regarded as an exceptional personality was probably provided by his election to the Beefsteak Club in 1739, when he was twenty-eight. The 'Sublime Society of Steaks' had been founded four years earlier by John Rich, the manager of the Covent Garden Theatre. Its exclusive membership, limited to twenty-five persons, included many distinguished representatives of the nobility, the arts, and the stage—such as Garrick, Hogarth, Kemble, and the Dukes of Argyll and Leinster. Once a week, at Rich's Theatre, the members met together and dined in accordance with a prescribed ritual, all wearing large, round, beribboned hats. The conversation on these occasions was knowledgeable, witty and brilliant.

We know very little about Saunders Welch's wife, except that she was 'an amiable woman', and that she died young, leaving him with two infant daughters. Before her death she made him promise that he would never remarry. He kept to his undertaking, says Miss Hawkins, 'but against his judgment and inclination', and thereafter, as a widower, he lived 'a life of blameless morality'. The daughters were brought up at their father's house by a governess; Anne, the elder, was plain and intellectual and remained a spinster to the end of her days, whilst her sister Mary, beautiful and empty-headed, eventually married the fashionable sculptor Joseph Nollekens.

In 1746 Saunders Welch was appointed High Constable of Holborn. This was an ancient office of growing importance, although in London, like most of the other public positions, it had become tainted by inefficiency and corruption. The High Constable was an officer of the hundred; his duties were part-time and unpaid, but there was a procedure by which he could be reimbursed for his legitimate expenses. In general, he stood on an intermediate level between the justices and the petty constables; he served for a term lasting from one year to three years, or even longer. He was responsible for the supervision of the petty constables in his area, the maintenance of public order, the suppression of brothels, the regulation of ale-houses; and, in addition, he had a number of administrative functions. High Constables were usually drawn from the middle classes; in towns they were usually wealthy tradesmen.

The High Constable of Holborn had the special duty of accompanying condemned criminals on their final journey to the gallows at Tyburn, and Saunders Welch soon became a familiar and popular figure in these processions. John Thomas Smith had met people who could recollect seeing him, 'dressed in black, with a large, nine-storey George the Second's wig, highly powdered, with long flowing curls over his shoulders, a high three-cornered hat, and his black baton, tipped with silver at either end, riding on a white horse to Tyburn with the malefactors'.

It seems reasonable to suppose that Welch had a tendency towards showmanship; his delight in dressing up is confirmed by Miss Hawkins, who relates that his dinner clothes were frequently decorated with gold and silver. Another of his foibles, apparently, was his inclination to use long words. Boswell tells how Dr. Johnson and Sir Joshua Reynolds one day attended Welch's office when he was examining a youth from the slums. 'Welch', says Boswell, 'who imagined he was exalting himself in Dr. Johnson's eyes by using big words, spoke in a manner that was utterly unintelligible to the boy; Dr. Johnson perceiving it, addressed himself to the boy, and changed the pompous phraseology into colloquial language.' Afterwards, when Dr. Johnson and Sir Joshua Reynolds were discussing the incident, the former, in some amusement, referred to Welch's 'swelling diction'.

Despite these frailties in his character, however, Welch was universally beloved, and was never happier, according to John Thomas Smith, 'than when he was rendering assistance to those of his numerous friends who stood in need of it'. It is not difficult to understand the feelings of affection and mutual respect which arose almost instantly between Henry Fielding and Saunders Welch when their work brought them into such close contact at the Bow Street Office. Eventually, on the 6th December, 1753, Henry wrote to the Earl of Hardwicke, the Lord Chancellor:

My Lord,
    As I hear that a new Commission of the Peace is soon to pass the Great Seal for Westminster, give me leave to recommend the name of Saunders Welch; as well as to the next Commission for Middlesex. Your Lordship will, I hope, do me the Honour of

believing, I should not thus presume, unless I was well satisfied
that the Merit of the Man would justify my Presumption. For this
besides a universal Good Character, and the many eminent services he hath done the Public, I appeal in particular to Master
Lane*; and shall only add, as I am positive the truth is, that his
place can be filled with no other more acceptable to all the Gentlemen in the Commission, and indeed to the Public in General . . .

Lord Hardwicke by then had sufficient confidence in Fielding's judgment to accept his proposal without hesitation, and
so, on the 13th February, 1755, Saunders Welch was appointed
a Justice of the Peace for Middlesex. In the same year—the
records do not supply the exact date — he also became a
magistrate for Westminster.

During his long and active spell as High Constable of Holborn—he had, in fact been sworn in for that office on the 2nd
July, 1746—Welch had acquired an unrivalled knowledge of
the mentality and method of the London criminals. Basically,
he agreed with Henry Fielding's assessment of the causes of
crime. In a letter, written in 1753, he condemned excessive
luxury coupled with idleness and low morals; criminals were
encouraged, he said, by 'the bad example of too many in
higher stations'. He criticized, too, the inadequacy of street-
lighting and the general inefficiency of the watchmen.

In 1754, a year before he became a magistrate, Saunders
Welsh published a pamphlet entitled *Observations on the
Office of Constable*. This was an instructional handbook for
petty constables and was remarkable for the fact that, written
at a time when the peace officers had fallen into such abject
disrepute, it foreshadowed the notion of the citizen-policeman,
confident, trusted and reliable—the very concept which was
adopted a century later when the professional British police
force came into being.

In respect of their general demeanour Welch gave petty
constables the following advice, 'Let the service of the public
be the great motive of all those actions which regard your
office; this, properly attended to, will keep you from all offici-
ous, wanton acts of power'. It was essential that they should
not be provoked by the ill manners and scurrilous reflections
of those with whom they came into contact in the performance

* John Lane was a well-known Master in Chancery.

of their duties; 'Avoid passion and resentment,' he warned. He was against the use of force; 'I advise never to strike,' he said, 'except it be absolutely in your own defence; but striking at all, if possible, should be avoided, for the sword of justice, not the arm of the constable, was intended for punishment.' And they must always be on their guard against the activities of 'low solicitors', who would be constantly preying on them, waiting to seize upon any act of irregularity or recklessness.

Another pamphlet, which Saunders Welch wrote some years afterwards, was called *A Proposal to Render Effectual a Plan to Remove the Nuisance of the Common Prostitute from the Streets of this Metropolis*. Nothing was being done for the welfare of the harlot, he said; usually she was bailed out by a trading justice, and then convicted and sentenced either to a whipping or to a month's imprisonment. Like John Fielding, he recommended that reformatories should be established for girls who had been rescued from prostitution, but he also suggested that the law should deal far more sternly with those at the root of this evil, the brothel-keepers. Prostitutes, he said, fell into two distinct categories; firstly, there were the women who chose that way of life because they were avaricious and lazy: and secondly, the young girls who had been seduced or abandoned, and had been driven on to the streets by hunger and want. His aim was twofold, 'to provide a decent and comfortable maintenance for those whom necessity or vice hath already forced into that infamous course of life, and to maintain and educate the children of the poor who are either orphans or are deserted by wicked parents'.

It was strangely fortuitous that two men such as John Fielding and Saunders Welch, both of whom held views on social reform well in advance of their day should have come together at the Bow Street Office in succession to Henry Fielding.

CHAPTER ELEVEN

JOHN FIELDING AT THE HELM

ON the 14th October 1754, six days after the death of Henry Fielding, the following notice appeared in the *Public Advertiser*:

Whereas many thieves and robbers daily escape justice for want of immediate pursuit, it is therefore recommended to all persons who shall henceforth be robbed on the highway or in the streets, or whose shops or houses shall be broke open, that they give immediate notice thereof, together with as accurate a description of the offenders as possible, to JOHN FIELDING ESQ., at his house in Bow Street, Covent Garden. By which means, joined to an advertisement containing an account of the things lost (which is also taken in there), thieves and robbers will seldom escape: as most of the principal pawnbrokers take in this paper, and by the intelligence they get from it assist daily in discovering and apprehending rogues.

And if they would send a special messenger on these occasions, Mr. Fielding would not only pay that messenger for his trouble, but would immediately despatch a set of brave fellows in pursuit, who have been long engaged for such purposes, and are always ready to set out to any part of this town or kingdom on a quarter of an hour's notice.

It is hoped that the success of this plan will make all persons for the future industrious to give the earliest notice possible of all robberies and robbers whatever.

A similar advertisement, in almost identical terms, was printed at regular intervals in the *Public Advertiser* from that time onwards.

At first glance it might appear that John Fielding was losing sight of the fact that he was only a justice for Westminster and Middlesex. However, there was nothing improper about his offer to send his thief-takers to 'any part of this town or kingdom'. A private citizen had the right then, as indeed he has in the present day, to arrest a person who had committed a felony. In fact, John's scheme accorded with the official policy of the time, that the prosecution of criminals, and even their capture, was a matter for the individual rather than the State.

The Bow Street police force was still composed of about half-a-dozen unpaid volunteers. It will be remembered that the Privy Council in the autumn of 1753 had voted Henry Fielding an allowance of £600 to cover the costs of his final plan to exterminate robbers from the streets of London. By the winter of 1754 this sum had all been expended, and John submitted a request for a further grant to finance his continued policing arrangements. In November 1755 he received another £200, in the form of an *ad hoc* payment rather than an annual subsidy. A year later he was obliged to write again saying, 'the £200 granted about this time twelvemonth to defray the expenses of Mr. Fielding's plan for apprehending robbers and preventing other disorders in or near the Metropolis is now totally expended in that service'. He enclosed the detailed accounts, showing a total outlay of £262 19s. od., and he asked for payment of the deficit of £62 19s. od. in addition to a further £200 for the coming year. 'And your Lordships may be assured that no pains shall be spared', he said, 'to make it answer for the good purposes for which it is granted.' The Privy Council had such a respect for his ability, or else were so devoid of any alternative ideas, that they acceded to his request.

On the 12th October, 1757, John Fielding submitted his accounts for the previous twelve months, but again they showed that he had overspent his grant, this time by a margin of £53. However, he could claim, 'from Michaelmas 1756 to Michaelmas 1757, almost every highwayman, street-robber, house-breaker and mail-robber that has made his appearance has been apprehended, executed, transported, or is now in custody'. He went on to suggest that for the future he should receive an annual payment of £400, 'no very extraordinary sum', he said, 'when 'tis considered what a security it is to the lives, properties and peace of His Majesty's subjects in the Metropolis'. In his usual, methodical manner John specified exactly how the £400 would be spent. At Bow Street there were to be four peace officers, paid £10 a year each, who would remain on call day and night to pursue criminals to any part of the kingdom; they would have two pursuit horses, costing a total of £40 a year for their upkeep. Also on constant duty at Bow Street would be an Orderly Man, at a salary of £20, and a Register Clerk, at a salary of £10, 'to take all informations and descriptions of suspicious persons, robbers and things stolen.' £60 annually would be spent on printing 'advertisements, cautions, handbills, etc.', and finally there was to be a float of £200 for 'the common occurrences and expenses on every other account'.

John Fielding's accounts for the years 1755–56 and 1756–57 are preserved in the British Museum; they afford a revealing insight to the multifarious activities of the Bow Street officers during these periods. There are trivial, routine tasks such as, 'going around Berkeley Square and that neighbourhood to examine the deficiency of the lights', 'suppressing some illegal performances at the Little Theatre by the desire of the Lord Chamberlain' and 'attending fraudulent auctions'. More adventurous duties included the breaking up of a riot at the Drury Lane Playhouse and 'pursuing Watts, a house-breaker, to Bristol'. A considerable part of their time was spent in the role of detectives; 'dragging the ponds to find the clothes of Cannicot's wife that was murdered', 'opening a pavement on suspicion of murder', and 'enquiring after a person supposed to be a French spy'.

At any rate, John's proud boast of the effectiveness of his Bow Street force was borne out by Canon John Brown, who wrote in his *Estimate of the Times:*

> We have recently seen the salutary effects of a new kind of police . . . by which the reigning evil of street-robbers hath been almost wholly suppressed.

The process by which the Bow Street house became the premier justices' office in the Metropolis was haphazard and ill-defined. Theoretically, there was no reason why any other Westminster or Middlesex magistrate should not have formed his own private police force, and even applied for a government subsidy to cover the cost; but it would seem that the Fielding brothers and Saunders Welch were the only justices who were prepared to play a purposeful and energetic role in

the fight against crime. In consequence, there was no opposition and no rivalry; Bow Street reached its predominant
position, not in competition, but by default.

Early in 1755, John Fielding and Saunders Welch submitted a joint memorial to the Government suggesting that
they should be paid salaries for their services as magistrates.
Their request was favourably considered and it was agreed
that they should each be granted an allowance of £200 a year
out of the Secret Service Fund, John's salary being increased
later to £400 a year. This money, however, was not very
readily forthcoming, as there is a letter in the British Museum
from John Fielding to the Secretary of State for the Home
Department, dated the 5th February, 1756, in which he com-
plains that both he and Saunders Welch were still awaiting
their initial payments. He wrote again on the 14th October,
1756, pointing out that the second instalments had become
due at Michaelmas, that is on the 29th of the previous month.

Bow Street continued to levy the regulation scale of fees
which were prescribed for a justice's work, but John Fielding
once told George Grenville that they were collected in 'the
most disinterested way', and were merely sufficient to pay the
expenses of the Office. In fact, John had grave doubt about
the suitability of a system of unpaid justices in the Metropolis, where the duties, if properly performed, were of such
an exacting nature. He was probably the first person to propose the creation of stipendiary magistrates, who 'should be
attentive by day and night to all information of fraud and
felony, and be vigilant and indefatigable in the pursuit of
offenders'. He favoured a magistrate in London receiving a
substantial salary for, as he put it, 'his being handsomely sub-
sisted will take away the temptation of making a gain out of
the paltry quarrels of the poor and thereby increasing the
poor's rates. And, indeed, it ought to remove every temptation
that dishonours the magistracy, and must in time free such
men from the scandalous imputation of "trading justice",
raise the dignity of the employment, and make it an object
worthy of acceptance, nay, meriting the study of the best of
men'.

John Fielding also put forward an even more revolutionary
proposal. He suggested in 1758 that the principal magistrates

in the Metropolis should all be qualified lawyers, 'and if such a one be bred to the Bar, the better', he said, 'for he ought to have a competent knowledge as well of the common, as the Crown law; the former to assist the poor with his advice, and the latter to bring offenders to justice, to give notice to the legislature of the defects of any penal law (which is easier discovered in the execution than in the framing of the law), and prevent himself and the officers from falling a prey to that swarm of low and hungry solicitors who are always lying in wait to take advantage of their errors; and the more knowledge he has of human nature, the better, as it will enable him to detect and unravel the dark clues of guilt'. By the time he wrote these words, John had learnt from his own experiences, and from those of Saunders Welch, how very vulnerable legally-unqualified magistrates would always be, even if they were men of outstanding ability, against the wiles and subterfuges of the Newgate attorneys. Probably he compared their position with that of an erudite lawyer, such as his predecessor, Henry Fielding, whose skill and training had protected him from the snares and pitfalls which were constantly laid before him.

The Metropolis needed five or six of such qualified and salaried magistrates, in John's opinion, and each of them should have his own office where he would be in regular attendance. He considered that it was of paramount importance that justices should officiate at their offices for set hours, and he reorganised the routine at Bow Street so that at least one magistrate was on duty each day from 10·00 a.m. until 2·00 p.m., and again from 5·00 p.m. until 9·00 p.m. Indeed, no-one worked harder than John himself; he confessed some time later that during those years he had been obliged to live 'in a constant contention with the refuse of creation; and to be so incessantly employed in this labour, as not to have leisure to converse with friends, or to enjoy, with any degree of comfort, the common necessities of life'. He described his own assignment at the Bow Street Office as being 'a station full of difficulties, full of perplexities, and full of dissatisfactions'.

The newspapers of that period bear witness to the constant activity of the Bow Street magistrates. For example, the

Public Advertiser reported on the 18th of October, 1754, that Saunders Welch had led a night raid on Blackboy Alley, as a result of which about forty men had been arrested. These prisoners were brought before John Fielding the following day, and after an examination lasting from ten o'clock in the morning until six o'clock in the evening he committed the majority of them to Bridewell and to the New Prison as 'loose, idle, and disorderly persons'.

Whereas Henry Fielding's policing arrangements had been principally confined to the streets of the Metropolis, John cast his net further afield to embrace the approach roads into London, where the highway robbers were then reigning supreme. He never approved of the national idolatry for the highwaymen, which seemed to him to be both degrading and illogical. In his view they were simply robbers on horseback, in search of an easy prey, 'What cowardice,' he wrote, 'to attack ladies, and unarmed persons, with pistols at their heads.'

Early in 1755, before John knew the measure of the financial support he could expect to receive from the Government, he published his *Plan For Preventing Robberies Within Twenty Miles of London*. He proposed that people whose houses were situated between five and twenty miles from London should club together, paying a subscription of two guineas a year each to their appointed treasurer. Whenever a highway robbery occurred in the neighbourhood of one of the subscribers, he would immediately ascertain all the particulars and would hire a horse and a messenger to carry a report to the Bow Street Office. Care should be taken, John pointed out, to find out the name and address of the party who had been robbed, 'for it sometimes happens when a highwayman is apprehended that the prosecutor not being found, the former escapes justice and is let loose again on the public'. On his way to Bow Street, the messenger would stop at every alehouse, public inn and turnpike in order to issue descriptions of the highwayman and his horse. When an account of the robbery had reached Bow Street, the magistrates would decide, at their discretion, whether to send out police officers in immediate pursuit, or merely to insert a notice of the details in the *Public Advertiser*. All the expenses incurred would be met by the relevant treasurer from the funds in his possession.

John was aware that the success of his plan would depend to a large extent on people reading his notices. 'The ale-house keepers, stable-keepers who let horses for hire, and pawnbrokers should constantly read the advertisements inserted by Mr. Fielding in the *Public Advertiser*', he said. 'The first would then never harbour a rogue; the second would never furnish a highwayman with a horse, without knowing it enough to detect him and save the horse; and as to the latter they have already found so many advantages from what is here recommended that nothing further need be said.' He was always at great pains to point out that although he made immense use of the *Public Advertiser*, he himself had no financial interest in the paper.

John Fielding and Saunders Welch found it difficult to work together harmoniously at the Bow Street Office. This is not altogether surprising as they were both men with strong and diverse personalities. They were both individualists; and further, their approach to their work was completely different, Fielding being totally preoccupied, and Welch enjoying a vast range of interests outside his magisterial duties.

The trouble between them seems to have come to a head about 1760, for there is an undated letter in the British Museum from Saunders Welch to the Duke of Newcastle, probably written around that year, in which he complained bitterly about John's behaviour. He alleged that John had treated him 'when in office, and under his own roof . . . in a manner too opprobrious to repeat, and too offensive for any but the ill-deserving to bear'. He continued, 'so far did Mr. Fielding forget himself as to descend to ill language such as he would have reproached in a criminal before him'. In the same letter Saunders Welch attributed John's hostility to a mistaken belief that Welch was attempting 'to supplant and injure him'.

It may have been partly because of the ill-feeling between the two magistrates that it was decided that Saunders Welch should set up his own subsidiary office, firstly at his house in

Long Acre, and thereafter at Litchfield Street, which connects
Charing Cross Road with St. Martin's Lane.

From 1763, Westminster had three principal magisterial
offices, Bow Street, Litchfield Street and the Guildhall. Bow
Street dealt with most of the more serious cases, whilst
'Saunders Welch's attention', according to John Thomas
Smith, 'was for the most part confined to the abandoned
women and pickpockets who frequented Hedge-lane, the Haymarket, Cranbourne-alley and Leicester-fields; the last of
which, from the rough and broken state of its ground, and the
shadow of a lofty row of elms which then stood in the road in
front of most of the houses on the eastern side, was rendered a
very dangerous part to pass, particularly before the streets
were paved and publicly lighted'. In addition, Saunders
Welch covered the Mary-le-bone area and Tyburn. After an
execution at Tyburn, says Mr. Smith, the offices at Bow Street
and Litchfield Street were 'thronged by gentlemen who had
lost their watches and pocket-books, or ladies who had been
robbed of their velvet cardinals or purses'. The Guildhall, an
unimportant office, was manned by the Westminster justices
of the peace, sitting in rotation.

A continual source of regret to John Fielding was the low
standing with the public of the Bow Street thief-takers. The
word 'police', as describing the peace officers, was not commonly used until the latter part of the eighteenth century,
and at that time it was applied in its wider sense, embracing
the whole of the civil administration; Samuel Johnson's
dictionary, compiled about 1750, defines 'police' as, 'the regulation and government of a city or country so far as regards
the inhabitants'.

John wanted the civil administration to be respected. 'The
police of an arbitrary government differs from that used in a
republic', he wrote, 'and a police proper for England must
differ from both, as it must always be agreeable to the just
notion of the liberty of the subject as well as the laws of the
constitution.' He had an inherent regard for the system, in
theory at least, as employed in this country. 'Let the weak or
wicked laugh at or abuse this police as they please', he said;
'every true Briton must have this satisfaction to reflect, that
no private person whatsoever, no watchman, beadle, constable,

or magistrate can unjustly deprive him of his liberty or property, with impunity.'

Gradually the citizens of the Metropolis were beginning to
appreciate that the brand of justice administered by the
magistrates at Bow Street was of an entirely different order to
that which appertained in most other magisterial offices. But
they did not have the same growing appreciation of the Bow
Street police, Fielding's set of 'brave fellows' on whom he
depended so much. Perhaps this was due principally to the
unfortunate reputation which the thief-takers had acquired
in the preceding years.

The most notorious thief-taker of all was Jonathan Wild,
the original of Peachum in *The Beggar's Opera*. Wild was
born at Wolverhampton in 1682 and started life as a buckle-
maker's apprentice. He came to London as a young man, and
due to his extravagant manner of living he was imprisoned
for four years for debt, during which time he made a number
of useful contacts in the underworld. Soon after his release he
built up a gang of thieves, pickpockets, and highwaymen, all
of whom he supervised personally with such success that he
was described in the *Newgate Calendar* as being 'The Prince
of Robbers'. However, Wild was not content to be a gangster-
chief and he also set himself up as a master thief-taker. He
used to contact people who had just been robbed, offering to
recover their stolen property for them, provided no questions
were asked. For this purpose he opened a broker's office near
the Old Bailey, at which he collected all the proceeds of the
thefts committed by his men. In addition, he used to carry
out his own arrests; in the trials of the period he featured
repeatedly as the principal prosecution witness who had often
been responsible for the apprehension of the prisoner. Such
was his audacity that in 1723 he applied to the Lord Mayor
and Aldermen for the freedom of the City of London, 'in
return for his services to justice'.

Finally, Wild was tried at the Old Bailey in February, 1725,
on a charge of assisting in the escape of a highwayman. Despite
his spirited defence, based on a contention that he had always
been on the side of law and order and had, in fact, been instrumental in securing the executions of upwards of sixty-seven
criminals, he was convicted and sentenced to death. He was

hanged at Tyburn on the 24th May, 1725, before an infuriated mob who, according to the account in the *Newgate Calendar,* 'treated this offender with remarkable severity, incessantly pelting him with stones, dirt, etc. and execrating him as the most consummate villain that ever disgraced human nature'.

There were many other bogus thief-takers who, encouraged by the lure of large-scale rewards, did not hesitate to indulge in perjury, fraud, and indirect murder. John Fielding was as much opposed to the insidious blood-money system as Henry had been before him, and he contended that it would be more economical, and far more efficacious, for the Government to devote their resources to the creation of a centralised, Metropolitan peace-keeping organisation, based on the Bow Street police force.

The disrepute of the thief-takers, and the abomination in which they were held by the public, were intensified by the activities of four rascals, McDaniel, Berry, Egan and Salmon, who were convicted at the Old Bailey in February, 1756, of a conspiracy to procure two other persons to commit a robbery. The evidence for the prosecution showed that they had been practising as 'thief-takers' since about 1740; their usual method being to induce some simpleton to join them in committing a crime, and then to denounce him to a magistrate and collect the appropriate reward. On at least one occasion their deceived accomplice had been hanged. Eventually, in the summer of 1754, they had persuaded two young men called Kelly and Ellis to take part in a faked robbery at Deptford, in which Salmon had masqueraded as the victim, and McDaniel had appeared on the scene and carried out the arrests. Kelly and Ellis were convicted at the Kent Assizes, but afterwards the full truth of the incident was revealed. McDaniel and his gang were convicted and sentenced to be stood in the pillory and to be imprisoned for seven years.

A month after the trial when McDaniel and Berry were exhibited in a pillory near Hatton Garden they were nearly lynched by the mob, and had to be rescued by prison warders and peace officers. In spite of this, however, Egan and Salmon were placed in a pillory at Smithfield three days later. Again there was a riot, in which Egan was killed and Salmon so severely injured that he died on his return to Newgate Prison.

John Fielding was deeply distressed by a rumour that these four men had been associated with the Bow Street police. He felt it necessary on three separate occasions to publish the following denial in the *Public Advertiser*:

Whereas there are a body of honest and faithful men, commonly called thief-takers, who have been employed for several years by the late Henry Fielding, Esq., and the present Mr. Fielding, which said thief-takers have, by their great diligence and bravery, broke, apprehended and brought to justice some of the most desperate gangs of street-robbers that ever existed, to the great hazard of their lives, they having been wounded at different times, and one of them having lately lost an arm, which in all probability will cost him his life; it was thought proper at this juncture to distinguish these persons, who have real merit to the public, from the set of wretches, Stephen McDaniel, John Berry, etc., who by assuming the character of thief-takers have not only brought that employment which, when not abused, is a very laudable one, into disrepute, but have committed the most horrible abuses on the public that were ever heard of; and it must be observed that this most wicked gang never were employed by any magistrate as thief-takers.

It has been suggested that the Bow Street thief-takers of this period were in receipt of some sort of concealed salary from the Government, but no such payments have been discovered in any of the official accounts. It is more likely that, however praiseworthy their courage, skill and devotion to duty, they were being recompensed very largely from the rewards which followed automatically upon the termination of a successful prosecution. Whether they were inspired by a heightened sense of public spirit, or were merely adventurous, civil mercenaries, it would be very difficult to say.

It may be worth noting that neither Henry nor John Fielding ever claimed any special powers for their thief-takers above the authority of an ordinary member of the general public. The common law allowed any person to arrest an offender who was committing, or had committed a felony; indeed, the arrest could be carried out on reasonable suspicion, provided that a felony had actually been committed. This right of arrest under the common law did not extend to misdemeanours—virtually all the less serious types of offence—

E

unless the offender was causing a breach of the peace, either
by making an affray, or by using violence to an individual.
Henry and John Fielding both conceived their Bow Street
officers as being a small group of highly-trained private
citizens, merely carrying out the delegated responsibilities of
their fellows.

In spite of the general antipathy towards thief-takers, Londoners were gradually, almost grudgingly, beginning to
acknowledge the efficiency of the new policing arrangements.
In February, 1756, the *Public Advertiser* published this
comment:

It is remarkable that, by the spirit that has lately been infused
among the peace officers, and by the bravery of Mr. Fielding's
people, within a month this town has been freed from numbers of
pickpockets, from no less than twenty pilfering shoplifters, one
gang of house-breakers, two very extraordinary horse-stealers, and
two very different gangs of street-robbers.

CHAPTER TWELVE

A SEAT OF JUSTICE

AN official such as the police magistrate may seem a functional inconsistency to a person who has been inured to the modern British judicial process; for the basic principles of the remoteness and the impartiality of the Bench necessitate that the magisterial duty should be entirely separate from the initial investigation of crimes, and the pursuit and apprehension of criminals. However, this division of responsibilities was slow to develop and, indeed, the justice of the peace was originally intended to maintain the law actively and physically, rather than to merely enforce its provisions in the detached tranquillity of a secluded courtroom.

The disparate nature of the two aspects of a justice's responsibilities were emphasized when Henry Fielding began to conduct the proceedings in the Bow Street Office on the pattern of a superior court of law, and to preside over them as a member of the judiciary. But, even then, his incongruous role as a part-policeman and a part-judge did not, apparently, evoke either criticism or comment. In spite of his blindness, John Fielding often used to visit the scenes of crimes to carry out his personal enquiries. Horace Walpole, describing a burglary at the London home of Lord Harrington says, 'Fielding is all day in the house, and a guard of his at night'.

As might be expected, Saunders Welch, with his long experience as a high constable, continued to devote a great deal of his time to police work even after he was appointed a magistrate. A particularly daring arrest, which he discharged single-handed, has been recounted by John Thomas Smith. Information was received that a well-known footpad, who had always managed to evade arrest, was hiding in an upstairs room of a house in Rose Street, Long Acre. Saunders Welch decided he could take no chances with the man. 'After hiring the tallest hackney coach he could select, he mounted the box with the coachman, and when he was close against the house, he ascended the roof of the coach, threw up the sash of a first-floor window, entered the room and actually dragged the fellow from his bed, out of the window, naked as he was, on to the roof of the coach.'

We have no descriptions of Saunders Welch in his office in Litchfield Street, but it is a reasonable presumption that he followed the procedures which Henry Fielding had initiated at Bow Street. Boswell has said that Welch 'kept a regular office for the police . . . and discharged his important trust, for many years, faithfully and ably'. According to Boswell, Dr. Johnson, 'who had an eager and unceasing curiosity to know human life in all its variety, told me that he attended Mr. Welch in his office for a whole winter, to hear the examination of the culprits; but he found an almost uniform tenor of misfortune, wretchedness and profligacy'.

As far as John Fielding is concerned, there are a number of objective accounts of his cases at the Bow Street Office, which clearly demonstrate his fairness, his courtesy, and his extremely judicial approach to the matters before him. He had, too, an infinite knowledge of the underworld and a perception of human behaviour which caused him to be greatly feared by the criminal fraternity.

Dr. Thomas Somerville has told how he once travelled on a coach from York to London, and one of the other passengers, a man called Mathewson, was arrested a day later for forgery. So efficient were John Fielding's arrangements (by that time he had become 'Sir John') that within a few hours he had traced all the people who had been on the coach. Dr. Somerville himself was contacted by a Bow Street officer in the gallery of the House of Commons and was asked to attend at the Office immediately. He complied with this summons and he has left the following description of what took place:

I was so much amused and interested with the appearance of Sir John Fielding, and the singular adroitness with which he conducted the business of his office, that I continued there for an hour after the removal of Mathewson, while Sir John was engaged in the investigation of other cases. Sir John had a bandage over his eyes, and held a little switch or rod in his hand, waving it before him as he descended from the bench. The sagacity he discovered in the questions he put to the witnesses, and a marked and successful attention as I conceived, not only to the words, but to the accents and tones of the speaker, supplied the advantage which is usually rendered by the eye; and his arrangement of the questions leading to the detection of concealed facts, impressed me with the highest respect for his singular ability as a police magistrate.

Thereafter, Dr. Somerville became a frequent spectator at the Bow Street Office in common with a great many others, among whom was the Duke of Kingston. Probably John Fielding's most professional critic was Samuel Curwen, an experienced American judge who, following a visit to Bow Street, expressed the opinion that the blind magistrate was 'as eminent a character in the juridicial line as perhaps any man in the civilised world'.

Sir John Fielding was becoming a familiar figure in the life of London, and the cases which came before him were widely reported. In 1764, Signor Giovanni Casanova, the Italian adventurer, appeared at the Bow Street Office as a result of a complaint against him by one of his jilted mistresses that he had threatened her with violence. He has described what took place in his memoirs:

At the end of the room I saw a gentleman sitting in an armchair, and concluded him to be my judge. I was right, and the judge was blind. He wore a broad band round his head, passing over his eyes. A man beside me, guessing I was a foreigner, said in French, 'Be of good courage; Mr. Fielding is a just and equitable magistrate.' When my turn came, the clerk of the court told Mr. Fielding my name, so I presume. 'Signor Casanova', said he, in excellent Italian, 'be kind enough to step forward. I wish to speak to you.' I was delighted to hear the accents of my native tongue, and making my way through the press I came to the bar of the court.

The incident ended happily enough, as Casanova gave an undertaking not to assault the lady and he was bound over, with two sureties, to keep the peace.

The nature of John Fielding's work, coupled with his somewhat aloof disposition, were not calculated to win him universal popularity. He reacted to venomous gossip in his customary oversensitive manner. During the summer of 1758 he inserted a notice in the *Public Advertiser,* commencing:

Whereas several gross, scandalous, and malicious reports have been industriously spread within these last few days, with an

intention to injure Mr. Fielding's character, without the least
shadow of a foundation, such as his being committed to Newgate,
suspended as a magistrate, etc.

He went on to offer a reward for any information which would
reveal the author of these rumours. A few days later, he wrote
to the Duke of Newcastle complaining about 'the evil consequences of mob malice against a public magistrate'.

Nevertheless, the Bow Street Office was gradually gaining
in stature and growing in authority. It had achieved a reputation for stability in an atmosphere of lawlessness and confusion, and for probity in a general climate of incompetence,
graft and corruption. The regular Bow Street magistrates
were beginning to attain a public image in their judicial
capacity. When James Boswell and two young companions
were composing a joint letter to David Hume, the philosopher, in March 1763, they emphasized the sincerity of their
recollection that he had spoken some disputed words by
saying, 'we are ready to make oath either before Sir John
Fielding, or Mr. Saunders Welch that we heard you utter that
very expression'.

Four months later, Boswell had had occasion to pay a personal visit to the Bow Street Office. This was after an altercation with the landlord of his lodgings in Downing Street,
who had accused him—quite falsely as it happened—of taking
the maid into his room during the night. The indignant
Boswell was determined to vacate the house forthwith and he
consulted his friend, James Coutts, the well-known Scottish
banker, to enquire how much rent he was legally bound to
pay under the circumstances. The following entry appears
in Boswell's journal, dated July 6th, 1763:

By the advice of Mr. Coutts, I went to Sir John Fielding's, that
great seat of Westminster justice. A more curious scene I had
never beheld: it brought fresh into my mind the ideas of London
roguery and wickedness which I conceived in my younger days
by reading The Lives of the Convicts, and other such books. There
were whores and chairmen and greasy blackguards of all denomi-
nations assembled together. The blind Justice had his court in a
back hall. His clerk, who officiates as a sort of chamber counsel,
hears all the causes, and gives his opinion. As I had no formal

complaint to make, he did not carry me in to the Justice, but told me that as my landlord had used me rudely, although I had taken my lodging by the year, I was only obliged to pay him for the time that I had lived in his house.

To those familiar with the daily cavalcade of applicants at any of the magistrates' courts in the heart of London today, it will be of interest to observe that even as far back as 1763 people with a grievance or a problem were beginning to turn to their local magistrate for advice.

John Fielding received his knighthood on the 1st October, 1761. The pleasure which he experienced on gaining this distinction might have been tempered by the knowledge that he himself had asked for it. For, in December 1757, he had written to the Duke of Newcastle on a matter which, he said, was of the most delicate nature and required a good deal more than candour. He pointed out that his situation rendered him 'obnoxious to many bodies of people, who have been the objects of justice and whose wicked and oppressive designs have been by my vigilance obstructed'; he instanced sharpers, gamesters, publicans, pawnbrokers, journeymen, and thieves. Finally, he set out his proposal:

I think that if His Majesty would be graciously pleased to confer the same honor on me as he did on Sir Thos. Duveil, it would greatly conduce to my own safety, strengthen my power and add much to my influence. And, as it would be a public testimony of being protected and approved by my Royal Master, it would prevent mob insolence and facilitate the execution of any future plan I might be so happy to contrive for the public good.

At that time there can have been few men who were serving the Government so unselfishly and for such a small return as John Fielding. In his undefined and unofficial position he was frequently consulted by Ministers about forthcoming legislation, and his views, even when they were not acted upon, were usually treated with great respect. When Lord Barrington, the Secretary of State for War, sent him the draft of a new Recruiting Bill, which would have introduced a form of compulsory service, John replied with a warning that such a system would be unacceptable to the British people. He suggested that he should call on Lord Barrington to discuss the

Bill, 'for my situation and experience in life', he said, 'rather enables me to see inconveniences than to remedy them'.

It appears from the records of the Westminster justices that John Fielding succeeded a magistrate called Bartholomew Hammond as Chairman of Westminster Sessions in the spring of 1763; he delivered his first Charge to the Grand Jury on April 6th of that year. He remained as Chairman for a long period, but the exact date of his relinquishment of the appointment is difficult to ascertain as all the relevant documents are now missing. It can be assumed that John, an ardent upholder of the essential dignity of the law, was one of the leaders in the agitation of the Westminster justices to be provided with a proper courthouse for their Sessions, so that they might discontinue their use of the disreputable Hell Tavern. This object was achieved within a year of John Fielding becoming their Chairman when the Earl of Northumberland, at that time the Lord Lieutenant of Middlesex, purchased a building for them in King Street, Westminster, immediately adjacent to the Parliament Square, and converted it at his own expense into a Westminster Sessions courthouse.

In addition to his work at Bow Street, John Fielding took his duties as Chairman of Westminster Sessions very seriously. He once admitted to George Grenville that the Westminster magistrates were 'not men of the first repute', and he made every effort to improve their standing and to increase their self-respect. In 1764 he submitted a memorandum to the Secretary of State, complaining of the behaviour of three typical trading justices, one of whom, he said, was executing his office in different alehouses, borrowing money from gaolers and constables, and encouraging litigation amongst the poor. All three men were subsequently removed from the Westminster Commission. On the other hand, he tried to build up a spirit of camaraderie by arranging periodical dinners for the Westminster magistrates whenever he could persuade the Treasury to bear the cost.

In 1765, the justices of Westminster were accorded a peculiar honour by the king when they were given permission, in the words of the Annual Register, 'to distinguish themselves by wearing the arms of Westminster, with the emblems of magistracy, on a gold shield, fastened to a riband hanging down the breast'. The purpose of this innovation was, apparently, 'for the better securing of their persons, and to procure a more ready obedience to the laws'. This privilege fell into disuse many years ago, but it has never been officially rescinded.

By this time, John Fielding had added to his appointments on the Commissions of Middlesex and Westminster, by becoming a justice of the peace for the counties of Essex, Kent, Hertfordshire and Surrey. It is likely that he never really accepted the idea that either he or the Bow Street Office could be circumscribed by any arbitrary limits of jurisdiction. It was not that he was avid for power, or had visions of establishing a private empire; rather, he saw the fight against crime as a single campaign, which would have to be waged on an extraterritorial basis. At Bow Street he kept a register of crimes and criminals which he made available to justices all over Britain. 'There is a correspondence settled with many of the active magistrates in the country, at all distances', he wrote, 'who constantly give notice to Mr. Fielding when they have committed any desperate rogue or suspicious man, especially if a stranger in that country; by which means they are often furnished with material to bring such offenders to justice.' This is one more instance of John Fielding's farsightedness, for the first official Criminal Records Office in this country was not set up until as recently as 1869.

John Fielding's notices in the *Public Advertiser* demonstrate the scope of his authority and the variety of his problems. He went out of his way to issue preliminary warnings because, as he said, 'preventing offences is not only a more agreeable office to the magistrates, but a more useful one to the public, than the punishing of offenders'. When there was an outbreak of rowdyism at the Covent Garden and Drury Lane theatres, he published an edict that he would spare no pains 'to punish to the utmost extremity of the law, all those who shall for the future be found guilty of thus disturbing and annoying the rest of the audience'. When in the long, harsh winter of 1759–1760 large crowds of obstreperous skaters were assembling every weekend in St. James's Park to destroy the peace of the Sunday morning, John threatened, but not too seriously, that he would send out a Press Gang to round up some of the young men 'for serving their country against the French upon the frozen lakes of Canada'. On a more serious note, he warned the public against taking part in the 'wanton cruelty' of the ancient Shrove Tuesday custom of cock-baiting.

The Bow Street magistrates had assumed a wide and general responsibility for the preservation of law and order in and around London. In the summer of 1764, the *Public Advertiser* announced that the magistrates had under consideration, 'ridding the fields and places adjacent to the Metropolis of those swarms of loose, idle, and disorderly people who daily assemble therein'. Subsequently, a series of raids were made by the constables, and numbers of vagrants were arrested and taken to the Bow Street Office.

John Fielding had prepared his own master-scheme for the curtailment of crime. He presented it to the Duke of Newcastle in April, 1761, and in an accompanying letter he said, 'I have drawn out so simple and yet so exceptional a plan of police, as must infallibly secure peace and good order to the Metropolis, and do immortal honour to your Grace.' An abstract of his plan survives among the Liverpool manuscripts in the British Museum. At the start of the abstract, John gave his opinion that, 'the causes of the frequent robberies and other disorders in or near the City of London' were two-fold: firstly, the separated and weakened state of the civil power and, secondly, the absence of a proper force at the turn-pikes near London to pursue robbers and to prevent their escape.

In order to achieve a measure of centralisation, John proposed the appointment of five or six special, legally-qualified magistrates who would all be justices for Middlesex, Westminster, Surrey, Herfordshire, Kent and Essex. They would be paid a fixed salary and would, therefore, 'act without fee or reward', and each would have his own office in different parts of London, at which he would attend for regular hours every day and every evening. To perpetuate the supremacy of Bow Street, John went on to suggest that there should be 'a centre or principal office' situated at Covent Garden. The fees from these various offices would be collected into a single fund and would be used to cover such essential expenses as rents, and the wages of clerks and messengers.

With regard to policing arrangements inside the town, John proposed that the constables should be organised on a unified, metropolitan basis, rather than remaining the responsibility of the individual parishes. He also suggested that during the autumn and winter, foot patrols, each consisting of a constable and a messenger from one of the magistrates' offices, should be sent out 'between the hours of five and ten in the fields about London'. He was in favour of maintaining the system of 'keeping the watch', but he would have preferred to see two watchmen, instead of one, at every watch-post so that they could perform periods of alternate duty.

Another radical proposal in Sir John Fielding's scheme was the stationing of a regiment of Light Horse in the vicinity of London with the special task of providing sentinels at all the turnpikes. As soon as a robbery occurred, the nearest turnpike would report it to Bow Street 'for transmission to the other offices'. He realised that this suggestion would meet with strenuous opposition but, he said, 'as any person whatever, by the laws of this kingdom, may pursue and apprehend felons, no fair objection can be made to the placing of the above troops for the purposes above-mentioned as they are intended to co-operate with, and act under, the civil power'.

Since so many crimes were hatched in public houses, John considered that magistrates should exercise more care in the granting of licences. He also suggested that street-lighting should be improved by fixing lamps on the outside of the footway, rather than on the sides of the houses.

Whatever the Duke of Newcastle might have thought of the scheme, he certainly took no steps to implement any of its proposals. However, it will be seen in later chapters that many of John Fielding's ideas formed a basis for the future developments of the magistracy and the system for the maintenance of law and order in London.

Meanwhile, Fielding continued his campaign against the highwayman. He was constantly urging the keepers of stables to make adequate enquiries before hiring out their horses to strangers, and he offered to supply them at regular intervals

with printed handbills, giving the descriptions of every highwayman and his horse which had been recently notified to the
Bow Street Office. He also provided armed guards for stage
coaches travelling on the more dangerous routes. The *Public
Advertiser* recounted in April, 1771, that a certain coachman
had been held up frequently just outside London by one
particular robber. Eventually he took one of the Bow Street
officers with him on his journey. The report continued, 'They
were attacked near Highgate by the same villain, who rode up
to the coach door, presented his pistol and demanded money;
the guard fired and shot away part of the jaw and chin of the
highwayman, who fired into the coach, but happily missed
them all; he was secured and carried to an hospital.'

In 1768, John moved out of Bow Street and rented a large
house in the village of Brompton, very near the present position of the South Kensington Underground Station. Henry
Fielding's elder son, William, was then twenty and had gone
to sea, but Allen, Henry's younger son, was still at school.
Probably the vivacious Mary Ann Whittingham, John's
adopted niece and another member of his household, was
living at home at the time pursuing her studies. William was
destined to become a barrister and a magistrate like his father,
although his career was impeded by a severe stroke when he
was about thirty. Allen became a clergyman and the husband
of Mary Ann, with whom he had grown up in the relationship
of brother and sister. They were married in 1783, when his
father and her uncle were both dead. One can imagine the
delight of the Fielding half-brothers if they had been alive
to witness this happy union between their two families.

CHAPTER THIRTEEN

THE END OF AN ERA

JOHN FIELDING was certain that the depredations of the London criminals would never be checked until the roads were adequately lit and efficiently patrolled. The first of these deficiencies was partially rectified in the spring of 1764 when the Treasury spent a large sum of money on paving and lighting many of the streets of Westminster; but, as far as the second was concerned, the Government remained unconvinced that the necessary expenditure could be justified.

It was true that, from time to time, small, mounted patrols were sent out by the Bow Street Office on specific missions. These were paid for out of the annual grant made by the Treasury for general policing arrangements, and the exact details were enumerated by John in his expenditure accounts; for instance, an item dated the 16th September, 1756, reads: 'for two men and two horses patrolling the roads to Ranelagh during the season'. However, this was only scratching at the surface of the problem and fell far short of the size and extent of the scheme John had in mind. His suggestion that cavalry should be stationed at the turnpikes on the approaches to London had aroused no favourable response from the authorities, probably because they were obsessed with the constitutional problems involved in the employment of the army in such a role.

John continued to agitate and eventually, in the autumn of 1763, the Government made him a small grant, to be used in the formation of a horse patrol for an experimental period of about six months. The patrol, numbering eight men, first operated on the 17th October, 1763. Two days later, John wrote to George Grenville, the First Lord of the Treasury, saying, 'Sir John Fielding presents his most respectful compliments to the Right Honble. Mr. Grenville: it is with the greatest pleasure he acquaints him that the Horse Patrole, established through his means, gives infinite satisfaction to the public, especially those who inhabit the neighbourhood

of London, many of whom I have spoken with'. He went on
to ask for the enlargement of the grant to cover an additional
two men, as a total of eight had proved insufficient. Grenville acceded to this request and the allocation was increased
accordingly.

The members of the horse patrol were well-armed, but as
they had no official status they did not wear any uniform.
Each man was paid four shillings a night, plus his expenses.
They worked in pairs and their routes, which passed along all
the principal turnpike roads, covered an area bounded to the
north by Highgate, to the south by Clapham, to the east by
Greenwich, and to the west by Ealing. The *Public Advertiser*
announced that the men employed on the turnpikes had been
issued with horns so that they could summon the patrols in an
emergency.

Within a week of the commencement of the horse patrol,
Grenville received an anonymous note disparaging the entire
scheme and alleging that the new force was composed of professional murderers and thieves. Sir John was furious. In a
letter to Grenville, dated 1st November, 1763, he complained
of, 'the infamous falsehoods . . . calculated to prejudice you
against me, and thereby to rob me of the confidence, without
which my most earnest endeavours can do but little good'. Of
the patrol itself, he commented, 'I think it is proper to
acquaint you that no steps of that kind ever gave such general
satisfaction, and its good effects, I may say with truth, have
been already felt, but two robberies having been since committed by two footpads, who were detected and found to be
soldiers of the guards'. He then went on to list the names and
the occupations of the ten members of the patrol, which included a baker, a chandler, a publican, and John's own coachman. 'None of these were charged with murder or tried for
felony,' he said indignantly; in fact, several either were or had
been constables. He added, 'The labour of the horse patrol is
so severe and hazardous that I am rather surprised than otherwise that I have such proper persons to undertake it'.

John was perfectly justified in claiming the immediate success of the horse patrol, for during the months of that winter
the number of hold-ups and robberies on or near the metropolitan turnpike roads showed a considerable decrease. In

January, 1764, *Jackson's Oxford Journal* reported that, 'several gangs of thieves have lately left London to avoid Sir John Fielding's parties and have disguised themselves as gypsies'. But the Government still begrudged the money for the project and John experienced the utmost difficulty in extracting even the promised allocation. In reply to his continued exhortations that the horse patrol should be put on a permanent basis, Charles Jenkinson, the First Secretary to the Treasury, countered with the suggestion that the expenses should be borne by the individual counties rather than by the national exchequer. John replied that no county would be prepared to countenance such an idea.

On the 9th July, 1764, Jenkinson wrote to Grenville suggesting that the scheme might be continued for another three months. Grenville agreed and the horse patrol came to end in October, 1764, having operated for a period of one year at a total cost to the country of £1,014. 18. 0. From then on, John was only left with his two mounted pursuers, stationed at the Bow Street Office in readiness to deal with emergency calls.

Sir John Fielding also used to organise occasional foot patrols consisting of a body of constables under the command of one of the Bow Street Runners. During the summer of 1764, in a letter to Charles Jenkinson, he related how one such force had gone out 'into the fields near Tyburn and Tottenham Court Road, to search the ditches where footpads have lately infested'. In a fierce encounter two robbers were captured, one being seriously wounded; 'all which circumstances,' John added, 'might, I am convinced, be prevented. There is nothing I so sincerely lament as the want of an opportunity of convincing Mr. Grenville of the amazing importance of the police to the Government; for notwithstanding his most laudable resolution not to lay any permanent expense on the Crown that can be avoided, yet I am sure that he will never spare any necessary expense where the public good is the object.'

The Government turned increasingly to the Bow Street magistrates on all matters affecting the administration of public order. Indeed, without a regular police force there was no-one else who could advise them in times of civil unrest—

or upon whom they could cast the blame when the violence of the mob prevailed.

In 1765, the House of Commons attempted to arrest the decline of the home silk-weaving industry by passing a Bill which imposed a much heavier duty on imported silk. The measure was rejected by the Lords, amidst the mounting indignation of the weavers, who singled out the Duke of Bedford, one of the Bill's chief opponents, as the principal target for their anger. The Duke's coach was attacked as he was leaving Parliament after the debate and he himself was slightly injured; two days later his house was besieged by a large crowd and would undoubtedly have been wrecked, had they not been dispersed by a troop of cavalry.

For about a week, London hovered on the brink of an outbreak of widespread, anti-Government rioting, while Sir John Fielding and Saunders Welch, whose relationship was then extremely strained, continued to give a completely divergent prognosis of the situation; the former deeming it a trivial disturbance and the latter sensing a serious implication in what was taking place. As soon as the tension had subsided, the Government appointed a committee of enquiry to investigate the causes and the handling of the disorders.

The committee produced their report with a minimum of delay. They found that 'the beginning and continuance of these disorderly assemblies were in great measure owing to the remissness of several of the magistrates, and to their not exerting themselves properly in the execution of the laws against riots and riotous meetings'. Sir John Fielding, they stated, was 'particularly blameable', but they also censored the magistrates in general 'for not doing their duty in suppressing these tumultuous meetings'.

As has been mentioned previously, the justices of the peace were responsible for dealing with labour disputes, and this duty periodically fell to the lot of the Bow Street magistrates. Saunders Welch was possessed of the sort of honest and fearless personality which appealed particularly to the British working-man. When the journeyman-shoemakers were striking for higher wages in 1766, he attended one of their meetings and persuaded their leaders to meet representatives of the employers, to whom he observed, 'that as they had raised

De la Cour pinxit ad vivum.   T. Ryley fecit

Sir Thomas De Veil Knight,

One of his Majesties Justices of the Peace for the Counties of Midx.

Essex, Surry, & Hertfordshire the City & Liberty of Westmr.

the Tower of London & the Liberties thereof.

Published according to Act of Parliam. June 1741.   Sold by De la Cour Katharine Street in the Strand.

1. Sir Thomas de Veil, the first of the Bow Street magistrates

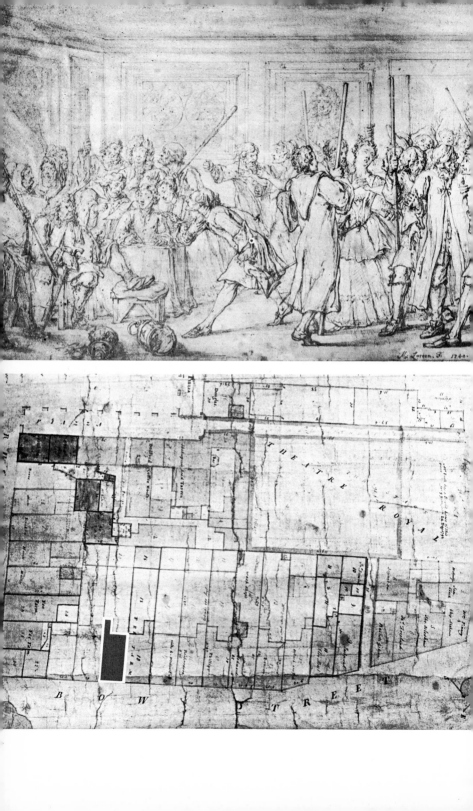

2. (above left) This drawing of 1740 by Marcellus Laroon, entitled 'Night Walkers before a Justice' has an added nineteenth-century caption, 'A French gentleman brought at night before the justice at Bow Street'

3. (bottom left) A plan in the Bedford Office Records shows the portion of Covent Garden which includes Bow Street and part of the Piazza. The names of the householders in Bow Street are given; 'Fielding' is unfortunately unclear; but the position of the Office is indicated by dark area surrounded by white line

4. (above right) Henry Fielding

5. (bottom right) Sir John Fielding in his Court

6. (*above*) Saunders Welch

7 & 8. (*right*) A letter from Sir John Fielding to Robert Palmer, dated June 14th, 1780, in the Bedford Office Records, indicates that the Bow Street Office had not been completely destroyed in the Gordon Riots, just over a week before, as had previously been believed

Brompton Place
June 14th

Sir John Fielding's respects to Mr
Palmer, & after a long fit of Illness
and a partial recovery, he has met
with a severe treatment from the
common people.

My lease is not of long duration
I should be glad to know from you
how far it can be extended by his
Grace, so as to justify my repairing
the old office which I am inform'd may
be easily done & which I would wish
to do immediately, in order to establish
the Public office.

In all cases relative to Myself
where you are to form the judgment. I make no
propositions, but rest satisfied on
your determination & am with
esteem your
Affectionate Friend.

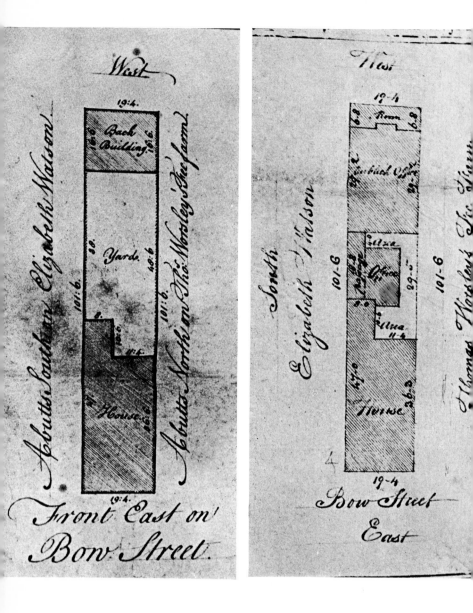

9. Small plan on the lease taken out by Sir John Fielding's executors for No. 4 Bow Street, on 10th April, 1781

10. Small plan on James Read's lease for No. 4 Bow Street, dated 27th May, 1811

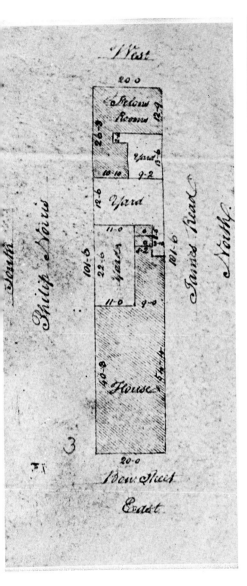

11. Small plan on James Read's lease for No. 3 Bow Street, dated 9th August, 1813

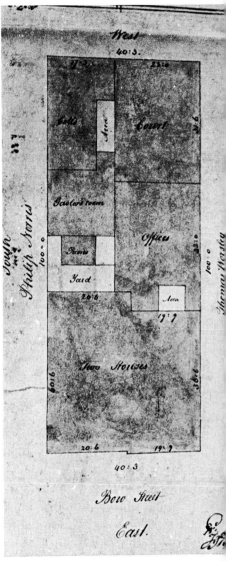

12. Small plan on the lease of 28th February, 1842, for Nos. 3 and 4 Bow Street, between the Duke of Bedford and the Receiver for the Metropolitan Police

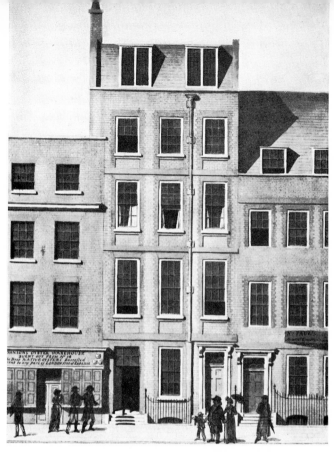

13. (*above*) A sketch of No. 4 Bow Street in 1825

14. (*below*) A sketch of the hotel, The Brown Bear, which stood opposite Nos. 3 and 4 Bow Street, and contained a strong-room for prisoners

the prices of their shoes on account of the increased value of provisions, they should consider that the families of their workmen had proportionate wants'. This simple advocacy proved successful and an all-round increase in wage-rates was arranged. John Thomas Smith, who has recounted this story, ends by saying that after the negotiations were concluded, the shoemakers 'carried Mr. Welch on their shoulders to his office in Litchfield Street, gave him three cheers more, and set him down'.

John, too, had his successes in settling industrial troubles. During the year 1768, he intercepted a large body of coal-heavers who were marching on the House of Commons, and persuaded them to abandon their protest and to send a dele-gation to discuss their grievances with him at the Bow Street Office. A few weeks later he acted as arbitrator when the tailors were staging a militant demonstration for higher wages. But probably his greatest triumph in this sphere was the part he played in bringing an equanimity to the labour relations of the weaving trade, which was to subsist, with only minor eruptions, until the commencement of the Industrial Revolu-tion. He achieved this by arranging for the representatives of the journeyman-weavers and the employers to meet together at Bow Street under his personal chairmanship, and to nego-tiate a new wage structure, which was later embodied in an Act of Parliament. Samuel Scholl, himself a weaver, writing of this agreement in 1811, said that John Fielding's name 'ought to be recorded in letters of gold, and inscribed on the hearts of present and rising generations, with the utmost gratitude, to the latest period of time'.

The most serious riots with which the Bow Street Office had to contend during this period were the popular demon-strations associated with the return to England of the out-lawed John Wilkes, after his four year, self-imposed exile in France. Not only did Wilkes flaunt the authorities by coming home, but he succeeded in getting himself elected to Parlia-ment as the Member for Brentford in March, 1768. Horace Walpole has described the wild scenes of rejoicing which en-sued in London after the ballot figures were announced:

All Westminster was in a riot. It was not safe to pass through Piccadilly; and every family was forced to put out lights; the windows of every unilluminated house were demolished. The coach-glasses of such as did not huzza for 'Wilkes and liberty' were broken, and many chariots and coaches were spoiled by the mob by scratching them ... In the city they attacked the Mansion House and broke the windows.

The disorders grew in intensity as the magistrates and the constables strove desperately to control the situation. When the Dowager Duchess of Hamilton refused to light up her house, it was attacked for three hours by an incensed crowd who smashed down the gates, doors and shutters, and tore up the pavement outside. The Austrian Ambassador was bundled from his coach, which was daubed with Wilkite slogans. Other houses were attacked and acts of hooliganism and violence were perpetrated in the streets.

The Government persisted in their view that the maintenance of order was primarily the responsibility of the civil power—in other words, the magistrates. After a week of rioting, Lord Weymouth, the Secretary of State, reproved Sir John Fielding because a wine merchant had sought the protection of the Bow Street police and, nevertheless, his house had been assailed by the mob. Lord Weymouth said that he thought it 'his indispensable duty to take notice of any remissness in a magistrate, upon whom so much of the public order and tranquillity depend'. John had previously informed him that the eighty Westminster constables were being taxed to the very limit.

Wilkes was due to appear before the Lord Chief Justice in the Court of King's Bench on the 20th April in order to surrender to his warrant of outlawry. A few days before the hearing, Lord Weymouth sent Sir John a directive to be read to the other Westminster magistrates, urging them to prevent a riot when Wilkes appeared, and assuring them that a military force would be available in any emergency. 'I need not add', he went on, 'that if the public peace is not preserved, and if any riotous proceedings which may happen are not suppressed, the blame will most probably be imputed to a want of prudent and spirited conduct in the civil magistrate.'

In fact, there were no disorders on the 20th April, but the following week the mob was out again in force when Wilkes went to Westminster Hall to appeal against the Order of Out-

lawry. On this occasion, too, there might have been no serious
incidents had not the news seeped out that he had been refused bail and committed to the Kings Bench Prison at Southwark. Sir John, his fellow magistrates, and the eighty Westminster constables were all standing by, and Saunders Welch
was directed to ride with Wilkes in his coach. As the coach
was about to cross Westminster Bridge, it was seized by the
crowd and driven off along the Strand to the City. However,
Wilkes had no wish to be rescued and gave himself up later
that same day. Lord Weymouth, of course, blamed the magistrates for this occurrence. When Wilkes was to appear on
remand ten days later, Weymouth warned Sir John that 'if
the same indecent contempt of this civil power shall appear
on this occasion . . . his Lordship will think it necessary to
make a strict enquiry into it'.

There was no further disturbance and after Wilkes had
been sentenced to twenty-two months' imprisonment, Lord
Weymouth condescended to offer his belated gratitude to Sir
John and the Westminster justices, 'for the most important
assistance you have given towards preserving the peace in
these times of shameful riot and disorder'.

Meanwhile, John Fielding was perfecting a project for the
universal interchange of information regarding offences and
offenders throughout the country. 'The favourite object of
my ambition', he called it, 'and the great end of twenty years
labour.' During the autumn of 1772, he began to circulate,
free of charge, to magistrates in every part of England a bulletin called *The Weekly or Extraordinary Pursuit;* this contained details of all the criminals who had absconded from
London. He also encouraged county magistrates to send the
Bow Street Office, 'an early account of those offenders that
have escaped justice from the county, with an exact description of their persons, and a proper warrant for their apprehension; which being filed at the above Office, will be ready
to be sent to any part of England.' The scheme met with an
enthusiastic response from the magistrates generally, and it
was used with great success in tracking down a number of
fugitive criminals. John wrote proudly that it had given
England 'an instrument of law enforcement superior to that

of any country in the world'. He compared the foreign, professional police forces, employed 'at immense expense to pry into the affairs of inhabitants and travellers in an arbitrary manner', with the 'manly police of England who could not effect the liberty of the meanest of His Majesty's subjects until he had been charged'.

At the beginning of 1773, John applied to the Government for an annual grant of about £400 to finance his new venture. This was eventually approved, the Secretary of State, the Earl of Suffolk, expressing the view that the demand seemed to be 'very moderate and equitable'. Thereafter, the weekly bulletin became a permanent institution; its name was altered later, first to *The Public Hue and Cry* and then to *The Hue and Cry*. On the formation of the Metropolitan Police in 1829, it became the *Police Gazette*.

Sir John's lease of the Bow Street Office was due to expire in 1787. However, on the 20th of February, 1770, he took out a new lease, extending his tenure from Michaelmas 1787 until Michaelmas 1797, at a continued rental of £10 per annum. He wrote to the Duke of Bedford the following month to thank him for this 'generous gift of an additional ten years to the lease of his house in Bow Street.' Sir John added that he knew his behaviour had recently been misrepresented to the Duke; this was a terrible mortification to him, 'as he is conscious that it was impossible for any man to be more sensible of a favour conferred on his family than he was of that princely generosity which His Grace showed to his late brother, Henry Fielding, or to be more attached, from principles of gratitude and respect, to your Grace's honour, welfare and interest' than he had always been.

In spite of the national reputation the Bow Street Office had acquired, it was still held by Sir John as a personal tenancy, and was paid for and maintained at his own expense. The cost of upkeep was considerable and made growing inroads into his modest salary. In 1774, he attempted unsuccessfully to obtain an appointment as Law Clerk to the Secretary of State; in his letter of application he remarked, 'For twenty years I have contentedly laboured for daily bread and have neither asked for anything or bettered my situation'.

During the final decade of his life, Sir John Fielding was frequently consulted by politicians, lawyers and reformers. He was one of the principal witnesses examined by a House of Commons Committee, set up in 1770, 'to enquire into the several burglaries and robberies that of late have been committed in or about the cities of London and Westminster'. John told the Committee of the appalling growth in juvenile delinquency. Young boys began as pick-pockets, 'but turn housebreakers when they grow up, in order to procure a great income to supply their increased expenses'. He said that thieves no longer took the property they had stolen to pawnbrokers and silversmiths; instead they 'now go to Jews, who melt the plate immediately, and destroy other things that might be evidence'.

In the course of his examination by the Committee, Sir John condemned the existing system of watch-keeping. 'The watch is insufficient', he said; 'their duty is too hard, and their pay too small'. He also criticized the maladministration of the Westminster Gatehouse—the common gaol for the City. 'When a magistrate commits a man to that gaol for an assault', he remarked, 'he does not know but he commits him there to starve.' Speaking about the quality of the Westminster justices, he said, 'It would be useful to have some persons of rank and condition in the Commission of the Peace for Westminster, who would give a dignity to the Commission'. Finally, he commented on the great number of brothels and irregular taverns which were opening up all over London. They were, in his opinion, 'another cause of robberies, burglaries and other disorders'. He suggested that prostitutes 'walking or plying in the streets for lewd purposes after the watch is set should be considered as vagrants and punished as such'.

Sir John had strong views on the necessity for penal reform. In the course of a letter to William Eden (later Lord Auckland), written in 1776, he expressed his doubts about the efficacy of the hulks. 'I begin to fear', he wrote, 'that collecting the rogues of different countries into one ship may, instead of begetting reformation, occasion friendships and connections which would be cemented by their fellow sufferings and make them unite when discharged.' During that same year,

Sir John was invited to advise the Government on the new Penitentiary Houses they were hoping to establish.

In May 1774, Sir John's wife had died at his home in Brompton. Three months later he remarried, to a Mary Sedgley, at the Kensington Parish Church. There is no reason for believing his second marriage was any less happy than his first.

While the Gordon Riots were ravaging London in June 1780, Sir John was lying seriously ill at Brompton. He never recovered completely and his death occurred on the 4th September, 1780, at the age of fifty-eight. The following day, the *Lloyds Evening Post* carried this announcement:

On Monday evening at eight o'clock died at his house in Brompton, near Knightsbridge, after a long and painful illness, which he bore with the utmost patience, Sir John Fielding, Knt., one of His Majesty's Justices of the Peace for the counties of Middlesex, Essex, Herts, Kent, Surrey and the City and Liberty of Westminster, whose abilities as a magistrate could only be equalled by his humanity as a man, and whose loss will be most severely felt by the public, but by none so much as the poor, to whom he was a warm and unalterable friend.

Another newspaper described him as 'a consummate magistrate who was universally allowed to have the head of a philosopher, the heart of a Christian and the hand of a hero'.

Sir John Fielding was buried in Chelsea Parish Church, at the side of his first wife, Elizabeth Whittingham.

Saunders Welch had ceased to work as a magistrate in 1776, when he had been advised to move to a warmer climate following a severe illness. According to Boswell, as a result of Dr. Johnson's intercession with the Secretary of State, Welch was granted leave of absence to go to Italy, and also received an undertaking that his salary of £200 a year would continue. He went abroad accompanied by his elder daughter, Anne, whom Boswell describes as 'a young lady of uncommon talents and literature'.

We have very little information about the closing years of Saunders Welch's life. He was still in Italy in February, 1778, as Dr. Johnson sent him a letter there, addressed to 'English Coffee House, Rome', in which he apologized for not writing sooner, but said that their long friendship had grown too solid to need general expressions of good will. 'When we meet', he continued, 'we will try to forget our cares and our maladies, and contribute, as we can, to the cheerfulness of each other.' It is apparent from the letter that Welch had by then recovered, for Dr. Johnson said, 'I suppose you propose to return this year. There is no need of haste . . . . After having travelled so far to find health, you must take care not to lose it at home'.

Saunders Welch died at Taunton Dean in Somerset, aged 73, on the 31st of October, 1784, predeceasing his old friend, Dr. Johnson, by a matter of a few weeks. He was buried at St. George's Church in Bloomsbury, where a mural monument to his memory was erected in the porch. Welch's death did not attract a great deal of attention in the newspapers; however, *The Gentleman's Magazine,* in a short obituary notice, paid a tribute to his 'skill, activity and integrity' as a magistrate.

Anne Welch, who never married, lived until 1810; her sister, Mary, Mrs. Nollekens, died in 1817. Both daughters always remembered their father with the deepest affection, the younger of the two showing her respect in an unusual manner, for John Thomas Smith has told us that, 'Whenever Mrs. Nollekens related any anecdote of her father, she always elevated her person by standing on her toes, at the conclusion of every extraordinary mark of his benevolence, courage, or sensible magisterial decision'.

CHAPTER FOURTEEN

THE GORDON RIOTS

On Friday the 2nd June, 1780, a vast crowd of some 60,000 people led by the fanatical, twenty-nine-year-old Lord George Gordon, set out from St. George's Fields to march on the Houses of Parliament. This marked the commencement of one of the ugliest and the bloodiest weeks in the history of London—a week which clearly demonstrated the helpless inability of the magistracy and the amateur constabulary to protect the ordinary, peaceful citizen from the frenzy of an incensed mob.

The pretext for Lord George's demonstration was a protest against the recent legislation for the removal of certain disabilities from the Roman Catholics. But, as far as the marchers were concerned, it might well have been any of a score of differing causes, some religious, some political, and some social, which had awakened their latent spirit of revolt; and it might have been any orator, any emblem, or any slogan which had set the human tide in motion.

At this time, three months before his death, Sir John Fielding was confined to his house in Brompton. The final reference to his activities in the State Papers occurs on the 24th November, 1779, and his previously-quoted obituary notice spoke of his having undergone 'a long and painful illness'. Saunders Welch, too, had long relinquished his magisterial activities; even if he returned to England, as he intended, during the year 1778, he seems to have spent the last years of his life in retirement.

During Sir John's illness, the work at Bow Street was carried on by Sampson Wright and William Addington, both of whom successively were to become senior magistrates at the Office, and to be rewarded for their services with the honour of a knighthood. The Middlesex justices' records show that they became particularly active in returning recognizances to Westminster Sessions from the month of October, 1779, onwards.

Sampson Wright registered his property qualifications as a Middlesex justice on the 4th September, 1769. He had probably been at the Bow Street Office for some years, for one of his cases there was reported by the *Public Advertiser* in November, 1774. William Addington registered his property qualification for Middlesex on the 13th July, 1774. He had commenced his life as a clergyman, but resigned his living to enter the army, where he rose to the rank of major. On Sir John Fielding's recommendation he became a magistrate, and his name appears in newspaper reports of proceedings at the Bow Street Office around 1775. At that time, he wrote a book on criminal law, which he dedicated to Sir John, and he also gained a not-inconsiderable reputation as a playwright.

Paul de Castro, in his book on the Gordon Riots, has referred to Sampson Ramsforth as being a third magistrate from Bow Street, who was very much in evidence at that time. Ramsforth was, in fact, the High Constable of Westminster and there is no evidence that he ever became a justice of the peace for Westminster or Middlesex.

The Gordon Riots began around midday when Lord George Gordon and the rabble which had accompanied him from St. George's Fields poured across Westminster Bridge, with banners flying and bagpipes skirling to the massive, oft-repeated cry of 'No Popery'. The mob surrounded the Houses of Parliament and intercepted Peers and Members arriving for the day's debates, smashing their coaches and treating them with mounting violence. When he received a report on the situation, Lord Stormont, the Secretary of State for the Home Department, sent an immediate appeal to the Secretary for War, requesting him to arrange for a military force to be held in readiness, 'in case the Civil Magistrate should find it necessary to apply for their assistance'.

For the entire afternoon and evening the surging crowds continued their violent demonstration, and eventually, at about 9 p.m., a party of infantry and cavalry arrived, accompanied by William Addington. However, in spite of their drawn swords the soldiers were unable to force their way through the crush outside the Houses of Parliament. Shortly before midnight, Lord Stormont sent an urgent message to the Bow Street and Litchfield Street Offices, and to Sir John Hawkins, the Chairman of the Middlesex magistrates; 'I am informed,' he said, 'that the tumultuous assembly of people continues before the House of Commons. I desire you to take immediately every legal method to keep the public peace, and that a sufficient number of Justices, Constables and Peace Officers attend tomorrow to secure to the Lords and Members a free access and regress from both Houses of Parliament.' In the light of what followed, this must rank amongst the most nonsensical edicts which have ever emanated from a Minister of the Crown.

Meanwhile, sections of the mob were burning and looting the Roman Catholic chapels attached to the Sardinian Embassy, near Lincoln's Inn Fields, and the Bavarian Embassy in Golden Square. Sampson Ramsforth, with the aid of a handful of constables, managed to detain one of the rioters at the Sardinian Chapel, but the man was immediately rescued by the crowd. Ramsforth returned to the scene later, supported by a force of a hundred soldiers with fixed bayonets, and a few of the Bow Street Runners, and he succeeded in arresting thirteen of the ringleaders.

In the early hours of the morning, the harassed Lord Stormont sent another message to Bow Street, Litchfield Street and Sir John Hawkins: 'I am at this moment informed,' he said, 'that a tumultuous set of people have broken into the Sardinian and Bavarian chapels. I desire you without delay to protect the said Foreign Ministers' houses, and to endeavour to prevent further outrages'.

The remainder of the night passed off with only sporadic outbursts of violence, and at daybreak on Saturday, the 3rd June, Horace Walpole wrote, 'I smile today, but I trembled last night. I knew the bravest of my friends were barricaded in the House of Commons and every avenue to it was impassible'. The public concern was increased by a widespread rumour that the troops were sympathetic to the mob, and had stated they would refuse to open fire on them if ordered to do so by their officers.

On the Saturday morning, every available magistrate and constable was on duty as the surly, mutinous crowds thronged the streets. The greatest number of people assembled in

Covent Garden, to see the thirteen prisoners from the previous night brought to the Bow Street Office under a strong military escort for their appearance before Justice Wright and Justice Addington. After a brief interrogation, one of them was released on bail and the other twelve were committed to Clerkenwell Gaol.

That evening the centre of the disturbance shifted from Westminster to the City of London, where a mob gathered in Moorfields intending to destroy the Roman Catholic chapels and the houses of suspected Catholic sympathizers in the vicinity. Two leading city merchants appealed to the Lord Mayor, Mr. Brackley Kennett, for the protection of their property, but he replied, 'I must be cautious what I do lest I bring the mob to my house. I can assure you that there are very great people at the bottom of this riot.' Mr. Kennett, a shady character, had graduated from brothel to tavern-keeping, and later became a prosperous wine-dealer. In the event, the crowds were dispersed by constables led by the Aldermen of the ward before they could do much damage.

Sunday, the 4th June, was a bitterly cold day, but this did not discourage the rioters, who were out on the streets at an early hour in the morning vaunting their blue cockades, now adopted as the insignia of Lord George Gordon's supporters, and chanting their battle-cry of 'No Popery'. Lord Stormont clung tenaciously to his theory that this was still a routine disturbance, which could be handled in the traditional manner by the magistrates and the constables—and, in the last resort, by the intervention of the military. During the morning he sent a message to the commanding officer of the Horse Guards in Whitehall, requesting him to give special protection to the houses and the chapels of foreign ambassadors; if there was the slightest trouble, he said, information should immediately be conveyed to Justice Addington. Stormont then sent long and detailed instructions to the magistrates of Middlesex and Westminster, informing them how he wished them to behave in this emergency.

Outbreaks of violence occurred all that day in different parts of London. In the City, houses, schools, and chapels were pillaged and furniture, pews and vestments were burned in the streets. On the direction of the Lord Mayor, the troops stood by and took no action. However, at Lincoln's Inn Fields, where another church was attacked, the rioters were driven off by a detachment of Guards from Somerset House.

Monday, the 5th of June, was warmer and the size and the temper of the crowds had become far more menacing. The Earl of Jersey was voicing a general apprehension when he wrote in a letter that day, 'London seems at present to be totally taken up with this blue cockade mob . . . the Guards are in parties quartered all over the town. The public seems much more alarmed, for the numbers on Friday were greatly beyond all former and common mobs'.

During the morning the thirteen prisoners were once again examined at Bow Street and the evidence against the majority of them was found to be extremely flimsy. When arrests are made at the height of a mass disturbance it is often very difficult to differentiate between the active participants on the one hand, and the inquisitive bystanders on the other. Most of the men were found to bear excellent characters, and several were actually of the Roman Catholic faith. At the close of the examination, ten prisoners were discharged and the remaining three were despatched to Newgate Gaol under a strong military guard.

That evening the tide of vengeance was directed, not only against known Roman Catholics, but also against any persons who had been associated with the prosecution of the thirteen men at Bow Street. A mob of five thousand pillaged and fired the house of Sampson Ramsforth, High Constable of Westminster, who had carried out the initial arrests. Justice Addington hurried to the scene with a detachment of thirty troops, but when he arrived the flames were burning fiercely and the crowds were deliberately preventing the parish engines from fighting the blaze. A number of these who had appeared as witnesses for the prosecution had their homes destroyed in a similar manner.

In the City, the principal targets for the violence were once again the homes of Catholics and Catholic chapels. At one stage Lord Stormont sent an angry message to the Lord Mayor, saying he had just received intelligence that, 'a great number of seditious persons are employed in demolishing different dwelling houses, and all this is done in broad day without the least interposition of the civil magistrate'.

There was still no cohesive plan for suppressing the disorders, and no centralised direction of effort. The Government, supine and evasive, continued to rely on the ability of the 'civil power' to achieve some sort of strategic miracle which would restore the situation. Understandably enough, the King felt uneasy; he warned Lord North, the Prime Minister, that 'This tumult must be got the better of, or it will encourage designing men to use it as a precedent for assembling people on other occasions'. In reply, Lord North assured him that the military forces in London were being increased and would remain in a state of instant readiness.

At midnight Lord Stormont took action. He wrote to the Secretary for War, asking for large reinforcements of troops, and in another letter to Lord Amherst, Commander-in-Chief of the army, he said, 'Some of the Civil Magistrates who have just been with us here, give us as their clear opinion that it will be impracticable to keep the Publick Peace unless there is a very considerable Body of Horse which they can call in to their assistance'. Lord Amherst immediately ordered his reserves of cavalry at Southwark and Canterbury to move into London.

An exchange of notes on the Tuesday between Charles Jenkinson (later the first Earl of Liverpool), the Secretary for War, and Lord Amherst, revealed the unsatisfactory and incongruous role of the military in performing their anti-riot duties. They were permitted, said Mr. Jenkinson, 'to act only under the Authority and by the direction of the Civil Magistrate. For this reason they are under greater restraints than any other of His Majesty's subjects'. He went on to assert that there had been several instances during the prevailing disturbances where a magistrate had either summoned troops to his assistance and disappeared before their arrival, or else had waited for them to come, but had refused to give them any instructions. Lord Amherst replied, 'I see in its fullest extent the mischief that must arise from such conduct in the Civil Magistrates, and have written in the strongest terms to the different offices'.

That day was the most violent since the riots had started, as the mob came out armed with cutlasses, clubs and pole-axes. The Earl of Jersey described the scene in the morning when the crowds were 'parading in triumph in different parties thro' all the streets, threatening the houses and lives of those who they have understood to be the most in earnest in passing the Bill, and the Guards (Horse, Foot and Light Horse) sent in pursuit of them without any effect. They are got to such a pitch of confidence that I cannot conceive any way of bloodshed being avoided tonight . . . these three days they have spent in pulling down houses, chapels and papist schools, the magistrates standing by, even the Lord Mayor, and not ordering the soldiers to act'.

Lord Jersey's presentiment of bloodshed was soon borne out. Five hundred rioters marched on the Archbishop of Canterbury's palace at Lambeth, but were driven off by troops before they could mount a direct assault. Another large party tried to force their way through St. James's Park to attack the Queen's House; they were intercepted by a troop of Horse Guards who threatened that, if anyone were to come any closer, they would open fire without waiting for a magistrate's authority. The greatest crowds surrounded the Houses of Parliament where there were repeated scuffles, and at one stage the position became so serious that a detachment of cavalry, under the direction of Justice Hyde, drew their swords and charged the demonstrators. All day there were spasmodic attacks on the homes of Roman Catholics in various parts of London.

Meanwhile, the House of Commons, to whom many people looked for a lead in suppressing the disorders, passed a series of lame resolutions condemning the behaviour of the mob, and hurriedly adjourned until the following Thursday morning.

At five o'clock in the afternoon, Justice Hyde decided that the time had come to clear the throngs from the vicinity of the Houses of Parliament. Accordingly, he entered Palace Yard and read a proclamation under the Riot Act; then, after waiting for an hour, he ordered the cavalry to charge. The infuriated mob broke up and swarmed into St. Martin's Street, where Justice Hyde had his London home. In a short space of time all his private possessions were burning in the street, and his house had been smashed up and set alight. An ensign and thirty soldiers appeared and tried to clear the area, but as there was no magistrate available who could empower them to use their muskets they were forced to withdraw.

In the evening, the King again wrote to Lord North expressing his exasperation with the conduct of the House of Commons and the magistrates. 'Allowing Lord Geo. Gordon, the avowed head of the tumult, to be at large', he said, 'certainly encourages the continuation of it . . . I fear without more vigour that this will not subside, indeed, unless exemplary punishment is procured it will remain a lasting disgrace, and will be the precedent for further commotion.'

By nightfall the mob had completely lost its reason. Masses of men and women poured through Holborn and Snow Hill to Newgate, intent on rescuing the three prisoners who had been committed from Bow Street on the previous day. When the Keeper refused to release the men, his house was fired and an all-out assault was commenced on the prison. Some people battered down the doors and the windows; others scaled the prison walls with ladders; wardens and constables were attacked and beaten; and the three hundred prisoners were liberated from their cells. To add to the confusion the flames spread out from the Keeper's house and soon the whole prison was blazing fiercely. 'At length the work of ruin was accomplished', said an onlooker, 'and while the gaolers and turnkeys were either flying or begging for their lives, forth came the prisoners, blaspheming and jumping in their chains. The convicts were taken to different blacksmiths in the neighbourhood.'

Bow Street, too, was filled with a surging crowd, and Sir John Fielding's clerk, Nicholas Bond, considered their attitude so menacing that, leaving Macmanus, a Bow Street Runner, in charge of the Office with two constables, he hurried away to summon the help of the military. Giving evidence later against a sailor, William Lawrence, who was executed for his part in the affair, Macmanus said:

I stayed in the house near three hours. I saw a great crowd of people; they filled all Bow Street and all the streets leading to it; some of them had clubs, others sticks, iron bars and choppers. I saw in particular the prisoner, Lawrence. I saw him constantly

close to the door. Suddenly there was a cry, 'Newgate, Newgate,
Newgate', when many of the people went away.

About nine o'clock that evening, Macmanus went on, the
mob returned, probably fresh from the sacking of Newgate
Gaol, and once more assembled outside the Bow Street Office.
'Numbers who had clubs in their hands came to the door', he
said, 'shouting, "Damn you! We will have it down presently"!' Helped by the constables, Macmanus chained and
barricaded the door; then the three of them escaped out of
the back of the house.

Macmanus, who seems to have been the only Runner available, went home to fetch his cutlass and his pistols. He arrived
back in Bow Street at about ten o'clock the same evening and
found the crowds still surging about the office. 'The windows
were all broken', he said, 'the wainscoting torn down, and
many fires alight in the street where the furniture was burning.' The landlord of The Brown Bear, a tavern on the opposite side of the road, was adding to the havoc by supplying the
demonstrators with free liquor. The odds were too heavy for
Macmanus to interfere and he was obliged to become a passive
spectator. The work of destruction continued without inter-
ruption until around three o'clock the following morning,
when the mob stormed off to ravage other buildings.

It has always been assumed that the Bow Street Office was
totally demolished by the rioters. Dr. Johnson, in a note to
Mrs. Thrale, spoke of it being left in ruins; and William
Fielding, Henry's elder son, said in 1816, 'I remember the
night when the house of my uncle, Sir John Fielding, was
destroyed by the mob.' However, a letter has now come to
light in the Bedford Estate Records which indicates that the
damage was not nearly so great as was thought.

The letter in question was written by John Fielding, at
his home in Brompton, on the 14th June, 1780, to the Duke of
Bedford's agent. In the course of it he says, 'My lease is not of
long duration. I should be glad to know from you how far it
can be extended by His Grace, so as to justify my repairing the
old Office, which I am informed may be easily done, and
which I would wish to do immediately in order to establish
the Public Office'. It seems probable, therefore, that the house

itself was never set on fire, but only the furniture, clothing and papers, which were taken from it and burnt in the street.

Many other homes were sacked that night, including those of Lord Mansfield, the Chief Justice of the King's Bench, Dr. Markham, the Archbishop of York, and Alderman Bull, an ex-Lord Mayor of London. The mob also attacked Lord North's house in Downing Street, but they were driven off by a squadron of Dragoons. Fleet Prison and the New Prison were besieged and the Keepers of both establishments opened their gates to the crowds, who then released all the prisoners.

Two ladies have left descriptions of the scenes in different parts of London during the early hours of that morning. Susan Burney, who watched the proceedings from the roof of her father's house in Leicester Fields said, 'Our Square was as light as day by the bonfire from the contents of Justice Hyde's house, and on the other side we saw flames ascending from Newgate, a fire in Covent Garden, which proved to be Justice Fielding's, and another in Bloomsbury Square, which was Lord Mansfield's'. Lady Anne Erskine, whose point of observation was further to the east, in Clerkenwell, saw her house surrounded by fires. 'The scene was truly horrible,' she said, 'for the flames around had got to such a height that the sky was like blood with the reflection of them.'

By Wednesday, the 7th of June, any semblance of order or control had vanished. The London mob, reinforced by hooligans and other lawless elements from the surrounding counties, was running amok, looting, pillaging, burning, and extorting money from householders under threat of violence. Families barricaded their homes and armed themselves in readiness for any eventuality, and several banks in the City were issuing muskets to members of their staff. That morning the Attorney-General called on the King and advised him that the only way of dispersing the rioters was by the use of military force, without having recourse to the civil magistrates. At much the same time, Lord Stormont was upbraiding the justices of the Litchfield Office for their persistent absence from the principal centres of trouble.

King George III wasted no time in issuing a proclamation which set out that owing to the behaviour of the mob it had become necessary 'to employ the military force, with which

F

we are by law entrusted, for the immediate suppression of such rebellious and traitorous attempts, now making against the peace and dignity of our Crown, and the safety and lives and properties of our subjects.' He had, therefore, he said, given orders to the army to use the utmost force against the rioters. This was virtually a declaration of martial law, and Lord Amherst began immediately to dispose his forces for action. In fact, the royal proclamation reached the City of London just after the Lord Mayor and the Aldermen in the Court of Common Council had agreed to send a petition to the King, entreating him to give way to the demands of the rioters.

All that day the scenes of violence continued over the whole of London, the houses and offices of the magistrates suffering particularly severely. There were also further attacks on prisons, both the Fleet and the King's Bench being set on fire. The worst outrage was the attack on the Holborn Distilleries, when numerous buildings were gutted and vast stocks of spirits were looted by the drunken crowd.

In the evening the first serious clashes occurred between the rioters and the troops. Several attempts to capture the Bank were broken up by the accurate small-arms fire of the infantry; and in a skirmish on Blackfriars Bridge the troops inflicted heavy casualties on the mob with their muskets and their bayonets. Gradually the army and the Militia—who were now fully mobilised—gained the upper hand. Even so, at midnight Lord Amherst felt obliged to warn the Government that all his available forces had been committed, and he was left without any reserves whatsoever.

In the early hours of Thursday, the 8th June, there was bitter fighting in the City when cavalry and infantry were called in to repulse another massive onslaught on the Bank by a huge crowd, many of whom had equipped themselves with firearms.

The troops continued in action without a break for the whole of that day, endeavouring to disperse the mob and to attack them in small groups. This strategy proved so successful that, by the afternoon, the secretary of one of the largest insurance companies in the City felt confident enough to declare, 'The riots seem to be in a fair way of subsiding and we are now under military law, and our magistrates—our scoundrel magistrates—are superseded by a more absolute authority'. The magistrates were being blamed on all sides, but, surprisingly enough, little or no censure appears to have been levelled at the House of Commons, which had re-assembled that morning to discuss the crisis, and had promptly adjourned again without passing a single resolution or making any authoritative pronouncement.

The constitutional position at this stage was none too clear. The soldiers were taking their prisoners, not to the justices, but before a special Court-Martial, which was in constant session, to be examined by a military Judge-Advocate. The Privy Council considered the situation at a meeting attended by all the judges, and agreed, without resolving the issue, that there should be no official proclamation of Martial Law, and that the civil courts should remain open, but that the military should be empowered 'to act at their discretion'.

Thursday night was comparatively peaceful, the streets being extensively patrolled by parties of soldiers. On Friday, the 9th June, when the fighting was very nearly at an end, the Privy Council issued warrants for the arrests of Lord George Gordon and the principal ringleaders of the rioting. Gordon was seized and committed to the Tower on a charge of High Treason. The following day Lord Jersey made a detailed tour of inspection of London and, on its conclusion, sat down and wrote, 'Quiet now seems to be the idea of everybody and the mob is crushed'.

CHAPTER FIFTEEN

IN THE IMAGE OF BOW STREET

THE aftermath of the Gordon Riots was a period of consider-able heart-searching for the people of London. During that perilous week they had experienced a moment of truth in which it had been clear beyond all doubt that the ancient, parochial system of peace-keeping would always be completely ineffectual in dealing with a violent and widespread disorder.

After the last of the rioters had been dispersed, there was a brief interval of military control before the troops handed back the surveillance of the streets to the constables and the watchmen. The residents of the Metropolis relished this re-spite from lawlessness to the full. On the 14th June, 1780, the *Public Advertiser* commented:

> The cities of London and Westminster were never so well guarded nor so peaceable. In the night time there is not the least noise in any of the streets, but everything is profoundly still. No nocturnal revellers break lamps or knock down watchmen; no midnight shrieks of prostitutes; no hideous noise of rattles from the old men; no disturbances at the door of roundhouses . . .the late riots were shocking in their effects, but should a vigilant and regular police be established, nothing of the kind can happen in the future.

The article went on to urge the householders to organise their own armed patrols and to enforce the law themselves. Indeed, in the summer of 1780, several voluntary peace-keeping associations were being formed for the protection of the public, but Lord Amherst pointed out that it was unlaw-ful for these groups of vigilantes to carry arms.

In retrospect, most of the blame for the escalation of the Gordon Riots was attached to the magistrates and the con-stables. 'The miserableness of the Westminster police', said a pamphlet, 'has become obvious, and inherent in that weakness is a danger to the whole country.' Another writer asked, 'Will you, my Fellow-Citizens, still submit to the necessity of calling in the King's Troops on every occasion? Will you subject yourselves to the Danger of having your dearest Privileges invaded by a military Power over whom you have no control?'

In 1781, Sheridan rose in the House of Commons to demand a full enquiry into 'the defective state of the magistracy', but this proposal was rejected by the Government, the Solicitor-General describing the Gordon Riots as 'a single instance of a defect in the civil power which, in all probability, would never occur again'. It is doubtful if this sanguine view was shared by many of the more thoughtful London citizens.

While the ferment of discussion continued, Sir John Fielding's house in Bow Street was being re-built. The rating ledger for the parish of St. Pauls, Covent Garden, from Easter Day 1780 until Easter Day 1781, still shows Fielding as the occupier although his death had occurred in September 1780; for the whole of that period, in fact, the premises were most probably uninhabited. In the ledger for the year commencing on Lady Day (March 25th), 1781, the name of the occupier is left blank, but a side-note discloses that a rate of £3 3s. od. had been collected. On the 10th April, 1781, William Addington and Kempe Brydges, acting as executors for Sir John Fielding's estate, took out a new lease for ten years from Michaelmas 1797 when the current lease was due to expire, until Michaelmas 1807. The rent was to remain at £10 a year 'in consideration of the Damage . . . sustained by the late riot which happened in June last past and the expense and charges which the (executors) will be at in repairing and reinstating the premises'.

The name of Fielding's successor, Sampson Wright, first appears as occupier of the house, in the rating ledger for the year commencing on Lady Day, 1782, by which time the building must have been partially or fully restored. Sampson Wright made himself personally responsible for the enquiries centring around the activities of Charles Price, known as 'Old Patch', one of the most notorious swindlers who ever operated in London during the eighteenth century. Price, an expert in the art of disguise and also in cloak-and-dagger tactics, eluded the Bow Street police for many years before he was eventually captured. At the beginning of the pursuit, in the year 1784, an advertisement appeared in the Press, headed

'Public Office Bow Street', and the text of the announcement, which concerned one of Price's accomplices, began: 'Whereas a woman answering the following description stands charged with felony; whoever will apprehend her and bring her before Sir Sampson Wright at the above office, shall receive £200 for her commitment....'

Almost exactly five years after the Gordon Riots, the Government introduced the London and Westminster Police Bill, a far-reaching, reformative measure, 'for the further prevention of crimes, and for the more speedy detection and punishment of offences against the peace'. The Bill incorporated many of the proposals which had been propounded by Sir John Fielding, but it also contained several clauses of which he would have been highly critical.

The broad effect of the new plan was to form the whole of London—including the City—into a single 'District of the Metropolis' which would be divided, for administrative purposes, into nine separate divisions. Each division was to have its own Public Office, presided over by a resident, stipendiary magistrate, and all the fines, forfeitures, and penalties he collected would be used to defray the general expenses of the office. In addition, each division would have its own force of twenty-five fit and able men, properly armed and equipped to act as full-time, salaried petty constables, and to carry out regular patrols both mounted and on foot.

The petty constables were to have far wider powers than the parish peace-officers. They would be able to arrest any person in possession of articles which they had 'probable grounds to suspect'; they could enter into licensed premises at any hour of the day or night without a warrant; and they were given a special power of control over pawnbrokers and publicans.

One of the most controversial features of the Bill was the placing of the entire newly-created District of the Metropolis under the supervision of three commissioners of police, appointed and paid by the Crown. These commissioners would act as 'general comptrollers and superintendents of the whole establishment', and as such would have complete authority over both the stipendiary magistrates and the constables and watchmen in the various divisions.

Finally, the old system of statutory rewards for successful prosecutions was to be abolished, but the commissioners of police would be enabled to make financial grants in their discretion, to any person who had been instrumental in bringing about an arrest or securing a conviction.

On the 23rd June, 1785, the Solicitor-General, Sir Archibald Macdonald, introduced the London and Westminster Police Bill in the House of Commons. He said that it would be a useless waste of time and words to dwell upon the necessity for this measure. 'No person,' he went on, 'can feel himself unapprehensive of damage to his person or property, if he walks in the street after it is dark; nor could any man promise himself security, even in his bed. Robbery and villainy are becoming so daring that they are . . . perpetrated openly, with undisguised violence in the most populous places, and frequently before it is near dark.'

Dealing with the position of justices of the peace, the Solicitor-General said he was sure that 'public business of any sort will never be adequately and effectually performed, unless those to whom the performance is committed, are paid for their trouble, except in the case of persons eminent in rank and fortune, whose regard for the public, together with the absence of any other pressing avocations, might induce them to do business gratuitously'. The present system was resulting in corruption, inattention and neglect. 'The corruption naturally arises', he commented, 'from the situation of persons engaged in a troublesome employment, who will inevitably contrive some means of paying themselves.'

The total cost of the new establishment, said the Solicitor-General, would amount to about £20,000 a year, about double the expense of the existing system; but most of the increase would be met from the legal fees at the new Public Offices, together with an increased toll on the turnpikes adjacent to London. Also, there would be a considerable saving from the abolition of parliamentary rewards, a proposal which had the strong support of Bow Street magistrates—he referred to Bow Street as, 'the only Office in the Metropolis, that bore any resemblance to an Office of police'.

The new Bill awakened an immediate storm of antagonism. The justices in the Metropolis bitterly resented the creation of stipendiary magistrates, both from motives of personal jealousy, and because some of them genuinely believed that the employment of professionals would seriously undermine the long-established voluntary system. The City was filled with indignation about its inclusion in the scheme, and the Press was generally hostile. A large number of people saw an inherent danger in the appointment of the three government-nominated commissioners of police, who would be invested with arbitrary powers and would command their own, independent, armed police force.

Within a few days, a meeting of Middlesex justices condemned the Bill as 'inexpedient and totally unnecessary', and the Surrey justices passed a resolution to the effect that the existing laws were 'sufficient for all the purposes of protection and security to the public'.

On the 29th June, the Sheriffs of London presented at the Bar of the House of Commons a petition from the Lord Mayor and the Aldermen, who comprised then, as they do today, the magistrates of the City of London. The petition expressed apprehension 'of the mischievous and dangerous effects of a law which, under colour of correcting abuses, over-turns the forms established by the wisdom of our ancestors for the regular administration of justice'. It concluded by urging the House to reject the Bill and thus to relieve the City of the dread 'of being reduced under the scourge of such a system'.

In the ensuing debate, one alderman contrasted the Bow Street Office with the offices set up by trading justices. 'Everyone knew', he said 'there was a regular Office in Bow Street, under the countenance of, and paid by (the) Government, but then there were a great many persons who had got into the Commission, that set up Offices of their own, for the mere sake of trade, and of getting money by business of office,' but, he contended, there were no trading justices in the City of London and consequently, their magisterial offices were not in need of reform.

Eventually the Government yielded to the mounting opposition and withdrew the Bill, at the same time promising to introduce a new and amended version during the following Session. This was, in fact, never done. In 1786, a measure very similar to the original Bill was enacted by the Irish Parliament in Dublin, and it was noted that after the creation of police commissioners, the magistrates, relieved from their control of the peace-officers, began to apply themselves more regularly and more diligently to their judicial functions.

The abandonment of the London and Westminster Police Bill left the magisterial system and the policing arrangements in the Metropolis exactly as they had been. The only real innovation to combat the growth of crime in the decade between 1780 and 1790, was the revival by Sir Sampson Wright, soon after his appointment as senior magistrate at Bow Street, of Sir John Fielding's highway patrol. Wright succeeded where Fielding had failed in obtaining the financial support of the Government. The Treasury papers disclose a series of regular payments for the scheme commencing on the 22nd August, 1783.

During the winter of 1789, there was an alarming increase in the number of violent robberies which were perpetrated in the heart of London, and on the 25th April, 1790, Sir Sampson Wright introduced an armed foot patrol to tour the streets of the Metropolis from dusk until midnight. A few months later, the Government agreed to finance this force as well, and in consequence it was placed on a permanent basis. More will be said about the operations and payment of the foot patrol in a later chapter.

It was Sir Sampson Wright who was responsible for founding in 1786 *The Weekly Hue and Cry,* later to become *The Public Hue and Cry.* This was an elaboration of John Fielding's weekly bulletin of information to county justices known as the *Weekly or Extraordinary Pursuit.* The new paper consisted of four pages and was published twice a week. It contained accounts of crimes, descriptions of criminals and stolen property, and reports of the examinations of suspects at Metropolitan magistrates' offices; the back page was always devoted to a list of the names and particulars of deserters from the army, a large proportion of whom used to drift into the underworld.

During this period, there were several changes in the composition of the Bow Street Bench. In 1785, the somewhat disreputable individual, Nicholas Bond, became a magistrate;

F*

he had started life as a journeyman carpenter, had then become a Bow Street Runner, and had finally been appointed as
Clerk to the Office. The Webbs have described Bond as 'an
illiterate, ignorant man'; he must have had a strong mercenary
tendency as well for he used to charge fees to newspaper re-
porters attending at Bow Street, as a result of which *The
Times* ceased to publish any accounts of cases there. Sampson
Wright died in 1792 and his place as senior magistrate was
taken by his colleague, William Addington. The vacancy for
a third magistrate was filled at that time by Richard Ford,
who preserved the connection between the Bow Street Office
and the theatre as he was a son of the co-manager of Drury
Lane.

In the years that followed the Gordon Riots, the corruption
of the Middlesex justices became more prevalent and more
blatant, though the venality was largely confined to the areas
of the county which lay within the Metropolis. Edward Sayer,
writing in 1784, attributed the difference in quality between
the urban and the rural magistrates to 'the absurdity of applying the same form of government to two very different subjects—to the various and intricate affairs of a city as well as
the simple and unembarrassed regulations of a county'.

The reason for the sudden deterioration in the standards
of the Middlesex justices was undoubtedly due to the fact that
in 1781, Sir John Hawkins, who had been Chairman of the
Middlesex Sessions since 1765, was replaced in that appointment by the reprobate banker William Mainwaring, who was
also elected to the Chairmanship of Westminster Sessions.
Whatever the defects of his character, Sir John Hawkins was
essentially a man of honour and he had striven incessantly to
improve the reputation of his magistrates. There were then
about 900 persons in the Middlesex Commission out of whom
about 170 had taken their qualification oaths. Only a small
group—probably the elite of the Commission—attended to
the judicial and executive business of Quarter Sessions at
Hicks Hall.

Soon after assuming his joint office, William Mainwaring
persuaded the Government to pay him a secret salary of £350,
which was later increased to £750. He quickly gathered about
him at Middlesex Sessions a small clique who were as un-

scrupulous as himself, and between them they founded an era of over forty years' debased administration. During the initial period they set the pattern for their subsequent behaviour by shamelessly bestowing most of the patronage appointments on themselves, their friends, and their families. Mainwaring actually conferred the richest prize of all, the Treasurership of the County, on his son G. B. Mainwaring, and he also arranged for a number of the accounts, controlled by Sessions, to be transferred to his own bank which was then in a somewhat precarious financial condition.

It was, perhaps, inevitable that the rot which had started at the top should have contaminated the whole of the Middlesex Commission. Justice Blackborough was a typical example. A Committee reporting on his conduct in 1790, said that he had 'threatened the constables that if they took thieves or prostitutes in (his) tenements, he will protect his tenants and if they interrupt them, they will be punished.' Blackborough, according to the Committee, had also habitually taken bribes from publicans in exchange for granting them licences.

A few years earlier, the inhabitants of Mile End, in a forthright statement, had declared, 'when we see individual justices prostituting the dignity of their stations to procure themselves a livelihood, opening offices in different parts of the town for the purpose of administering justice in the way of trade and striving and contending against each other for business . . . we cannot but draw the conclusion that to the magistrates of such a description, depravity and dissipation is as essentially necessary for the advancement of their interests as is a flow of business to the traders of any other class'.

In 1792 the Government endeavoured once again to reform the system when they gave their full support to the privately-sponsored Middlesex Justices Bill, a measure which has provided the organisational basis for the magistrates' courts of the Metropolis ever since. This new Bill omitted the two proposals which had aroused the greatest hospitality in the 1785 measure, for it did not suggest the creation of police commissioners, and it had no application to the City of London. In other respects it followed the earlier, abortive Bill with only minor modifications.

The Metropolis was to have an establishment of seven

Public Offices (originally it was intended that there should only be five), shaped in the image of Bow Street; each of which would be manned by three stipendiary magistrates, appointed by the Crown at an annual salary of £400. An important feature was that the magistrates would sit for regular hours, and would attend to all the business from their own localities. All the fines imposed and the fees received at these Public Offices would be paid into a special fund which would be used to defray the general administrative expenses. Every Office would have its own force of not more than six salaried constables, paid at the rate of 12/- per week, whose work would be similar to the routine duties of the Bow Street Runners.

The provision of buildings and equipment for the seven Public Offices was to be the responsibility of the Secretary of State for the Home Department. There would be two of them in Westminster, at Great Marlborough Street and Queen's Square; four in Middlesex, at Hatton Garden (Holborn), Worship Street (Finsbury Square), Lambeth Street (Whitechapel) and High Street (Shadwell); and one in Surrey, at Union Street (Southwark).

The Bill also included a controversial clause under which the salaried constables were empowered to arrest and to bring before a stipendiary magistrate, any 'suspected persons and reputed thieves' found wandering in the streets. The magistrate, if he deemed that the prisoner had had 'an intent to commit a felony', could then deal with him under the Vagrancy Acts and impose a sentence of up to six months imprisonment with hard labour.

On the 16th March, 1792, Francis Burton, a private Member, sought leave of the House of Commons to present the Middlesex Justices Bill. He began by saying that, 'Gentlemen, from their own observation, must be acquainted with the blessings which this country enjoys from the fair administration of the important office of a Justice of the Peace. In London, however, the case is different and excepting the office in Bow Street and the administration of magistracy in the City . . . these blessings are inadequately, if at all experienced'.

Burton continued, 'Those who are robbed of trifles, or slightly injured in their persons, if at a considerable distance from Bow Street, put up with their injuries rather than involve themselves in the trouble of a prosecution of the offenders'. Not only was London inflicted with justices who used their authority as a trade, he said, but there was also a deficiency of proper magistrates' offices.

Dealing with the conduct of the proposed Public Offices, he suggested that one of the magistrates should be present from nine in the morning until a late hour in the evening, and that two of them should always be available in the principal part of the day. As each magistrate would have a salary, he would be 'placed in a situation in which he could have no other interest than the upright discharge of his duty'.

Henry Dundas, the Secretary of State for the Home Department, seconded the motion and assured the House that the new magistrates would be granted no additional powers. He went on to speak of 'the alarming increase in pickpockets' in London, and said that these thieves had become so numerous and so audacious that no person could walk the streets in safety.

On the 17th April, Mr. Dundas moved the Second Reading of the Bill. It was immediately criticised by William Mainwaring, whose corrupt practices as Chairman of Sessions have already been noted, and who had entered Parliament as Member for Middlesex in 1785. He called the Bill 'a cold, feeble measure that might do some little good but a great deal of mischief'. He was intensely suspicious of the method proposed for the appointment of the stipendiary magistrates and considered that this would give the Crown 'a prodigious deal of patronage and that too, in the most exceptional way'.

This last argument was taken up by the influential Charles James Fox, who also feared that, although the King would have the nominal appointment of the new magistrates, their selection would really be controlled by the Secretary of State who had also been responsible for nominating the former magistrates in the Metropolis. 'What security is there', he asked, 'that he who appointed these trading justices, who are now said to be unworthy of their station, will appoint men of better character or capacity to succeed them? . . . I do not think it in the last degree likely that these persons will be better than their predecessors.'

Richard Brinsley Sheridan was another opponent of the

Bill. He predicted that magistrates drawing a salary from the Government would be robbed of all independence, and he even suggested that they might be dismissed from office if they voted wrongly at an election. He was convinced, he added, that 'this system of police is nothing more than a system of influence'.

However, in spite of the powerful weight of criticism, the Bill was read a second time and was then passed to Committee where it again met a withering attack from Fox. This time he concentrated on the enormity of creating a body of salaried magistrates, perpetually influenced by the Government, in substitution for the gentlemen who had always performed their duties 'without deriving any emolument for it'. These unpaid justices 'being under no particular obligation to the executive power', he said, 'can have no interest in perverting the law to oppression'. He condemned the proposals for introducing a new principle 'the effect of which no man can foresee'.

A study of the various debates on the 1792 Bill in the House of Commons reveals the interesting fact that almost the whole of the discussions centred on the justices in their peace-keeping, rather than in their judicial capacity. It was assumed by all the speakers that the stipendiary magistrates would be recruited from the same sources which had provided the trading justices and not, as Sir John Fielding had proposed thirty years before, from qualified lawyers at the Bar. In setting up the seven Public Offices the Government were, in fact, creating a new type of court to replace the travesty of justice which was taking place in the magistrates' private houses; it is a little surprising that no one suggested that neither the men who were going to administer the reformed system, nor their clerks, should be required to have had even a minimal legal training.

The Bill was read for the third time on the 23rd May, and in due course it was passed into law, for a trial period of three years, as the Middlesex Justices Act of 1792. Later on its provisions were placed on a permanent basis and the stipendiary magistrates with their Public Offices became an integral part of the English legal establishment.

The position of the Bow Street Office, which was not mentioned at all in the Middlesex Justices Act, became more anomalous than ever after 1792. The house continued to be held on personal leases by successive senior magistrates until 1842, whereas, from the outset, the new Public Offices were the property of the Home Department. Again, the Bow Street magistrates went on drawing their salaries from a secret service account, while the magistrates at the Public Offices were paid an identical stipend from the Consolidated Fund.

In common with the magistrates, the constables attached to the Public Offices had had their powers and their functions specifically enacted by statute, but the Bow Street Runners and the Bow Street Patrols had no constitutional status whatsoever.

A slight move towards uniformity was achieved in 1793 when the Secretary of State authorized the fees collected at Bow Street to be handed over to the Government, like the fees from the Public Offices; by which means, he said, 'it was intended to put this (Bow Street) Office upon the same Footing as the Seven Offices with regard to applying the Fees and the ordering of its Expenditure, as nearly as could be done without an Act of Parliament'.

Apart from this, the Bow Street Office retained the unique independence of its magistrates and its private police force, fettered by no statutory restrictions and encumbered by no territorial limitations. The Government apparently accepted this without question, as did Parliament—and as did the British people.

CHAPTER SIXTEEN

THE LONDON OF 1797

THE Report of a Select Committee on the Police of the Metropolis in 1797 gave full details of the establishment at the Bow Street Office at that time.

The three stipendiary magistrates, Sir William Addington, Richard Ford and Nicholas Bond each received a salary of £400, in addition to which Addington was paid £300 a year 'in lieu of fees, emoluments etc.' There were four clerks at salaries from £80 to £160, an office-keeper, a housekeeper and a messenger were each paid £35 a year; and at the bottom of the salary scale was an assistant jailer, employed at 7/- per week.

The Bow Street police consisted of six Bow Street Runners and sixty-eight Patrols. For economy, one of the Runners was also employed as the official office-keeper.

An exhaustive account of the state of crime, the magistracy, and the peace-keeping forces in London at the end of the eighteenth century was provided by Patrick Colquhoun in his *Treatise on the Police of the Metropolis,* the first edition of which was published in 1797.

Colquhoun came from Glasgow. After a few years as a teacher in Virginia he returned to his home town, where he established himself as a successful merchant and acquired a considerable reputation as a municipal reformer. He was Provost of Glasgow for two years before travelling south to London, where he settled for the rest of his life.

When the seven statutory Public Offices were set up in 1792, Patrick Colquhoun became one of the stipendiary justices—known as police magistrates—and he was posted to the Office in Worship Street, Finsbury Square. Although the Home Department had announced that applicants for these new appointments need not necessarily be sitting justices, most of those who were chosen were, in fact, already members of the Middlesex or the Westminster Commissions. The selections made in the first year were, by all accounts, a motley assortment. Apart from Colquhoun, they included three clergymen, three barristers, two starch-dealers, two city Councillors, two ex-Members of Parliament, an army major, a former Lord Mayor of London, and the Poet Laureate. Most of them had relied for their nominations on influence, jobbery and patronage rather than on their individual attributes, and it is probably true, as Robert Peel alleged in the House of Commons in 1825, that in general, from their previous occupations they had been utterly unqualified to perform the duties of magistrates.

A comparison between Henry Fielding's description of the state of crime in 1751, and that which was drawn by Patrick Colquhoun in 1797, leads to the inevitable conclusion that the passage of forty-six years had made little or no improvement in the situation.

London, said Colquhoun, was 'the receptacle of the idle and depraved of almost every country, and certainly from every quarter of the dominions of the Crown'. The criminals were working with impunity and there was no security of life or of property. He went on, 'In vain do we boast of those liberties which are our birthright, if the vilest and most depraved part of the community are suffered to deprive us of the privilege of travelling upon the highways, or of approaching the Capital in any direction after dark, without danger of being assaulted, and robbed, and perhaps wounded or murdered ... if we cannot lie down to rest in our habitations without the dread of a burglary being committed, our property invaded and our lives exposed to imminent danger before the approach of the morning'.

The answer to the problem, Colquhoun thought, was 'a well regulated and energetic police, conducted with purity, activity, vigilance and discretion'. But even then there would remain the basic deficiencies in the criminal law and procedure, in the penal system as a whole, and in the public morality and conscience.

On a sociological level Colquhoun, like Henry Fielding, considered that the spread of dishonesty was partly attributable to the 'vicious and immoral behaviour' of the poorer classes, and to their 'improvident and even luxurious mode of living'. They ate expensive food, they succumbed to the temptations of fraudulent lotteries, they frequented public houses and gaming saloons; and they neglected their children and reared them to become thieves and prostitutes.

Once more echoing the views of Henry Fielding, Colquhoun deplored the system whereby those who had been injured by criminal offences were obliged to prosecute the culprits at their own expense. 'When robberies or burglaries have been committed in or near the Metropolis', he said, 'where the property is of considerable value, the usual method is to apply to the City Magistrates, if in London, or otherwise to the Justices at one of the Public Offices, and to publish an Advertisement offering a reward on the recovery of the articles stolen and the conviction of the offenders.' But, he complained, many persons who suffered small robberies avoided the trouble and the cost of discovery and prosecution, and others did not know what to do. In any case, he added, 'No hardship can be so great as that of subjecting an individual, under any circumstances whatsoever, to the expense of a public prosecution carried out on behalf of the King'. He asserted that private prosecutions were often so ill-prepared and so badly presented that the prisoner had little difficulty in securing an acquittal. The Acts which authorised the payment of the prosecution costs were interpreted differently by various courts, and to obtain recompense for loss of time, the prosecutor had to plead poverty.

Colquhoun went a stage further than Henry Fielding in that he recommended the institution of Public Prosecutors for the Crown, working under the Attorney-General. This suggestion acquired the backing of the liberal-reformer Jeremy Bentham, but it was not until many years later that some such system was officially adopted.

It was, perhaps, in his chapter on the peace officers, that Colquhoun made his most important and far-reaching proposals. He repeated the sweeping criticisms of the existing system which had been made so often before. There were then over 2,000 watchmen in the Metropolis, he said, guarding the lives and properties and the inhabitants of its 8,000 streets, lanes, courts and alleyways. Their rate of payment varied between $8\frac{1}{2}$d. and 2/- a night. In general, they were aged and feeble 'and almost, on every occasion, half-starved, from the

limited allowance they receive'. They were also subjected
perpetually to bribery and intimidation by the thieves, housebreakers, burglars, receivers and prostitutes in their areas.

To guard the Metropolis there was, in addition, a force of
about 1,000 constables. This figure included the 50 full-time
salaried constables at Bow Street and the seven Public Offices,
but these, said Colquhoun, could expect small assistance
from the parish constables who had very little time to devote
to their parochial duties during their twelve months in office.
Lastly, there was the Bow Street Patrol consisting of sixty-
eight men under the personal direction of William Addington.

Colquhoun suggested that the entire system should be reorganised and that the nucleus of a professional police force
should be set up in every parish, to work in collaboration with
the local, unpaid forces. The whole of the police establishment should be controlled by a Central Police Board. He
appealed for the office of constable to be more highly regarded
by the public. 'It is an honourable profession to repel by force
the enemies of the State', he said. 'Why should it not be
equally so to resist and to conquer these domestic invaders of
property, and destroyers of lives who are constantly in a state
of criminal warfare?' He asserted that the absurd prejudice
against the constables had been the chief reason why so many
'unworthy characters' had filled this office. At best, they were
ill-supported and poorly rewarded for the risks they ran and
the services they performed.

Neither the theory of a preventive police force, nor of the
separation of the magisterial from the policing functions, had
ever been put forward in Britain before. Colquhoun sum-
marized the reasons for his proposals in the preface to the
sixth edition of his *Treatise*, published in 1800, when he said:

Police in this country may be considered as a new science, the
properties of which consist not in the Judicial Powers which lead
to Punishment, and which belong to the Magistrates alone, but
in the Prevention and Detection of crimes, and in those other
Functions which relate to the Internal Regulations for the well
ordering and comfort of Civil Society.

Turning to the magistracy, Colquhoun stated the total
number of officiating justices in London was about 270; this

figure included the twenty-six aldermen in the City of London and the twenty-four police magistrates at Bow Street and the seven Public Offices. He added that the task of investigating criminal offences was mostly carried out by the aldermen and the police magistrates. The Public Offices had jurisdiction over Westminster, Middlesex, Surrey, Kent and Essex which afforded 'considerable advantages in the prompt detection and apprehension of offenders'. Unfortunately, said Colquhoun, great inconvenience was caused by the fact that the aldermen had no powers outside the limits of the City of London, and the police magistrates had no authority inside those limits. 'The whole difficulty', he suggested, 'resolves itself into a mere matter of punctilio, founded perhaps on ill-grounded jealousy or misapprehension, which a little explanation would probably resolve.'

The defects in the procedure for bringing defendants to justice had not, apparently, altered very much since the time when Henry Fielding had written his own treatise. When a magistrate had committed a prisoner for trial, said Colquhoun, he still retained a very good chance of avoiding conviction. 'His first hope is that he shall intimidate the Prosecutor and Witnesses by the threatening of the gang with whom he is connected; his next, that he may compound the matter or bribe or frighten the material witnesses so as to keep back evidence or induce them to speak doubtfully at the trial, though positive evidence was given before the magistrate, or, if all should fail, recourse is had to perjury, by bribing the Receiver or some other associate, to swear an alibi.'

Elsewhere in the *Treatise*, Colquhoun remarks that 'the adroit thief often escapes from his knowledge of the tricks and devices which are practised through the medium of disreputable practitioners of the Law'. He acceded to Henry Fielding's view that the full details of a prisoner's bad record should be admissible in evidence as part of the prosecution case, for if that were done the hardened criminal would be distinguished in the eyes of the jury, from the novice in crime. Far too many prisoners, said Colquhoun, were being prematurely released by Proclamations or by Royal Pardons, without any reference to the committing magistrate 'who may be supposed to have accurately examined' their backgrounds and their characters.

Colquhoun was in favour of rewards being given for information in respect of offences, and for successful prosecutions. If criminals were to be detected, he said, some persons must risk their health and their lives to bring them to justice. Without a power to grant financial recompense, 'a Magistrate is placed in the situation of a person pledged to work without tools or implements of labour, by which he can in any respect, accomplish his purpose'. But under the system of fixed awards, defending counsel usually sought to impress on a jury that the prosecution's witnesses had a pecuniary interest in giving their evidence; it would be preferable, Colquhoun suggested, if the trial judge had a complete discretion to decide who should receive a reward, and what amount should be given.

After sitting as a police magistrate for five years, Patrick Colquhoun had acquired a considerable knowledge of the habits of the underworld of London. He blamed the prevailing state of lawlessness on the absence of an efficient police force, and also on the lack of sufficient attention to the 'employment, education and morals of the lower orders of the people'.

'It is impossible', Colquhoun wrote, 'to reflect upon the outrages and acts of violence continually committed, more particularly in and near the Metropolis, by ravagers of property and destroyers of lives in disturbing the peaceful mansion, the castle of every Englishman and abridging the liberty of travelling on the Public Highways, without asking—why are these enormities suffered in a country where the Criminal Laws are supposed to have arrived at a greater degree of perfection than in any other?'

Colquhoun provided an interesting summary of the types of people who became thieves, highwaymen, and burglars, in and around London. A small minority, he said, were either educated men who had been lured by indolence 'to indulge in gambling, debauchery and dissipation, and having become impoverished, have recourse to the highway to supply their immediate wants', or else they might be tradesmen who had ruined themselves by gambling and extravagant living. A greater number were 'Servants, Hostlers, Stable and Post-Boys, and Persons who being imprisoned for debts, assaults or petty offences, have learned habits of idleness and profligacy in gaols'.

The ranks of the criminals were constantly swelled by the many guilty prisoners who were acquitted at their trials, and the convicts who were discharged from the hulks and the prisons at the end of their sentences. In the past few years, said Colquhoun, no less than 11,934 persons had been released, for one reason or another, from the eight different gaols in the Metropolis. At that time, of course, there were no prison after-care or welfare services, and he gave a grim picture of the lot of the released prisoners, which made it almost inevitable that they should relapse into crime:

Without friends, without character, and without means of subsistence, what are these unhappy mortals to do? They are no sooner known or suspected than they are avoided. No person will employ them, even if they were disposed to return to the paths of honesty; unless they make use of fraud and deception, by concealing that they have been the inhabitants of a prison or the Hulks. At large upon the world, without food or raiment and with the constant calls of nature upon them for both, without a home or any other asylum to shelter them from the inclemency of the weather, what is to become of them?

The criminal fraternity, according to Colquhoun, was becoming far better organised. The most daring and strong-minded of the thieves were forming themselves into gangs or societies, to which they only admitted members who were as audacious and resolute as themselves. 'Robbery and theft, as well in houses as on the roads, have long been reduced to a regular system. Opportunities are watched and intelligence procured, with a degree of vigilance similar to that which marks the conduct of a skilful General, eager to obtain an advantage over an enemy.' Before breaking in a house, these gangs carried out a careful reconnaissance; very often one of the servants was enrolled as an accessory, or else a former servant might be asked about the exact location of the most valuable property. 'The same generalship is manifested in the nocturnal expeditions of these criminal associates upon the highways,' Colquhoun declared. They found out the routes and the times of the patrols, and they took infinite trouble to discover the movements of those travellers who would be carrying money or valuables. The pickpockets had also grown more cunning, he said, and so had the footpads, whose outrages 'are too often marked with those acts of cruelty and barbarity which justly render them objects of peculiar terror'.

Patrick Colquhoun was convinced that one of the best ways of fighting the thieves was by attacking the receivers. The trade of a receiver of stolen goods, he said, was at that time extremely profitable. Many footpads, housebreakers, and highwaymen had made their arrangements with some receiver even before they carried out a theft and then the stolen articles could be disposed of at speed; plate could be melted down and visible indentification marks obliterated. He suggested that there should be compulsory registers of dealers, pawnbrokers, watch-makers, silver-smiths, stable-keepers, and cheap lodging houses. Also, because a number of hackney-coachmen assisted the thieves in conveying stolen property, all hackney-coaches should be off the streets by midnight unless the coachman was in possession of a special justices' licence. And lastly, of course, there should be a proper force of police, assisted by a trained, efficient body of watchmen and patrols.

The continual growth of the Port of London, particularly in connection with the rich West Indies trade, had opened up a new and lucrative arena for the pilferer and the thief. 'The trade of the Port of London', wrote Colquhoun, 'is at present, far, very far, beyond that of any other port in the world. 13,500 vessels (besides numerous river-craft) arrive there each year, bringing and carrying away from £50,000,000 to £70,000,000 worth of goods.' The plunder of this merchandise was immense; not only the labourers unloading the ships and the prowlers on the wharfs took part in this wholesale pilfering, but gangs of river-pirates sailed the Thames every night to raid the unprotected craft riding at anchor. He urged a general tightening up in the law to combat this menace, and the institution of a special police office at each of the dock-yards with a force of marine police at its disposal.

Among the social evils of the day Colquhoun singled out public houses, pawnbrokers' shops, and gaming saloons for particular denunciation. Until recently, he said, it had been considered a disgrace for a woman to be seen in the tap-rooms of alehouses, but now these were filled increasingly with men, women and children. In such places thieves and criminals received asylum and boys and girls of tender years were 'to be found engaged in scenes of lewdness and debauchery'. Pawn-brokers' shops were frequently resorted to by the poor on the slightest pretext, to dispose of their clothing or their house-hold goods, 'rather than forego the usual gratification of a good dinner or a hot supper'. As for gaming saloons, 'the accumulated evils arising from this source', he declared, 'are said to have been suffered to continue, from a prevailing idea that Persons of Rank and their immediate asociates were beyond the reach of being controlled by laws made for the mass of the People, and nothing but capital offences could attach to persons of this condition of life'.

Colquhoun estimated that there were 50,000 prostitutes in the Metropolis.* A pamphlet published twenty-one years later made the number 'at least 40,000', and the writer added, with scarcely-credible prudishness, 'Every fifth unmarried woman is a —, the blood flys to my face and my pen drops from my fingers when I think of the word which rigid truth calls upon me to use here.'

On the subject of punishment, Colquhoun was extremely critical of the British penal system, which placed such em-phasis on deterrence through severity. There were more than one hundred and sixty different offences which were punish-able with hanging; 'It requires little penetration', he said, 'to be convinced that a criminal code, so sanguinary in its pro-visions, must in the nature of things defeat (its) ends'. In his opinion the increase in the crime-rate was directly attribu-table to the fact that so many comparatively minor offences carried the death penalty; in consequence the injured forbore to prosecute, juries went out of their way to acquit, and judges put forward too many recommendations for mercy. He pointed out that in several of the countries of northern Europe the scale of punishment was far less severe, and yet the incidence of crime was considerably lower.

* Both this estimate and the one which follows were probably using the generic term 'prostitutes' to cover all women of loose morality.

At that time an increasing proportion of the prisoners under sentence of death were being reprieved and transported to the convict settlements in New South Wales and Van Dieman's Land—Colquhoun puts the reprieve-rate as high as four-fifths. He gave an interesting table showing the results of trials at the Old Bailey between April 1793 and March 1794. During that period a total of 1,060 prisoners were tried, out of whom 493 were convicted and 567 acquitted. Only sixty-eight prisoners were actually hanged; of the remainder, 169 were transported, and the rest were either whipped or imprisoned, or both.

Patrick Colquhoun's views on the punishment of criminals were undoubtedly influenced by the new, humanitarian teaching of the political philosopher Cesare Beccaria, whose important work on the subject had been published in 1764; his views on the preservation of law and order were greatly affected by the writings of the two Fieldings. In his treatise, Colquhoun referred to Henry Fielding as 'that able and excellent magistrate', and went on to say:

Those who contemplate the character and conduct of this valuable man, as well as that of his brother, the late Sir John Fielding, will sincerely lament that their excellent ideas and accurate and extensive knowledge upon every subject connected with the Police of the Metropolis, and the Means of preventing crimes, were not rendered more useful to the Public. It is to be hoped, however, that it is not even yet too late.

CHAPTER SEVENTEEN

THE BOW STREET POLICE

ON the 5th March, 1785, the *Morning Herald* published a humorous poem by a clergyman, containing the couplet:

> Like Bow-street runner—most uncivil—
> Bringing theft to light.

This is the earliest reference yet discovered of the term 'Bow Street Runner', which does not seem to have come into general use until the beginning of the nineteenth century.

Very little is known about the first Runners; partly because their methods were deliberately kept secret, and partly because they preferred their identities to be unknown on account of the public hostility towards thief-takers. It was not until the closing years of the eighteenth century that the Runners lost their anonymity, and then their names became household words, and their exploits a favourite subject for discussion in the home, the tavern, and the coffee shop.

The numerical strength of the Runners was surprisingly small. Even in 1797, when they had become firmly established, the Report of the Select Committee on Finance put the number of Bow Street 'Officers' at six—although Patrick Colquhoun, writing in the same year, gave the figure as eight. Just over thirty years later, in 1828, the chief clerk at Bow Street told a House of Commons Committee that the Office had eight 'principal officers', and he went on to mention individually their names and the duties on which they were then employed.

At first the Runners performed their thief-taking in their spare time. However, it was soon realized that this was a fairly lucrative pursuit, both from the point of view of official reward-money, and also from the unofficial payments which were received from the employers who had hired them privately. Under Sir John Fielding, they became full-time professionals and received a salary—or more exactly, a retainer—of 11/6d. a week; this was later increased, firstly to a

guinea, and then to 25/-. In addition, they received an allowance of 14/- a week for expenses, but they still relied for their
principal remuneration on their private hirers. Some idea of
the amount they could earn is provided by the fact that
Townsend, the best-known Runner of all, is supposed to have
left an estate worth £20,000 on his death in 1832; while John
Sayer, his colleague and contemporary, is said to have amassed
a fortune of some £30,000.

Most of our knowledge of the lives and the adventures of
the Bow Street Runners derives from the period after the
death of Sir John Fielding; indeed, a great deal of it is based
on the anecdotes of Townsend himself, for he became, in the
latter part of his life, a very garrulous and probably a none too
reliable old man. Another valuable source of information on
this subject is the journal of Henry Goddard, which was first
published in 1956, based on his original manuscripts and skil-
fully edited by Mr. Patrick Pringle. Goddard started with a
Bow Street patrol; in 1826 he was promoted to become an
officer at the Great Marlborough Street Public Office, and in
1834 he was transferred back to Bow Street as a Runner. However fascinating the account of his day-to-day activities, it is,
perhaps, a matter for regret that he did not live in the previous century so that his journal might have covered an
earlier, hidden period.

One of the first recorded examples of the swift and thorough
manner in which the Runners handled their cases is given
in the *Annual Register* for 1775. In July of that year a burglary was committed at a house of a Mr. Conyers at Epping, and
a large quantity of plate was stolen. The enquiries were placed
in the hands of the Bow Street Office and Runners were sent
out immediately to every street, lane, and corner where
persons suspected as melters of plate were supposed to reside
—but with no result. Later on, Sir John Fielding received a
message that a coach had been seen behaving suspiciously in
the vicinity of the burgled house. Fortunately the coach-
number had been noted and it was possible for Sir John, with
the assistance of the Coach Office, to trace the owner, who
reported that both his coach and his coachman were missing.
As soon as the coachman returned, he was apprehended and

taken to Bow Street. At first he protested his innocence but eventually he made a full confession, disclosing the location of the house where his accomplices were waiting with the stolen property. The Runners organised a raid forthwith and on entering the house they found 'Lambert Reading in bed with his girl, ten loaded pistols lying beside him and the greatest part of Mr. Coynyer's plate'.

The Bow Street Runners had no uniform, their only token of office being a small baton surmounted by a gilt crown. This emblem became widely known and respected and usually provided a sufficient means of identification. Goddard has told how in 1831 he wished to question the driver of a cab which was travelling down Regent Street. 'I ran to the head of the horse,' he said, 'took hold of the bridle and holloa'd, at the same time showing my brass staff to the driver to stop.'

The senior magistrate at Bow Street was responsible for the appointment of new Runners as they were, in fact, his own private force and were answerable almost exclusively to himself. They do not seem to have been recruited from men of a common background. For instance, Vickery had been a harness-maker, Bond a carpenter, and Townsend is said to have started life as a costermonger or a coal-heaver. Others became Runners very early in life—Ruthven joined the force at the age of seventeen. It was generally believed that before Townsend went to Bow Street he had accumulated an immense knowledge of the London underworld by frequently attending trials at the Old Bailey.

Although all the Runners were of equal rank, and in theory a new assignment was given to the first officer to become available, several of them became specialists in certain branches of their work. For many years, from about 1790, Townsend and Sayer used to attend at the Bank of England for ten days in every quarter when the dividends were being paid out; they each received forty guineas a year for this service. Vickery was constantly employed by the Post Office, both for security and for the investigation of frauds; while Keys was an expert on coining and forgery. Bond and Donaldson were hired regularly by Covent Garden and Drury Lane theatres to prevent crimes and disorders during the performances. Donaldson became extremely knowledgeable on the identities and the methods of the leading London pickpockets, and he used to mingle with the crowds entering and leaving the theatres crying out, from time to time, 'Take care of your pockets'. Bond was ruthless in dealing with members of the audience who created a disturbance; on one occasion a gentleman from Soho Square complained to the Bow Street Office that he had been sitting in the pit at Drury Lane 'applauding and booing' when Bond had seized him by the collar and ripped open his shirt. From the beginning of the nineteenth century there was also a Runner on duty in the lobby of the House of Commons during all Parliamentary sittings.

Perhaps the strangest task performed by the unofficial Bow Street force was the protection of the monarchy. This duty originated after George III had been attacked by a mad woman called Margaret Nicholson in 1786; she was only one of the many who had managed to enter the various palaces when the Royal Family were in residence. Initially this important responsibility was allocated to Townsend and Macmanus, and on the death of the latter he was succeeded by Sayer. The king paid each of his bodyguards the sum of £200 a year. Giving evidence before the House of Commons Committee in 1828, the chief clerk at Bow Street said that George IV was generally attended by Townsend and Sayer on his visits out of London. It appears that the monarchy had a high regard for the efficiency of the Runners, as Goddard has told how William IV instructed him to tail his troublesome young cousin, the Duke of Brunswick, in the spring of 1836, and indeed, asked him to report personally on any discoveries he made.

The principal functions of the Bow Street Runners were, of course, connected with the pursuit and the apprehension of criminals. This work was performed as a routine duty in and around London, and they were also available for private hire, and to give their assistance to magistrates in any part of England. If a person applied to the Bow Street Office for help, said the chief clerk in 1828, the question of payment was 'very little considered'. He went on, 'If the magistrates thought it an offence of that magnitude that required their immediate

attention and assistance, an officer would be sent'. Nevertheless, the Runner on a private hiring was usually paid at the
rate of a guinea a day, plus fourteen shillings a week travelling expenses; in addition, if his investigations proved successful, he would expect a substantial reward, though Townsend
complained that a great many employers were 'rather mean
on that subject'.

Goddard gives an example of the private hiring of a Runner
in 1835. A gentleman had travelled up to London from
Southampton in his post-chaise to report a burglary which
appeared to have also involved an attempted murder. He was
seen in the Bow Street Office by Sir Frederick Roe, the Chief
Magistrate, and Mr. Hall, one of his assistants, who both
listened carefully to his statement. 'After consulting it over
for a few minutes,' says Goddard, 'Sir Frederick turned his
eyes and pointing towards me said to the applicant, "There is
the officer that I and my brother magistrate intend sending
down to Southampton in so grave a matter". Accordingly I
was instructed to proceed by that night's mail.'

When a Runner was privately hired to investigate a case
outside the jurisdiction of the Bow Street magistrates, he
would have to contact the local justices without whose authority he was unable to make an arrest. Normally, as the justices were responsible for clearing up the crimes committed
in their areas, they were only too ready to co-operate. It
was by no means unusual for county magistrates to apply
direct to the Bow Street Office for help, indeed, if a case was
at all complicated they would have little hope of solving it
without some sort of professional assistance. Goddard mentions an instance when a murder in the country was reported
to the Secretary of State for the Home Department who, at
once, referred the matter to the magistrate at Bow Street.

Sometimes, however, the activities of the Runners were
frustrated owing to the dishonesty or jealousy of the county
justices. This was particularly so in the coastal districts of
Kent where a number of magistrates were believed to be in
league with the gangs of smugglers. Once when Ruthven was
sent down to arrest some smugglers, he was told by the chief
magistrate before he left Bow Street, 'On your arrival in Kent,
it will be your duty to apply to some magistrate to back the

warrants and be sure you do not apply to one of the magistrates at the Cinque Ports, lest the object you have in view be thwarted by the party giving information to the persons accused'. There was an occasion when Goddard was threatened with arrest by the Mayor of Dover, unless he handed over some papers which he had discovered on a prisoner in the town gaol.

It was customary for the Runners to work singly or in pairs, and their operations were by no means confined to Britain. Townsend informed a House of Commons Committee, 'I went to Dunkirk in the year 1786 to fetch over four that were hanged', and the chief clerk at Bow Street said in 1828 that Salmon and Ruthven had just returned from the Continent where they had been 'in pursuit of persons who have absconded with property belonging to their employers in the City'.

There can be no doubt of the danger of the Bow Street Runners' lives, nor of the audacity which they invariably displayed in the course of duty. Armstrong once fought an armed highwayman on a roof-top in Chatham and eventually overpowered him by throwing him down into the street below. Another time Armstrong was attacked by five robbers in Spitalfields and severely injured. Sayer said of Macmanus, after his death, that when he had been compelled to fight, his existence appeared no object to him, even when he had lost 'rivers of blood'. The stories of Townsend's bravery are numerous. Captain Grownow, who knew him personally, has written, 'To the most daring courage he added great dexterity and cunning; and was said, *in propria persona,* to have taken more thieves than all other Bow Street Officers put together. He frequently accompanied mail-coaches when the Government required large sums of money to be conveyed to distant parts of the country.'

In an age when the magistrates and the parish constables had neither the aptitude, the experience, nor the facilities for investigating serious offences, the Runners were laying the foundations of the modern processes of criminal detection. The meticulous enquiries, the detailed search for clues, the methodical piecing-together of the available evidence; all these were apparent whenever the Bow Street Officers were working on a case. Goddard once matched the casing of a discharged bullet with a mould and several unfired bullets he had taken from a suspect. 'I occupied myself for some time,' he wrote in his journal, 'in looking at the discharged bullet; and on comparing it closely with the others, I discovered a very small round pimple on all the bullets. In looking into the mould, there was a very small hole hardly so large as the head of a small pin and this I found accounted for the pimples.' He immediately consulted a gun-smith who confirmed the accuracy of his deduction.

The Runners were severely censored for acting as intermediaries between the thieves and their victims for the recovery of stolen property. It was alleged that agreements were frequently concluded by which, in exchange for a reward and an undertaking not to prosecute, the owner would regain possession of his belongings. Sir Richard Birnie, the Chief Magistrate at Bow Street at the time, told the 1828 House of Commons Committee that he did not believe that such practices ever occurred, but the Committee were unable to accept this opinion. They reported their view that, 'compromises had repeatedly taken place by the intervention of police officers . . . . It has been distinctly asserted to your committee by officers that they have had the sanction of higher persons of their establishment for engaging in such negotiations.' The Report went on to instance two recent occasions, in each of which a bank had been robbed of a large amount of money and had paid the thieves £1,000 in order to recover their losses; on another occasion a similar amount had been given for the return of some Bonds. In all these cases the settlements were accompanied by promises not to prosecute.

The factor which provided the most serious grounds for suspecting the probity of the Bow Street Runners was their eligibility for a financial award in the event of a conviction under the old 'blood-money' system. Lavender estimated that he and his colleagues only received an average of from £20 to £30 a year each from this source. Townsend explained this low figure in more detail: 'The usual way of distributing the £40 on a conviction is,' he said, 'that the Recorder gives the prosecutor from five to fifteen or twenty pounds, according to the circumstances, and the apprehenders the remainder; that comes, perhaps, to three or four pounds apiece though the world runs away with the ridiculous idea that officers have £40.' Nevertheless, Townsend declared on another occasion, 'I have, with every attention that a man could bestow, watched the conduct of various persons who have given evidence against their fellow creatures for life or death, not only at the Old Bailey but in the circuits . . . they (the officers) are dangerous creatures; they have it frequently in their power—no question about it—to turn the scale, when the beam is level, on the other side—I mean against the poor, wretched man at the bar. Why? This thing called nature says profit is in the scale . . . for, God knows, nature is at all times frail, and money is a very tempting thing.'

Another branch of the Bow Street police was the foot patrol which, as has been mentioned in a previous chapter, was set up as a regular formation by the senior magistrate at the Office, Sir Sampson Wright, in 1790, and which was developed by Sir William Addington when he took over from Wright two years later. Full details of the establishment, duties, and payment of this force were given in the 28th Report of the Select Committee on Finance in 1798. At that time the foot patrol was sixty-eight strong and was divided into thirteen parties, each consisting of a captain and four or five men. 'Eight of these parties,' said the Report, 'are employed patrolling the different roads leading to the Metropolis to prevent robberies and detect offenders; and the other five parties are employed in the same way in different streets in the town.'

The members of the foot patrol did not wear uniform but they were well armed, the captains carrying a carbine and a pair of pistols, and each man being equipped with a cutlass. They commenced their duties at dusk and continued until midnight, or even later. Every morning the captains reported to the magistrate at Bow Street, 'to bring before him any offenders that they may have apprehended and to relate any offences they may have heard of, or any other occurrences that may have taken place during the course of the night'.

Like the Runners, the foot patrols were appointed by the Chief Magistrate* and it was to him that they owed their en-

* The Senior Magistrate or Chief Magistrate was still an unofficial appointment.

G

tire allegiance. 'Besides their nightly duty these men perform,' the Committee said, 'they are constantly under the direction of the magistrates and are also employed upon all occasions when the six officers are not sufficient for the business of the Office.' Probably members of the foot patrol welcomed these opportunities to act in the capacity of Runners, for at such times they were allowed to keep the full amount of their hiring fees. The Report continued, 'They are also employed to keep the peace upon all public occasions; at processions, meetings etc. when the whole body are collected and receive instructions from the magistrate for discharging the duty of the day. They attend His Majesty to the Houses of Parliament and other public places, the theatres, ancient music, opera etc.'

The captains of the foot patrol were paid at the rate of five shillings a night and the men at two shillings and sixpence a night. 'The original allowance for supporting this establishment,' said the Report, 'was £4,000 per annum; furnished from the Civil List Fund, but it does not now quite amount to that sum . . . from the irregularity of this money being issued, these men are frequently many months in arrear of their weekly allowance which, for many of them having large families and nothing but their allowances to support them, occasions much distress among them and, it is to be feared, a degree of energy is thereby lost to the public in their services.'

When Sir William Addington retired from his position as senior magistrate at the Bow Street Office in 1800, many people believed he would be succeeded by the energetic and farsighted Patrick Colquhoun, who had transferred from the Public Office at Worship Street to that at Queen's Square, Westminster, in 1797. However, the appointment was given to Richard Ford, one of the assistant Bow Street magistrates, who received a knighthood a short while later.

During the first years of the nineteenth century the number of highway robberies on the roads just outside London underwent a sharp increase. In 1805 Sir Richard Ford obtained the agreement of the Government for the revival of Sir John Fielding's horse patrol, though this time on a much larger scale and organised as a para-military uniformed force.

The new Bow Street horse patrol consisted initially of two inspectors and fifty-two men. They were heavily armed with cutlasses, truncheons and pistols, and their uniform comprised a black leather hat, a double-breasted blue coat with yellow buttons, a scarlet waistcoat, blue trousers, Wellington boots, steel spurs and white gloves. To emphasize their role as policemen, they were all sworn in as constables for Middlesex, Surrey, Kent and Essex, the counties in which they would perform their duties; and every patrolman, besides his more aggressive armament, carried a pair of handcuffs.

The horse patrol worked under the specific directions of the Bow Street magistrates. Like the foot patrol, they paraded at dusk and then split up into sections, each of which was allocated a beat with a far limit twenty miles from London. Whenever they encountered a coach or a horseman they were instructed to identify themselves by calling out loudly, 'Bow Street Patrol'. Their tour of duty finished at about midnight. The force was recruited from retired cavalry soldiers and was inclined to work with such military precision that their time-tables sometimes became known to the footpads and robbers. In fact, a highwayman was once captured in possession of a complete and accurate route-and-time schedule of the different patrols.

Members of the horse patrol were paid at the rate of 28/- a week, in addition to which each man received an allowance for the upkeep of his horse. For the first few years the overall cost of the scheme was in the region of £8,000 annually; however, the expenditure was not begrudged by the Government as it soon became apparent that the Bow Street police were drastically curtailing the activities of the highwaymen in the vicinity of London.

In his evidence before the Select Committee in 1828, Townsend made the following comment on the efficiency of the new arrangements:

There is one thing that appears to me most extraordinary, when I remember in very likely a week there would be from ten to fifteen highway robberies. We have not seen a man committed for highway robbery lately; I speak of persons on horseback; formerly there were two, three, or four highwaymen, some on Hounslow Heath, some on Wimbledon Common, some on Finchley Common, some on the Romford Road. I have actually come to Bow Street in the morning and, while I have been leaning over the desk, had three or four people come in and say 'I was robbed by two highwaymen in such a place; I was robbed by a single highwayman in such a place'. People travel now safely by means of the Horse Patrol that Sir Richard Ford planned. Where are the highway robberies now?

CHAPTER EIGHTEEN

THE TURN OF THE CENTURY

AT the beginning of the nineteenth century, the reputation of the justices of the peace throughout Britain was at an extremely low ebb. By then the magistrates 'of low degree' had largely vanished from the county Commissions, which had become, for the most part, a blending of the local gentry with the local clergy. Few of these people had been appointed for reasons of merit or suitability. 'They are selected', wrote Lord Melbourne, 'according to the peculiar notions and circumstances of each Lord Lieutenant'; and Lord Brougham remarked in the House of Commons, 'Some Lord Lieutenants appoint men for their political opinions: some for their activity as partisans in local contests.'

In rural areas the principal criticism of the magistrates was directed, not so much at their venality, as at their inefficiency and their authoritarian behaviour. With the growth of civic direction and the development of public amenities, the county rates were being constantly increased, and the inhabitants resented the enforced payments, arbitrarily imposed by an unrepresentative group of justices sitting at Quarter Sessions.

Resentment against the magistrates' autocratic powers reached its height in 1819 after the Peterloo Massacre. On August 16th of that year, a large gathering in Manchester, demonstrating in favour of parliamentary reform, was broken up by military forces acting under orders of the justices. In a sharp and bitter skirmish, eleven of the crowd were killed and many others wounded. A flood of anger immediately swept over the country, as speakers and pamphlets demanded that the ancient magisterial system should be drastically overhauled. Five years later, the atmosphere of bitterness still persisted and the *Morning Chronicle,* in an analysis of the situation, commented, 'We have ignorant petty tyrants, constituted to lord it over us'.

The Middlesex Commission remained in the disreputable control of William Mainwaring for thirty-five years until 1816 when, broken in health and generally discredited in character, he was obliged to resign his position as chairman. In 1814 his bank had failed and large sums of public money, which he had transferred to it, had been completely lost. Even after his father's departure, G. B. Mainwaring continued to hold office as Middlesex Sessions Treasurer, but he was unable to stifle the mounting disquiet regarding the suspected misappropriation of the county rates. As more and more defalcations came to light, resolutions came pouring in from meetings of ratepayers and parish officers demanding a full enquiry. Eventually in 1822, G. B. Mainwaring was obliged, in his turn, to retire.

A Committee of Enquiry was then set up to examine the administration of the county of Middlesex over the previous twenty years. The Committee's report showed that the apprehensions of the ratepayers were entirely justified; there had been a succession of fraudulent audits, unspecified payments, concealed salaries, and private agreements with contractors. Public records had been repeatedly suppressed 'for the purpose of preventing the discovery of irregular transactions'. It also came to light that some of the Middlesex justices were still making use of their Brewster Sessions to sell licences to publicans.

William Mainwaring had combined the chairmanship of the Middlesex and the Westminster Sessions, and the spirit of corruption had spread to the latter Commission as well. Besides the justices, the holders of other public appointments had been equally contaminated, particularly the high constables whose positions had deteriorated into an office subsidised by perquisites and bribes, and tenable for life. In 1794, the High Constable of Westminster had notified all the publicans in his area, by means of a circular letter, that if they would order a certain morning newspaper, in which he had a financial interest, he would recompense them by every means in his power. Since he was responsible for the inspection of their public houses, this was no empty promise.

Although the justices of the peace had fallen into such general disrepute, most people were reluctant to see them totally replaced by a body of salaried police magistrates. In 1821 G. B. Mainwaring, who was surely writing with his

tongue in his cheek, alluded to lay justices as the 'great unpaid'. They were, he said, 'a national, independent gratuitous
magistracy, giving their time, their learning and their efforts
to the preservation of the peace and the due administration of
the laws throughout the country'. He enquired scornfully,
'can any such a feeling prevail with respect to a stipendiary
body?' Sidney Smith voiced a more genuine fear five years later
when he wrote, 'What in truth could we substitute for the
unpaid magistracy? We have no doubt but that a set of rural
judges, in the pay of the Government, would very soon become corrupt jobbers and odious tyrants as they often are on
the Continent.'

Patrick Colquhoun had said that the new Public Offices
were formed in 1792 because of 'the pressure felt by the public
from the want of some regular and properly-constituted tri-
bunals for the distribution of justice . . . where the purity of
the magistrates and their regular attendance, might ensure
to the lower orders of the people, the adjustment of their
differences'.

The salaried police magistrates continued to be regarded
by many with grave misgivings, but the seven Public Offices
proved an immediate success and there was very little opposition when they were transformed into a permanent institution. As early as 1793 a Committee representing the
manufacturers at Spitalfields had sent the Secretary of State for
the Home Department an address of thanks for the appointment of the new magistracy, and acquainted him that 'great
benefits have arisen, with regard to the security of property
from the correct and regular manner in which judicial business has been conducted by the Magistrates of Police'.

After a few years, the Secretary of State began to receive
petitions from other parts of the country, especially from industrial areas, requesting him to give them stipendiary magis-
strates after the pattern of the Metropolis.

In 1800, an eighth Public Office was opened at Wapping
New Stairs, at the instigation of the West India merchants
who were gravely concerned about the continuance of robberies on the River Thames.

The police magistrates were paid the comparatively low
salary of £400 until 1821 when their stipend was increased to

£600. However, the pay was still insufficient to attract the most desirable applicants, and in 1825 Robert Peel, who was then Secretary of State for the Home Department, arranged a further increase to £800. Addressing the House of Commons on the 21st March, Peel said, 'When Police Magistrates were first appointed, it was the practice to select individuals to fill the office who, I must say, were utterly incompetent to discharge the duties which devolved upon them.' After mentioning the varied backgrounds of some of the men who had presided at Public Offices in the past, he went on to comment that 'the law had fixed no limitation with respect to the previous education of persons appointed to the office of magistrate, but he thought (the House) would be pleased to hear that limitation on that point had been prescribed by the Secretary of State'. He then disclosed that since 1812 all vacancies among the police magistrates had been filled by the appointment of barristers of at least three years standing. He implored the House to consider 'whether £600 a year, the present salary, is sufficient to induce a barrister to give up the emoluments of private practice and the hope of preferment in his profession, to undertake the duties of a magistrate, which requires their almost constant attendance'.

Peel told the House that the Public Offices were open from ten o'clock in the morning until eight o'clock at night. During these hours, two of the three magistrates at each office were usually on duty, so that their times for relaxation were very short. Henry Goddard, describing the routine at the Marlborough Street Office about three years later, stated that the magistrates held their sittings 'from eleven o'clock in the morning till three o'clock in the afternoon and again from seven to eight o'clock in the evening'.

Throughout this period it was never suggested, apparently, that Bow Street should be incorporated officially with the eight Public Offices; indeed, in 1821 a Member of Parliament put forward the rather doubtful proposition that the Bow Street Office 'was in the first instance erected by Royal authority'. At any rate, despite its independent status, Bow Street generally conformed to the regulations and usages of the other offices.

The magistrates at Bow Street received the same salaries

as the police magistrates. Various additional allowances were paid to the Chief Magistrate; Sir Richard Ford, for example, drew £500 a year for supervising the horse patrol and another £500 as 'Acting Magistrate for the Secretary of State's Office', which entailed assisting at all examinations conducted by the Secretary of State for the Home Department.

Sir Richard Ford died on the 3rd May, 1806, and was succeeded as Chief Magistrate by James Read, who was never knighted because, it is said, he declined to accept such an honour.

The lease of the property at No. 4 Bow Street, as it now became, expired in 1807. For some reason James Read did not take out a new lease until the 27th May, 1811. This provided for a twenty-one-year tenancy from Michaelmas 1807 until Michaelmas 1828 at a rental of £70 per annum—the first increase above the old £10 a year rent which had persisted ever since De Veil had signed his lease for the house in 1745.

The ground plan on Read's lease shows that considerable alterations had been made since 1781. The 'Back Building' had vanished, as had most of the yard, and these had now been replaced by a 'Publick Office' measuring 29' 2" by 19' 4". This was connected to the house by a passage, alongside of which were an office and an area.

For some time the Bow Street police had been inconvenienced by the lack of facilities at the Office for the detention of their prisoners. In 1797 the landlord of the Brown Bear, a somewhat disreputable tavern on the other side of the road, was paid the sum of £20 to provide a special strongroom for use as a cell. This was still being utilized in 1819 when Samuel Bamford and seven other radicals, known as the 'Manchester Rebels' were arrested and brought down to London for interrogation. Bamford has left the following description of their treatment:

We arrived in London about twelve o'clock and were immediately conveyed to Bow Street. We were placed in a decent room, our irons were immediately removed, and most of us wrote home to our families . . . afterwards we were conducted in couples to a room prepared at the Brown Bear public house opposite; where, after supper, the doctor amused ourselves and our keepers (who were about eight or ten police officers) with several recitations in his most florid style . . . . Mr. Perry, one of the Chief Officers at Bow Street, afterwards entered and apologised for having to submit us to what might be called a small inconvenience. It was customary, he said, to secure prisoners during the night, by a chain, and he hoped we should take it as a mere matter of form; we expressed our readiness to submit to whatever restraint might be deemed necessary. Small chains being produced, myself, Lancashire and Henley were fastened together and the other five in like manner secured, after which we continued our amusements during an hour or two and then went to rest on beds in the same room, still secured by chains to the bed post and to each other.

According to Henry Goddard, the Bow Street Runners also had a detention room 'with barred-iron windows and a very strong door' for the confinement of their prisoners in the Grapes public house alongside the office.

By the time James Read became Chief Magistrate, the premises at No. 4 Bow Street had become far too cramped for the requirements of the Office. In 1812 the Treasury made a grant of £1,295 for the conversion of No. 3 Bow Street, the adjoining house on the Russell Street side, to furnish additional accommodation. On the 9th August, 1813, Read took out a 16¼ year lease on No. 3, from Midsummer Day 1812 to Michaelmas 1828, at a rent of £90 per annum. This meant that the tenancies of both No. 3 and No. 4 would expire on the same day.

The ground plan on James Read's lease of No. 3 Bow Street shows that the house itself was slightly larger than No. 4, though the property extended back from the road for an identical distance. Behind the house there were three yards leading down to a building, designated as 'Felons Rooms'.

It was a measure of the authority of the Bow Street magistrates that during the early part of the nineteenth century, they took it upon themselves, whenever they had advance information concerning a duel, to send along their police officers to arrest the participants.

Duelling in England, as on the continent of Europe, was a revered pastime of the aristocracy. It would be no exaggeration to say that this illogical, puerile, and brutal manner of settling grievances was regarded as one of our most cherished hallmarks of chivalry and honour. In and around London there were recognised localities for these ritualistic combats; Leicester Fields, Chalk Farm, Wimbledon Common, Battersea Fields, Putney Heath, and the large space behind Montague House, the present site of the British Museum, were the most favoured places for a dawn meeting. And the highest in the land, the holders of the most responsible positions, were pleased to take part in one of the degrading spectacles. In 1789, the Duke of York fought Col. Lennox on Wimbledon Common; in 1798, Pitt fought Tierney; in 1809 Castlereagh fought Canning on Putney Heath; and in 1829, the Duke of Wellington, then the Prime Minister, fought the Earl of Winchelsea in Battersea Fields, and in the ensuing farce, after Wellington had taken the shot first and missed, Winchelsea spared the life of his distinguished challenger by deliberately firing into the air.

When a duellist killed his opponent, provided there had been no 'unfair usage', he was guilty of manslaughter, rather than murder. The early volumes of the *Newgate Calendar* contain accounts of many such trials which resulted in the defendant claiming Benefit of Clergy and escaping with no other penalty than a token burning of the hand. Duellists who were interrupted at the eleventh hour by police officers were merely bound over to keep the peace.

In 1806 Francis Jeffrey of Edinburgh agreed to fight a duel with the celebrated Irish poet Thomas Moore, as the result of some literary dispute. Moore has left an account of their meeting at the dawn of a summer's day in a field at Chalk Farm. He and Jeffrey were placed in position by their seconds, who gave them their weapons and withdrew. 'The pistols on both sides were raised', he says, 'and we waited the signal to fire, when some police officers, whose approach none of us had noticed, and who were within a second of being too late, rushed out from a hedge behind Jeffrey and one of them striking at Jeffrey's pistol with his staff, knocked it some distance into the field, while another running over to me, took possession also of mine. We were then replaced in our respective carriages and conveyed, crestfallen, to Bow Street.'

According to Moore's description, the incident continued in an agreeable manner. 'When we arrived at Bow Street', he states, 'the first step of both parties was to despatch messengers to procure friends to bail us . . . in the meanwhile, we were shown into a sitting room, the people in attendance having first enquired whether it was our wish to be separated, but neither party having expressed any desire to that effect, we were all put together in the same room.' They were then examined by the Chief Magistrate, James Read, who bound over the duellists in the sum of £400 each, and the seconds in the sum of £200 each. After these formalities, their pistols were returned to them and they were released. According to the convention of the times, honour was bloodlessly satisfied.

Two years later, another duel at Chalk Farm ended far more tragically, when a young army officer received a mortal bullet wound in his intestines. He was carried, doubtless in extreme agony, to a neighbouring house while frantic efforts were made to summon a surgeon. The victim was not fit to be moved and he died in about two hours. On that occasion, James Read had to go through the somewhat hollow formality at Bow Street of committing the victor and his seconds to stand their trial for murder at the Old Bailey.

It was inevitable that the Government should have placed more and more reliance on the Bow Street police, since they were the only effective civil force for keeping the peace in the Metropolis. Principally for this reason, the Bow Street magistrates developed gradually into unofficial Police Commissioners.

During his time as Chief Magistrate, James Read contended with two riots, both of which might have become a serious conflagration. The first of these occurred in the autumn of 1809 in the vicinity of the Bow Street Office. A year previously the Covent Garden theatre had been accidentally destroyed by fire, and as soon as it had been rebuilt the management announced that the price of the seats was to be increased. The reconstructed theatre opened on the 18th September 1809 with a performance of *Macbeth,* in which the leading parts were played by John Kemble and Sarah Siddons. A demonstration against the new prices commenced as soon as the curtain rose. The scene was described by a newspaper:

Mr. Kemble made his appearance in the costume of Macbeth amidst volleys of hissing, groans and catcalls. His attitudes were imposing but in vain. Not a word was heard save, now and again, the deeply modulated tones of the bewitching Siddons. On her entrance she seemed disturbed by the clamour, but in the progressive stages of the action, she went through her part with wonderful composure.

Eventually the tumult reached such proportions that the Bow Street police and the military were summoned; in the severe fighting which followed Read climbed on the stage and attempted to read a proclamation under the Riot Act. On succeeding nights the rioting continued. A large force of Runners and Patrols, under the leadership of Townsend, were stationed in the theatre during every performance. Their presence was bitterly resented by the agitators who paraded up and down with banners inscribed with messages like, 'Let not a British audience be intimidated by Bow Street Officers' and 'Britons be bold. Display your placards in spite of injustice and Bow Street blackguards'. The situation simmered for a few weeks with sporadic outbreaks of fighting and violence until the management yielded to pressure and restored their old charges.

The Burdett Riots in 1810 presented the authorities with a far more dangerous situation. Sir Francis Burdett, a radical politician and Member of Parliament for Westminster, was accused of violating the privileges of the House by causing one of his speeches to be published in a weekly journal. On the 5th April the Speaker issued a warrant for his arrest and a formal motion was passed by the Commons committing him to the Tower. Sir Francis was extremely popular with the London crowds, who regarded him as a champion of freedom and an upholder of the rights of the common people. When the Sergeant-at-Arms attempted to execute the warrant at Burdett's home in Piccadilly, he was refused admittance. A large mob formed quickly and started to demonstrate against the Government who, fearing a recrudescence of the Gordon Riots, immediately rushed all the available troops into London and mobilised the militia.

For several days Sir Francis' house was surrounded by soldiers and there were angry scenes between them and the protesting crowds, but these never developed into more than isolated skirmishes. On one occasion, when the military appeared to be losing control, James Read appeared and read a proclamation under the Riot Act. But the Government's precautions were more than adequate and the rioting never became widespread.

Eventually a mixed force of troops, Runners and Bow Street Patrols, led by James Read and Townsend, broke into the house and arrested Sir Francis. He was then taken to the Tower, accompanied by a huge military escort, amidst cheering crowds who continually chanted the slogan, 'Burdett for Ever'. The clashes between the troops and the mob continued until the beginning of June when Parliament was prorogued and Sir Francis Burdett was automatically released from captivity. No attempt was made to re-arrest him and he was allowed to resume his place in the House at the commencement of the next session.

James Read retired from his position as Chief Magistrate in 1813, and there was a break with tradition when his successor was selected, not from the remaining magistrates at Bow Street, but from one of the new Public Offices. Nathaniel Conant, who was appointed in Read's place—he received a knighthood soon afterwards—had been a Police Magistrate at Great Marlborough Street since its foundation in 1792. Samuel Bamford described him in 1819 as being 'an elderly and respectable looking gentleman', and from Bamford's account, the Secretary of State appeared to have employed Conant at his office in Whitehall to assist in the interrogation of prisoners charged with sedition.

Sir Nathaniel Conant remained as Chief Magistrate until he was forced to resign because of ill-health in 1820. During his last few months in office the Bow Street police added yet another distinction to their record for their gallantry, in attacking the Cato Street Conspirators.

On the 23rd February, 1820, a renegade ex-army officer named Thistlewood assembled a gang of some 25 cut-throats in a hayloft above a stable in Cato Street, Marylebone. That evening most of the leading Ministers of the Government were to dine with Lord Harrowby at his house in Grosvenor Square, and Thistlewood had arranged for one of his men to call there with a parcel while the dinner was in progress. It was planned that as soon as a servant opened the door, the rest of the gang would rush in and murder all the ministers present; the two Secretaries of State, Lords Sidmouth and Castlereagh, were to have their heads cut off and carried away as trophies. The conspirators then intended to set fire to London, to seize the Bank of England, and to proclaim a provisional government.

News of the plot leaked out and Lord Harrowby's dinner party was cancelled. A raid on the conspirators' hide-out in Cato Street was hastily organised by a detachment of Coldstream Guards, and a party of twelve Bow Street Runners and Patrols led by the redoubtable George Ruthven. This whole force was under the command of the sixty-year-old assistant Bow Street magistrate, Richard Birnie.

The small Bow Street contingent reached Cato Street first and, without waiting for the Guards, commenced their assault. Ruthven, at the head of his men, scrambled up the single ladder to the hayloft; a short, ferocious hand-to-hand encounter followed, in which Thistlewood killed one of the Runners with his sword and the heavily outnumbered Bow Street party were forced to withdraw. When the Guards arrived a full-scale attack was mounted on the hayloft and the conspirators were overpowered; a number of them including Thistlewood escaped, but they were arrested later the same night.

An editorial in the *Morning Chronicle* on the 25th February, 1820, commented:

Great credit is due to Mr. Justice Birnie and his officers for the promptitude and bravery with which they attacked the banditti with so inadequate a force. If they had waited to assemble more men so as to surround the house, the bustle of preparation might have got wind and put the ruffians on their guard . . . .

On Sir Nathaniel Conant's retirement, Richard Birnie shared in the general belief that he would be the natural successor; but in spite of the acclamation Birnie had received for his behaviour at Cato Street, Lord Sidmouth decided, once again, to promote one of the magistrates from the Great Marlborough Street Office, and he chose Robert Baker to fill the vacancy. It is said that when he heard of Baker's appointment,

Birnie remarked caustically, 'This is the reward a man gets for risking his life in the service of the public'.

A year after Sir Robert Baker had become Chief Magistrate, he had to handle the bloody rioting that occurred on the occasion of Queen Caroline's funeral. The Queen died on the 7th August, 1821, in Brandenburgh House, Hammersmith, at a time when the unpopular George the Fourth was staying at the Viceregal Lodge in Dublin. In her will, Caroline had expressed a wish to be buried in Brunswick, and arrangements were to embark her coffin at Harwich. Fearing that the mob would make the funeral an opportunity for a demonstration against the King, the Prime Minister, the Earl of Liverpool, issued secret instructions that the cortège should be diverted at Hyde Park on to a route through Paddington and Islington, and thus avoid passing through the City. Mr. Roger Fulford, the historian, has said, 'The decision to divert the procession from the City was Lord Liverpool's alone and the blame for taking a decision which he was incapable of enforcing must be his and his alone'.

In the event, the cortège was halted for an hour and a half at Hyde Park Corner while the crowd fought savagely with the constables to prevent the diversion from taking place. Eventually, Sir Robert Baker rode up with a squadron of Life Guards and led the procession forward along the altered route. From then on a running battle developed in which the soldiers several times opened fire, killing and wounding a number of demonstrators. By half-past one in the afternoon the mob had securely barricaded so many streets that Baker was obliged to go back on his instructions and to guide the cortège down Drury Lane to the Strand, and then through Fleet Street to the City.

The Government held, not unexpectedly, that Sir Robert Baker had been wholly to blame for the undignified disorders at the funeral. Furthermore, they alleged that he had shown a want of firmness in dealing with the mob; and it was said, at a crucial moment, when he had declined to read the Riot Act, Richard Birnie had come forward to do so in his stead.

In the welter of recrimination, Lord Sidmouth, the Secretary of State, decided to dismiss Baker from his position as Chief Magistrate. Apparently opinion was by no means unanimous regarding his responsibility, as four years later, in the House of Commons, a private member addressed the following words to Robert Peel, Lord Sidmouth's successor: 'I do not wish to allude to circumstances now gone by, and I hope never to be repeated, when an individual, Sir R. Baker, was removed from the magistracy, not by the Right Honourable gentleman opposite, but by another Secretary, contrary to the feelings and wishes of the whole body of the people'.

And so, in 1821, the ambitious and calculating Richard Birnie succeeded to the appointment which he had coveted for so long. The rise in his fortunes had indeed been spectacular. He had come down from Scotland as a penniless young man and obtained employment with a firm of saddlemakers in the Haymarket. In the course of his work he had pleased the Prince of Wales who had started to take an interest in his career. He had chosen as a wife the only child of a wealthy baker, and had acquired a reputation of diligence and respectability by his loyal service in the Militia and assiduous interest in parish affairs. Finally, he became a magistrate and graduated to Bow Street. For years past he had never lost sight of his ultimate goal.

Birnie was the last non-barrister to become Chief Magistrate; he was also the final holder of that position to act as an unofficial chief of police.

In 1821 the power and the influence of Bow Street were at their zenith. It was ironical, perhaps, that a man of Sir Richard Birnie's character and temperament should be destined to preside at the Office during a decline in its importance.

CHAPTER NINETEEN

THE FORMATION OF THE METROPOLITAN POLICE

A PUZZLED foreigner, writing about life in England at the beginning of the nineteenth century, remarked, 'The strange medley of licentiousness and legal restraint, of freedom and confinement—of punishment for what is done and liberty to do the same thing again—is very curious'.

Another symptom of this perplexing social attitude was the general antagonism, shared by all classes, to the concept of a professional police force in succession to the anachronistic, parochial system for maintaining law and order. It was generally believed that the establishment of a regular police would result in the suppression of public meetings and the curtailment of personal freedom. 'They have an admirable police force at Paris,' Lord Dudley reflected, 'but they pay dear for it. I had rather half a dozen people's throats were cut every few years in the Ratcliffe Highway than be subject to domiciliary visits, spies and the rest of Fouché's* contrivances.'

On the other hand, nobody doubted that the state of lawlessness in the country was rapidly growing out-of-hand. In 1812 even the compassionate reformer Sir Samuel Romilly expressed his concern at the increase in crime, and especially at the growth in offences of 'great atrocity'.

In this confused, contentious atmosphere, the Government set up a series of Parliamentary Committees which, over a period of sixteen years, argued and re-argued the practical and the social implications involved in the creation of a professional police force. After hearing evidence for nearly two years, one of the Committees reported in 1818 that, 'In a free country such a system would of necessity be odious and repulsive and one which no government could be able to carry into execution'. They added the ethereal sentiment, 'the police of a free country was to be found in rational and humane laws—

*Joseph Fouché was the Minister of Police in Paris from 1799 until 1802.

in an effective and enlightened magistracy . . . above all, in the moral habits and opinions of the people'.

There is no doubt that even amongst those who favoured the institution of a regular police, there was a considerable disparity of opinion about the exact form it should take. The Duke of Wellington, one of the foremost protagonists of the scheme, seems at first to have envisaged the police as an adjunct to the army, for in 1820 he urged Lord Liverpool, then Prime Minister, that he should immediately, 'Adopt measures to form either a police in London or a military corps which should be of a different description from the regular military force, or both'.

The 1818 House of Commons Committee had recommended that Bow Street should become even more the centre of peace-keeping operations and Lord Sidmouth, the Secretary of State for the Home Department, adopted their proposal. In 1821 he directed that, owing to the prevalence of crime in the heart of London, the Bow Street foot patrol should confine its activities to an area within five miles of the centre of the Metropolis. At the same time, he increased its strength to about one hundred men, and the whole force was placed under the control of an inspector. From then on, every evening sixteen patrols, each consisting of a conductor and four men, were sent out from Bow Street to tour the streets of inner London, while an emergency force remained in reserve at the Office.

In 1822 Robert Peel succeeded Lord Sidmouth as Secretary of State for the Home Department. During his six years as Chief Secretary for Ireland, from 1812 until 1818, Peel had established a regular Irish constabulary, nicknamed the 'Peelers', with extremely beneficial results, and he was determined to introduce a similar scheme in London. Soon after receiving his new appointment he set up a Committee under his own Chairmanship, to make recommendations with a view to 'obtaining for the Metropolis as perfect a system of police as was consistent with the character of a free country'.

However, Peel's ideas found no favour with his Committee, which reported that it would be difficult 'to reconcile an effective system of police with that perfect freedom of action and exemption from interference which are the great privileges and blessings of society in this country'. Further, they considered that 'the forfeiture or curtailment of such advantages would be too great a sacrifice for improvements in police'. The Committee suggested instead that there should be a Bow Street day patrol to operate in conjunction with the existing nocturnal foot and horse patrols; they also thought that the Bow Street Office, 'having no specific district assigned to it', should become the official criminal investigation headquarters for the whole of the country.

Robert Peel seized on the 1822 Committee's proposal for a new Bow Street patrol as a means of pressing forward with his ultimate design, whilst he awaited a more propitious moment before he raised the matter in Parliament again. Within a few months he had created a day patrol of three inspectors and twenty-four men to operate under the directions of the Chief Magistrate. This small force wore a uniform consisting of a blue coat, blue trousers, red waistcoat, and black felt hat. They were divided into three divisions, each consisting of an inspector and eight men. The first division assembled daily at 9 a.m. outside the Bow Street Office, and the other two met in various localities according to their instructions. Their duty was to tour the principal streets in the Metropolis until nightfall when they were relieved by the foot patrol.

There is no doubt that the introduction to London of its first uniformed professional police would, at that time, have aroused a storm of controversy had not Peel disguised his scheme as being simply an enlargement of the Bow Street forces.

In spite of the new arrangements instituted by Lord Sidmouth and Robert Peel, the peace-keeping procedures remained unaltered, and magistrates were expected to take part in both the physical apprehension of offenders on the one hand, and their subsequent examination and trial on the other. For example, one evening in 1822 information was received at the Bow Street Office that illegal gaming was taking place at a house in St. James's, and a raiding party was hastily organised consisting of Mr. Halls, a magistrate, the two Runners, Ruthven and Vickery, and eight members of the foot patrol. After battering down the street door of the gaming house, Mr. Halls supervised the arrest of about twenty people inside. The following morning at the Office he and another magistrate sat in judgement on the gamblers and, indeed, committed several of them to prison.

The aptitude of the parish constables and the watchmen had scarcely improved since the days of Henry Fielding. The police at the Public Offices of whom so much had been hoped, were having very little effect on the incidence of crime and were becoming increasingly subject to corruption. 'There was great service, great temptation, and little pay', said a magistrate in 1821. They received no recompense for wounds or injuries sustained on duty and their numbers were totally insufficient for their task. In the area of the Marlborough Street Office alone there was a contingent of eight professional police to deal with a locality of 270,000 inhabitants. Not surprisingly, the citizens of the Metropolis were taking the law into their hands; shopkeepers were forming private patrols to guard their premises during the night and householders were arming themselves against intruders. So many people had been killed and injured by domestic anti-burglar devices that in 1827 an Act of Parliament expressly forbade the setting of man-traps or spring-guns.

In London there was very little co-operation between the Bow Street police and the amateur peace-officers. A parish constable complained in 1828 of the attitude of the Bow Street force. 'I had to contend with innumerable difficulties,' he said. 'I saw a marked spirit of envy and a determination to do me all the injury they possibly could, as if I was undertaking something I had no business to interfere with.' On one occasion when he was on duty outside Drury Lane Theatre, he had been attacked by two of the Runners and 'dragged through the streets like a felon'. He reported the incident to the Chief Magistrate, Sir Richard Birnie, who 'chose to dismiss the complaint without having the case gone into, treating it as a squabble between officers'.

In 1828, soon after the Duke of Wellington had become Prime Minister, Peel appointed another Committee, the members of which he selected with the utmost care, 'to enquire into the cause of the increase of commitments and convictions in London and Middlesex, and into the state of the police of the Metropolis and of the districts adjoining'. The Committee soon reported their conclusion that, 'it was absolutely necessary to devise some means to give greater security to persons and property'.

On the strength of this Report, and the firm support for his views in the House of Commons and the House of Lords, Peel proceeded to draft his Bill for the formation of the Metropolitan Police. The feeling in the country was still largely opposed to such a scheme and all sorts of rumours began to circulate of the sinister uses for which this new force would be employed; it was even said that it would form a private army to place the Duke of Wellington on the British throne. On the other hand, there was a great deal of criticism of the parish peace officers. The *Quarterly Review*, commenting upon the proposed changes declared, 'There can be no doubt that the whole of the existing watch system of London and its vicinity ought to be mercilessly struck to the ground. No human being has the smallest confidence in it . . . their existence is a nuisance and a curse.'

On the 15th April, 1829 Robert Peel sought leave from the House of Commons to introduce his Metropolitan Police Improvement Bill. His speech, as reported in the volume of Hansard for the year, completely concealed the radical nature of his proposals and represented them rather as a modification of the prevailing system.

Peel began by reminding the House of the number of committees which had, during the past few decades, considered the methods of policing London, without producing any material improvements. He produced detailed statistics to show, not only the remarkable increase in criminality in London, but the fact that the conviction rate per head of the population was higher there than in any other part of England. 'Not less than one person in every three hundred and eighty-three,' he said, 'has been committed for some crime or other in 1828.' He went on to remark that many intelligent people had endeavoured to trace the cause of this phenomenon without arriving at any satisfactory conclusion. For his own part, he feared that one of the causes was the mechanical ingenuity of the age which enabled criminals 'to travel a great distance in a few hours and to use great caution in the selection of time and manner' of their offences. He also thought that the improved living standards in the country were the source of additional temptation to crime.

Reverting to the objects of his Bill, Peel said he was satisfied 'that so long as the present night-watch system is persisted in, there will be no efficient prevention of crime, nor any satisfactory protection for property or the person . . . The chief requisites of an efficient police are unity of design and responsibility of its agents—both of which are not only not ensured by the present parochial watch-house system but are actually prevented by it.' The remedy, he suggested, was to concentrate all the parochial police under one responsible and efficient head.

Peel continued by giving the House some examples of the total inadequacy of the policing arrangements in a number of London parishes. In the 'wealthy and populous district of Kensington', for instance, the inhabitants were dependent on the protection of six parish police officers, several of whom were not invariably sober. Other localities had no parochial police at all—Deptford with a population of around 20,000, was an example; here the inhabitants had been subjected to a succession of 'atrocious and sanguinary' crimes. 'Within the last few years,' said Peel, 'the indignation at those outrages has led to the formation of a voluntary night-patrol by the parishioners.'

The term 'watchmen', Peel asserted, had fallen into such disrepute that he intended to abandon it and to 'consider and speak of their substitutes as a species of night patrol'. All parochial control would be abolished and the new constables would be directed by a Board of Police, consisting of three magistrates who would have no more powers than those already possessed by the police magistrates at the Public Offices. The cost of the new formation would be met from a general police tax, which would replace the individual parish watch-taxes. At first, the reformed system would be introduced in a few central parishes but it would gradually be expanded. The settlement of the many details of his scheme would be 'annoying to the majority of the House', said Peel, and therefore he had decided to reappoint his 1828 Police

Committee in the form of a Select Committee for the purpose of discussing them.

In conclusion, Peel told the House that 'it is the duty of Parliament to afford to the inhabitants of the Metropolis and its vicinity, the full and complete protection of the law and to take prompt and decisive measures to check the increase of crime which is now proceeding at a frightfully rapid pace.'

It was a measure of the scant recognition of the extent of Peel's proposals in the House of Commons, that one Member asked him for a reassurance that the new constables would perform their duties by day as well as by night. In the event, the Bill was given a First Reading without a division. In due course, it had an easy passage through both Houses and received the Royal Assent on the 19th June, 1829.

Whether or not Robert Peel had ever envisaged a professional police force entirely independent of the traditional domination of the magistracy, must be a matter of opinion. Certainly in its origin the Metropolitan Police conformed to the established pattern, for their headquarters at 4 Whitehall Place was first instituted as a new Public Office, to be presided over by two magistrates—not three as Peel had once suggested—known as 'Commissioners of Police'. Their jurisdiction covered the whole of the Metropolitan Police District, an area which extended initially to a radius varying from four to seven miles from Charing Cross, excluding the City of London which was not incorporated into the scheme.

At one time, Peel was doubtful as to whether or not the Metropolitan Police ought to have a uniform. He then decided that they should wear a military-style jacket of red and gold, but this idea was soon abandoned, most probably because of the martial implications it was likely to evoke. Eventually it was settled that the uniform should consist of a blue cloth suit, with bright white buttons on the coat; a leather stock fastened with a brass buckle at the neck and showing the constable's number and division; a tall, chimney-pot hat of considerable weight, with a shining leather top; a pair of half-wellington boots; and a belt with a large metal buckle. The police were to be virtually unarmed but every man was issued with a baton and also, a strange relic from the era of the watchmen, with a rattle for use if he wished to summon assistance. The rattle was not replaced by the whistle until 1880.

Originally the new police comprised eight superintendents, twenty inspectors, eighty-eight sergeants, and 895 constables. The superintendents were mostly selected from retired sergeant-majors of the Guards, but Peel was emphatic that, as the force developed, all promotions should be awarded through the ranks. The available manpower was organised into six divisions, each of which had its own police station; the subsequent expansion was rapid and by May 1830, there had been an increase to seventeen divisions.

The payment offered to constables was 19/- a week, slightly less than the average, artisan wage-rate at the time. Sergeants were paid 22/6d. a week; inspectors, £100 a year, and superintendents, £200 a year. The two police commissioners received a salary of £800, similar to that of the police magistrates.

The fact that the Metropolitan Police, founded amidst an atmosphere of prejudice, suspicion, and hostility, grew into one of the most respected police forces in the world, must be largely due to the outstanding ability of the first Commissioners, a retired army officer, Colonel Rowan, and a barrister, Mr. (later Sir Richard) Mayne. These two, between them, moulded the concept of the unarmed, citizen-constable, equally conscious of his civic as of his peace-keeping responsibilities, which has been such a valued feature of the administrative life in this country ever since. A couple of the instructions to the police issued at the outset by Mayne may be quoted, as they set the pattern for the standards of behaviour he wished them to follow. A constable, he said, must have 'a perfect command of temper', and 'must never suffer himself to be moved in the slightest degree by any language or threats that may be used'. Next, 'The constables are to recollect on all occasions that they are required to execute their duty with good temper and discretion; any unnecessary violence by them in striking the party in their charge, will be severely punished.'

The code of discipline was rigorous and during the first nine years of the force, nearly 5,000 constables were dismissed for failing to fulfil its requirements.

On the 3rd November, 1829, the Duke of Wellington wrote to Peel, 'I congratulate you on the entire success of the Police in London; it is impossible to see anything more respectable than they are.' Peel replied, 'I am very glad indeed to hear that you think well of the Police. It has given me from first to last more trouble than anything I ever undertook . . . I want to teach people that liberty does not consist of having your house robbed by organised gangs of thieves, and in leaving the principal streets of London in the nightly possession of drunken women and vagabonds.'

The new police were essentially a uniformed body with no detective branch, although four officers in each division were allowed to wear plain clothes solely for the purposes of catching pickpockets and beggars. The Bow Street Runners and the police officers at Public Offices, none of whom have ever worn uniform, were kept in being to handle criminal investigation work, but they remained subject to the control of their own magistrates and were quite independent of the police commissioners. The horse patrol, too, was left in the hands of Sir Richard Birnie, the Chief Magistrate at Bow Street, who was an inveterate enemy of the new police and once declared publicly, 'I never saw a constable who was perfectly competent'. On another occasion, he remarked, during the hearing of a case, 'The fact is, the new policemen have such ridiculous instructions given to them by their superiors, who know nothing of the duties of a police officer, that they are not half so much to blame on these occasions as their superiors.'

A number of the Bow Street foot and day patrols were offered transfers to the new police; others were unceremoniously discharged without receiving either notice or compensation. The watchmen and parish constables, too, were disbanded in the whole of the rapidly-expanding Metropolitan Police District.

The tribulations of the new police in the early days were instigated as much by the general public as by the criminal fraternity. Many leading newspapers, including *The Times,* were utterly opposed to the new arrangements, mainly on the ground that the centralisation of control had bestowed an additional power on the Government. Less responsible journals delighted in the publication of invented or exaggerated accounts of the bad behaviour of constables on the beat. Brawls occurred almost nightly in which policemen were attacked and beaten up; and certain of the well-to-do are said to have ordered their coachmen to lash out at every constable they passed with their whips, and to drive straight at them if there was any attempt at interference.

In November 1830, Colonel Rowan felt constrained to issue the following directive to his men:

The Commissioners think it right again to caution every man in the Police Force, at a time when an attempt is being made to create a strong prejudice against them, that they should do their duty with every possible moderation and forbearance, and that they should not furnish a just ground of complaint against themselves by any misconduct.

The sustained campaign of reckless abuse and deliberately-fostered antagonism was bound to reach a climax. In fact, that moment came about in the dastardly affair of Cold Bath Fields.

A revolutionary organisation known as the National Political Union had announced their intention of holding a mass rally in Cold Bath Fields, near Holborn, on the afternoon of the 13th May, 1833. The Government, fearing an outbreak of violence, issued a proclamation declaring the meeting illegal and warning people not to attend. However, the N.P.U. persisted in plans, appealing to their supporters to turn out in force.

Although the Metropolitan Police had received no training in mob-control, they were ordered to deal with this situation which previously would have been entrusted to the military. Colonal Rowan supervised the arrangements personally. On the afternoon of the rally he assembled seventy of his men in Cold Bath Fields and stationed several hundred more in a nearby stable. When the meeting began, Rowan who was, of course, a justice of the peace, came forward and tried to read a proclamation under the Riot Act. He was howled down, and the massive crowd starting stoning the constables, a number of whom were injured.

At this stage Colonel Rowan called up his reserves who

endeavoured to break up the meeting with a truncheon-charge. The mob fought back savagely using missiles, bludgeons, and knives, and the heavily outnumbered police suffered innumerable casualties, one officer, P. C. Culley, being stabbed to death and two others severely wounded.

Certain sections of the Press for days afterwards were filled with accounts of police brutality during the riot. It was alleged that many of the constables had been drunk and that they had repeatedly used their boots and their truncheons against defenceless women and children. Amid the fervour of indignation the coroner's jury at P. C. Culley's inquest, in face of the law and the facts, insisted on returning a verdict that he had met his death through 'justifiable homicide'; and shortly afterwards, a jury at the Old Bailey acquitted a man on a charge of knifing a police sergeant, in spite of the clearest possible evidence of his guilt.

The Government would accept no responsibility for what had occurred at Cold Bath Fields and Lord Melbourne, the Secretary of State for the Home Department, tried to blame the police commissioners for the way the meeting had been handled. In deference to the climate of popular opinion, Melbourne appointed a Select Committee to examine the allegations of police brutality and improper conduct. After sitting for six weeks, the Committee was able to report that these charges were wholly unfounded.

Another Committee, in 1833, which had investigated further criticisms of the Metropolitan Police stated:

It was not to be expected that a new system of police, however perfect, could be introduced without many and strong objections from very obvious causes . . . and, perhaps, it is a matter for surprise that so great a change should have been accomplished without greater opposition than has been experienced.

It may be that in the months which followed that bloody afternoon at Cold Bath Fields, people were starting to realize the full extent of the metamorphosis which had taken place in the preservation of public order—how the constable with his truncheon at his side, had replaced the soldier, the musket, the sabre, and the bayonet. At any rate, the City of London established its own professional police force in 1839. The same year, an Act of Parliament permitted justices of the peace to form regular county constabularies if they thought fit; the creation of such forces was made compulsory in every county in 1856.

CHAPTER TWENTY

THE DEVELOPMENT OF THE UNDERWORLD

AROUND the middle of the nineteenth century two experienced sociologists, James Greenwood and Henry Mayhew, conducted their own, separate surveys of the underworld in the Metropolis. Their writings have provided a full, contemporary record of the nether side of London life as in the course of their researches, they visited the taverns, dens, hovels and alleys frequented by the criminal fraternity; and within this sordid environment, they interrogated the felons and the prostitutes at length about their backgrounds and habits.

Despite the improvements which had recently occurred in the quality of the magistrates and in the efficiency of the police, the vice and crime patterns were becoming firmly established, and were acquiring a new sophistication. 'We must not forget,' said Mayhew, 'that an increase of education and a growing intelligence, bring with them superior facilities for the successful perpetration and concealment of crime.'

Without doubt, a constant temptation to depart from the ways of honesty and virtue was caused by the appalling squalor and destitution in which many Londoners were obliged to live. Their houses were dirty, insanitary, overcrowded, and ill-repaired. 'I have seen grown persons of both sexes,' said an investigator, 'sleeping in common with their parents, brothers, and sisters and cousins, and even casual acquaintances of a day's tramp, occupying the same bed of filthy straw; a woman suffering in travail in the midst of males and females of different families that tenant the same room, where birth and death go hand in hand.'

For those without a home of any sort, there were the cheap lodging houses, most of which charged a set price of three pence a night. The principal object of the proprietors was to cram as many people as possible into the unventilated rooms. Two or three men or women were allocated indiscriminately to each of the bug-ridden beds, and others slept on palliasses, mattresses, and bundles of rags on the floor. In the dead of night, Mayhew was told, the breath of the occupants rose 'in one foul, choking steam of stench'.

The young lodgers, mostly thieves and prostitutes, were generally taken in for two pence a night. Sometimes as many as three or four dozen boys and girls shared one room. A prostitute describing her experiences at such place when she was only twelve said, 'There were very wicked carryings on. The boys, if any difference, was the worst. We lay packed in a full night, a dozen boys and girls squeedged into one bed. That was often the case, some at the foot and some at the top— boys and girls all mixed.'

It was estimated that there were about a hundred thousand vagrant children roaming the streets of the Metropolis; abandoned, ragged, and hungry, and snatching a miserable existence by alternately begging and stealing. Greenwood used to watch them crowding into Covent Garden when the market opened early in the morning. 'They would gather about a muckheap,' he wrote, 'and gobble up plums, a sweltering mass of decay, and oranges and apples that have quite lost their original shape and colour, with the avidity of ducks or pigs.'

Henry Mayhew interviewed an orphan girl who, at the age of eleven, had run away from the house where she had been in service, as a result of the frequent beatings she was receiving from her employers. After wandering about for a few days she had joined the flotsam and jetsam population of the London lodging houses, where she was soon seduced by a fifteen-year-old pickpocket. They had lived together as man and wife for three months until he was convicted and sent to prison. She had then discovered that she was suffering from a veneral disease and in order to obtain treatment, she broke a window and was sentenced to a month in the comptor. During her imprisonment she was cured, and on her discharge, friendless and desperate, she had become a juvenile prostitute.

An expert young pickpocket informed Mayhew that before he was sixteen, he had served thirteen prison sentences and had been flogged four times. 'If a boy has great luck,' he said, 'he may carry on for eight years. Three or four years is the common run, but transportation is what he's sure to come to in the end.'

Apart from the abandoned children and the orphans, there were numerous young criminals whose parents were professional thieves and who had been trained in dishonesty from their very infancy.

The lowest and the least skilled members of the criminal fraternity were the 'common thieves', who might be persons of either sex and of almost any age from six or seven upwards. They poured out into the streets of the Metropolis every morning to pick up their miserable and precarious livelihood. One of their main pursuits was pilfering from the stalls which stood on either side of the roads. Sometimes they worked singly: sometimes in groups, waiting for an opportunity when a stall-holder was preoccupied. They were also on the look-out for untended goods on display in the doorways and windows of shops, or on the pavements outside. And no loaded cart or carrier's wagon was safe from their depredations.

More daring common thieves, usually gangs of youths, would sometimes raid the tills of shops. The usual method of doing this was for one boy to seize the cap of another and to throw it into the shop. The owner, in the course of retrieving his property, would grab up what money he could from the till-drawer and run for dear life. As a variation they might climb on to the roofs of unoccupied houses to strip off the lead. And even if there were people in a house, some of these young thieves made a practice of breaking or lifting the kitchen window from the outside, and then inserting two sticks tied together with a hook at the end, to drag out any article within reach.

In the evening, drunken men were regular victims of common thieves, who used to loiter outside public houses in readiness for them to emerge. Children, too, sent by their parents to collect laundry or shopping, were an obvious prey for the ragged and hungry pilferers, especially when the light was fading or the streets were deserted.

The pickpockets were a band of highly skilled specialists. Usually they started very young, sometimes at the tender age of five, and they learnt their trade from their parents, their companions at low lodging houses, or from a recognized 'thief-trainer'. At the beginning of the tuition, they were taken to a room where a coat with a bell attached to it was hanging from a peg in the wall; the embryonic pickpocket then spent hours of practice in trying to remove some object from the coat pocket without ringing the bell. Next, the trainer walked up and down the room while the pupil endeavoured to extract a handkerchief from the tail of his coat. It was not until he was completely satisfied with the proficiency of his charge that the trainer allowed him to test his dexterity in the streets.

If a pickpocket was successful he might graduate from stealing gentlemen's silk handkerchiefs to attending fashionable gatherings in the West End and there, dressed as a clerk or a business man, he would employ his craft in stealing watches, wallets, and jewellery as he mingled with the crowds.

Pickpockets, like common thieves, often worked in groups, one member acting as a distractor by bumping into the intended victim or stopping to ask him the time or the way, whilst another was carrying out the theft. Sometimes a third member would be observing from a little way off, acting as a look-out with the additional duty, if his colleagues were discovered and chased, of accidentally impeding the pursuers or misinforming them about the direction in which the thieves had escaped.

Shoplifting in those days was almost wholly a female offence. The professional shoplifters, girls and women of varying ages, worked individually, in twos, or in threes. Usually they wore large cloaks or shawls to cover their movements and frequently they had a special pocket in the front part of their dresses, concealed under an ample crinoline. Their methods were simple in the extreme. They used to examine a number of items on the counter and then, having asked the shopkeeper to fetch something from a shelf, they would deftly remove one or more articles while his back was turned.

The professional housebreakers and shopbreakers had generally commenced their careers as common thieves, although sometimes a young boy was specially trained to enter premises through a fanlight or a small window in order to open a door for the other members of a gang. Fashionable houses were carefully watched for several weeks before being burgled. If possible, one of the thieves would become acquainted with a servant girl in order to find out from her the habits of the occupants and the location of the most valuable property. It was known, too, for a member of the gang to visit the house during the daytime so that he could inspect the lock on the front door. Most burglaries took place in the early hours of the morning, one man acting as lookout and two or three actually going into the house. Entry might be made by picking a doorlock, cutting or breaking a pane of glass, or even by one thief mounting on the shoulders of another and climbing through an open first-floor window.

Housebreakers did not use violence except in an emergency. However, most of them carried a life-preserver which usually consisted of a small ball attached to a piece of gut; this was fastened to the wrist and held in the palm of the hand. It was capable of inflicting very serious injuries.

In the case of large shops and warehouses, the thieves tried to smuggle one of their number inside during the daytime; he would emerge from hiding when the premises were closed for the night and let in his colleagues. A favourite method of raiding jewellers' shops was for a female accomplice to pose as a prostitute outside, in order to decoy police officers and other pedestrians away from the scene while the breaking in was taking place. As a last resort, if some constable continued to linger in the vicinity, the woman might pretend to collapse so that he would have to supervise her removal to hospital.

London was still afflicted with a large number of street robbers who were usually armed with a life-preserver or a bludgeon. Sometimes they would wait in a dark road until they saw a solitary passer-by; then they would knock him down and abscond with his watch and his wallet. They often operated with a woman who pretended to be a prostitute; it was her task to lure the intended victim into a secluded alley before the robbery took place.

Street robberies were also effected by garrotting. One man would hold the victim from behind, with an arm clasped tightly around his neck, while another went through his pockets. If a victim tried to cry out or to struggle, the garotter would increase the pressure on his arm so as to strangle him into insensibility.

The principal receivers of stolen property were the proprietors of the 'dolly shops' which were, in reality, unlicensed pawn-shops. These places, dark and dingy in appearance, were always overcrowded with junk of every description, especially men's and women's clothing, books, and furniture. The proprietor of a dolly shop would be willing to pay any sum from a couple of pence to a shilling for each article deposited with him; if it was not redeemed within a week he would acquire the ownership and be free to sell it. Items of more value such as silver and jewellery were generally disposed of through dishonest pawnbrokers.

Most thieves, especially housebreakers, made careful preparations for the immediate concealment of the proceeds of a crime. A cab would be standing by in the vicinity to rush the stolen property to a pawnbroker who would have a crucible ready over a slow fire for melting down any silver plate beyond the point of recognition. Other articles would be well hidden away until the search for them had been abandoned.

The River Thames had its own brand of thieves. The most numerous of these were the 'mudlarks', homeless, destitute boys and girls, usually ranging in age from eight to fifteen. These children would clamber on to the moored barges and throw overboard lumps of coal and pieces of iron from the cargoes; later, they would wade out to recover their spoil from the muddy shallows. Pilfering from ships in the London Docks was a recognized pastime even amongst those who were working on them legitimately, such as the sweeping-boys, the lightermen, and the dockside labourers.

Every night the river pirates set off in their small boats to pillage the vessels lying at anchor off the shore. Once on board they would carry out their raids with the utmost speed and then slip away again into the darkness.

There were also in the Metropolis the criminals whose stock-in-trade was guile, trickery, or a dishonest talent, like the coiners, the sharpeners, the forgers, and the swindlers.

In 1860 it was estimated that there were about 7,000 prostitutes walking the streets of London, about three-quarters of whom were addicted to stealing.

The most fortunate of these girls worked for themselves. Generally they took rooms at enormous rentals in the vicinity of the Haymarket, which was considered the central area for the casinos, theatres, and supper-houses. They caused very little trouble, but were apt to rob a drunken client if the opportunity arose. James Greenwood remarked that the attitude of the authorities to them was: 'As long as you create no public scandal, but throw a decent veil over your proceedings, we shall not interfere with you but shall regard you as an inevitable evil.'

Also around the Haymarket there were a number of 'accommodation houses', the proprietors of which were mostly worn-out prostitutes themselves. Any girl who did not possess her own premises could take in a client and hire a room for a short while or for the whole night. Naturally, the rents charged for this facility were very high, but these houses were always in great demand.

The 'introduction houses' worked on a different principle. They were run by professional procuresses with an intimate knowledge of the vice-life of the West End. On entering an introduction house, a man—and he might be a well known figure in the world of fashion or in one of the professions—would be offered a bottle of champagne while he discussed with the procuress the sort of companion he desired. She would then send out an agent to locate a prostitute for him, and, having supervised their meeting, she would arrange for them to adjourn to one of her own bedrooms or to the house of the prostitute, who would be expected in due course to hand over half the fee she received from her client.

A great many of the London prostitutes worked in brothels. Usually the brothel-keeper fed, clothed, and accommodated her girls in exchange for a proportion of the money they earned. Sometimes there was a communal room in which men could drink and talk until they had selected a girl; sometimes the prostitutes had to go out and pick up their own clients in the street.

Brothels, especially those in the poorer areas, often employed a thug to act as doorkeeper and to deal with clients who were reluctant to pay the price demanded by the prostitutes. Mayhew tells of a drunken gentleman who met a girl in the neighbourhood of Waterloo Bridge and went back to her room with her. In a moment of sobriety he tried to leave before the prostitute had either earned or received her fee. He found himself at the top of a darkened staircase with a large, powerfully built man armed with a bludgeon waiting for him at the bottom, and it was only after he had hurled a lamp at the thug and knocked him out that the gentleman was able to make his escape unscathed.

The most appalling feature of London prostitution was the increasing prevalance of 'dress lodgers', girls who, in the words of James Greenwood, belonged 'entirely and utterly to the devil in human shape' who ran the brothel at which they worked. It was estimated in 1869 that there were well over 2,000 dress lodgers operating in different parts of the Metropolis. These girls, for a variety of reasons, had fallen into the clutches of some brothel-owning harpy, who purloined most of their earnings and retained their services by brutality, threats, and terrorisation.

Mayhew persuaded a dress lodger to tell him her story. Her home, she said, had been at Matlock in Derbyshire, and at the age of sixteen she had come to London to stay with an aunt, for the purpose of visiting the Great Exhibition of 1851. On her arrival her aunt had been ill in bed and the girl had foolishly slipped out in the evening to take a look at the city. She became hopelessly lost in the labyrinth of strange streets and, seeing an open door, she knocked at it to enquire her way home. An old woman answered, asked her to enter, and persuaded her to drink a glass of gin. In the course of conversation the woman pretended to the girl that she was a close friend of her aunt. With extreme reluctance, the girl eventually succumbed to the suggestion that she should remain in the house for the night. She went on:

> Presently she asked if I wasn't tired, and said she'd show me a room upstairs where I should sleep comfortable no end. When I was undressed and in bed, she brought me a glass of gin and hot water, which she called a night-cap and said would do me good. I drank this at her solicitation, and soon fell into a sound sleep. The 'night-cap' was evidently drugged, and during my state of insensibility my ruin was accomplished.

After that, the girl had been too frightened and too ashamed to return to her aunt or to her home, and she had started to work for the old woman as a prostitute. Like most dress lodgers, she had no possessions of her own. She was kept indoors, a virtual prisoner, in the daytime and dressed up in gaudy clothes every evening to be sent out into the streets, under the constant surveillance of a professional watcher.

Another dress lodger, who was interviewed by Greenwood, had come into the power of the woman who kept her brothel by means of a simple subterfuge. She had been visited one day by a supposed detective who accused her, quite falsely as it happened, of robbing one of her clients during the previous night. The girl had protested her innocence and eventually, after a great deal of tearful pleading, the 'detective' had offered to hush up the matter for a payment of £10. The brothel keeper had loaned her this sum against an I.O.U. and a written undertaking by the girl that she would make over all her clothing and other possessions if she was unable to settle the debt. The woman had imposed her will on the girl ever since by constantly threatening to enforce the agreement and, having stripped her of all her belongings, to turn her out in the street.

Regarding the 'watchers', a prostitute told Greenwood, 'Sometimes it's a woman—an old woman, who isn't fit for anything else—but in general it's a man. He watches you always, walking behind you on the opposite side of the way. He never loses sight of you, never fear.'

Although London was still teeming with vice and crime, two significant improvements had resulted from the institution of a proper police force. Firstly, the use of firearms by criminals had fallen to minimal proportions. And secondly, there had been a gradual decrease in the number of young criminals. Henry Mayhew wrote in 1862:

We learn from the statistics of the constabulary of the Metropolis that juvenile crime has considerably reduced within the past ten years. Several of our police inspectors have laboured with untiring industry to reform the lodging-houses and to introduce cleanliness and decency, where immorality and filth formerly prevailed. And noble exertions have been made by Christian societies to illumine these dark localities with the light of Christian truth.

CHAPTER TWENTY ONE

LAST YEARS AT THE OFFICE

In November 1835, Charles Dickens, then a struggling, young journalist, published an article in the *Evening Chronicle* in which he described a scene that was re-enacted every afternoon at the Bow Street Office.

There were thirty or forty people, said Dickens, standing on the pavement and half across the road, patiently awaiting the arrival of the van which would convey the prisoners from the Office to their various gaols. When the van drew up at the door, the crowd thronged forward round the steps, leaving a narrow alley for the prisoners to pass through. The first people to emerge from the Office on that occasion were two sisters, handcuffed together, who had both been sentenced for prostitution, although from their appearance Dickens judged that the elder was no more than sixteen, and the younger 'had certainly not attained her fourteenth year'.

He continued: 'there were other prisoners—boys of ten, as hardened in vice as men of fifty—a houseless vagrant, going joyfully to prison as a place for food and shelter, handcuffed to a man whose prospects were ruined, character lost, and family rendered destitute by his first offence.'

When the show was over the crowd dispersed, while 'the vehicle rolled away with its load of guilt and misfortune'.

In his early days as a reporter Charles Dickens had actually attended hearings at the Bow Street Office and his account in *Oliver Twist* of the committal there of the Artful Dodger is undoubtedly factual. Noah Claypole, who had been sent along by Fagin to observe the proceedings, gained admittance to the court with difficulty:

He found himself jostled among a crowd of people, chiefly women who were huddled together in a dirty, frowsy room, at the upper end of which was a raised platform railed off from the rest, with a dock for prisoners on the left hand against the wall, a box for witnesses in the middle, and a desk for the magistrates on the right, the awful locality of the last named being screened off by a partition which concealed the bench from the common gaze and left the vulgar to imagine (if they could) the full majesty of justice.

The Court, says Dickens, smelt close and unwholesome; the walls were discoloured with dirt and the ceiling blackened. There was a dusty clock above the dock and an ancient, smoky bust over the mantel-shelf. Depravity and poverty, he adds, 'had left a taint on all the animate matter, hardly less unpleasant than the thick greasy scum on every inanimate object'.

Apparently the physical discomfort and the foetid atmosphere had been but little alleviated since the time, almost a hundred years before, when Henry Fielding and Joshua Brogden had laboured at the old Bow Street Office in 'the most unwholesome as well as nauseous air in the universe'.

The dignity of the court and the standards of justice had visibly deteriorated since the Fielding era, if the trial of the Artful Dodger is a genuine criterion. Directly the prisoner was shown into the dock, one of the magistrates enquired if he had ever been there before, to which the jailer replied, 'He ought to have been, a many times. He has been pretty well everywhere else. I know him well, your worship.' Shortly afterwards when the Dodger was making a statement in his defence, albeit a highly impertinent one, the clerk cut him short, exclaiming, 'There! He's fully committed! Take him away.'

Although this sketch occurs in a work of fiction, Dickens was always a most veracious writer; perhaps at times he over-defined his arguments for the sake of emphasis, but he was never guilty of deliberate distortion. Further, Dickens' experience of Bow Street coincided with the final phase of Sir Richard Birnie's term as Chief Magistrate, when he had become an offensive, irascible, and impatient old man. On one occasion, Sir Richard interrupted a barrister who was appearing before him, with the remark, 'I know you are paid for talking and must earn your fee'. To which he received the curt reply, 'I must say such conduct on your part justifies the opinion which is everywhere in circulation respecting your administration of the law'.

When Sir Richard Birnie died in April 1832, the *Morning*

Herald announced that the office of Chief Magistrate was to be abolished, and that the public functions connected with it would be carried out from then on by the two commissioners of police. However, this rumour proved to be unfounded and Sir Richard's successor, Frederick Roe, a police magistrate at Great Marlborough Street, was the first, and so far the only Chief Magistrate, to be honoured with a baronetcy instead of the customary knighthood.

Another famous Bow Street personality who died in 1832 was Townsend, the Runner. Such was his social stature during his closing years, that a few days before his death he had attended the King's levee and had chatted with the Duke of Wellington and the Marquis of Salisbury. He received an obituary notice in the *Gentleman's Magazine*, an unusual distinction at that time for a person of his humble background.

For a decade after the formation of the Metropolitan Police, the new force operated in a state of uneasy co-existance with the Bow Street Runners and the officers at the Public Offices. Londoners continued to scrutinize the activities of the regular police with hostility and mistrust,* especially on the rare occasions when they performed their duties in plain clothes. In 1833 an over-zealous constable named Popay, who was investigating a subversive organisation in Camberwell, managed to conceal his identity and to become a member of the group. When his stratagem was discovered, the horrified inhabitants of Camberwell addressed a petition of protest to the House of Commons, in which they complained they had found themselves to be 'living among spies seeking their lives', and stating that they were 'sorely feeling the taxes heaped upon them for the maintenance of those spies'. A Select Committee appointed to investigate the affair, reported that they solemnly deprecated 'any approach to the employment of spies, in the accepted sense of the term, as a practice most abhorrent to the feelings of the people, and most alien to the spirit of the constitution'.

*During this period the police were beginning to take over all the more serious prosecutions, instead of leaving them to private individuals—a system which had been so strongly criticized by Henry Fielding.

H*

The Government favoured the gradual elimination of the few remaining independent police formations, and their incorporation, wherever possible, into the unified official force. In pursuance of this policy, the Bow Street horse patrol was removed from the control of the Chief Magistrate in 1836 and was converted into the mounted section of the Metropolitan Police. The same year, a House of Commons Committee recommended that the police commissioners should have authority over all the police formations in London.

For some time an argument had raged over the necessity for the continued existence of the Bow Street Runners. Charles Dickens, one of their foremost detractors, asserted that they had grown into a sort of superstition with the public. 'There is a vast amount of humbug,' he said, 'about these worthies. Apart from many being men of very indifferent character, and far too much in the habit of consorting with thieves and the like, they never lost a public occasion for jobbing and trading in mystery and making the most of themselves.' On the other hand, there was a strong body of opinion which regarded the Runners as masters in the art of crime detection and, in consequence, as fulfilling an urgent national requirement. 'These men have been thief-catchers all their lives,' wrote a prominent business man, 'and know almost every thief in London and of what he is capable.'

However, the policy of the Government remained firm. On the 24th August, 1839, three Acts of Parliament received the Royal Assent; they provided, among their other clauses, for the incorporation of the Marine Police into the regular Metropolitan force, and for the total disbandment of both the Bow Street Runners and the special officers at the Public Offices. Neither the abolition of the Runners, nor the elimination of the only detective police in the country, evoked any comment from the daily Press.

It was not until 1842 that the Home Secretary authorised the Commissioners to appoint twelve plain-clothes detectives, to work from a small room at Scotland Yard and to operate anywhere in Britain. During the next twenty-seven years, this force was never increased to a total of more than fifteen men. Eventually, in 1869 Sir Edmund Henderson, the Commissioner, decided to institute a detective branch in every police division, but at the same time he wrote dubiously, 'There are many and great difficulties in the way of a Detective system; it is viewed with the greatest suspicion and jealousy by the majority of Englishmen and is, in fact, entirely foreign to the habits and feelings of the Nation'.

Gradually the detectives of the new Criminal Investigation Division were to learn that the only way of containing crime was to gain a thoroughly full knowledge of the underworld, and to consort with rogues and thieves, if need be, for the purposes of acquiring information. This was a method which had been perfected, like a great many others they adopted, by their discredited predecessors, the Bow Street Runners.

Two other links between the Bow Street Office and the police were also to disappear. In 1869, soon after the institution of the divisional detective branch, a Criminal Records Office was set up at Scotland Yard, to replace the Bow Street register of criminals which had existed since the time of Sir John Fielding. The *Police Gazette* continued to be produced at Bow Street, under the permanent editorship of the Chief Clerk, until 1883 when this too was transferred to Scotland Yard.

After the creation of the Metropolitan Police, the Bow Street Office was deprived of a measure of its former importance, but it retained its historical connections and it was still regarded as the principal magistrates' Office in London. In 1832 a new police station was opened on the opposite side of the road, and on the 23rd May, 1840, the Receiver for the Metropolitan Police requested the Duke of Bedford's permission to pull down and to rebuild the two adjoining houses in Bow Street 'long used as a magistrate's office'. On account of the vicinity of the market and the two theatres, he said, it was desirable that the Police Court should remain in Bow Street. Two days later the Duke consented to this proposal, but the Bedford Office Records do not disclose why the matter proceeded no further.

Apparently it was decided to continue using the Office in its existing condition, for on the 28th February, 1842, the Receiver for the Metropolitan Police took out a new thirty-one year lease on the property. The rent was to be £160 per annum and the tenancy was to run from Lady Day 1841 until

Lady Day 1872. The ground plan embodied in this agreement shows the two houses, numbers 3 and 4, amalgamated into one. The 'Felons Room' in the 1813 lease is now shown as 'Cells'; the yards behind No. 3 have become a 'Gaolor's Room', and the 'Publick Office' is called a 'Court'—in fact, the whole document is described as the 'lease of the Police Court'.

The term 'Magistrate's Court' had been officially sanctioned as a new name for the Public Offices by the Metropolitan Police Courts Act, 1839. This statute gave effect to many of the ideas which had been formulated by the Fieldings during the previous century; in particular, it envisaged the magistrates officiating as judges and administering justice in the manner of the superior courts.

From 1812 until 1839, the various Secretaries of State continued to fill any vacancies among the police magistrates by selecting barristers of at least three years standing, although in theory these appointments were still available to the legally-unqualified. The Metropolitan Police Courts Bill both raised the salary from £800 to £1,200 (Chief Magistrate £1,400), and introduced a statutory requirement that all police magistrates must be barristers with a minimum of seven years in practice. The latter provision was hotly debated in Parliament, one Member of the House of Commons protesting that 'no men to be met with in society were so utterly destitute of common sense as lawyers'; whilst another argued that the essential qualification should be increased from seven to ten years standing. *The Times* supported the second view on the ground that stipendiary magistrates should be 'men whose advanced years may be expected to exempt them from the caprices and impetuosities of youth'.

The Government decided to leave the requirement of seven years standing unaltered. When County Courts were established throughout England in 1846, it was enacted that the new County Court judges should require a similar minimum qualification and they were, in fact, granted salaries identical with those of the twenty-seven police magistrates.

The clause in the Metropolitan Police Courts Bill that aroused most hostility in Parliament was one which permitted police magistrates to try summarily cases of petty theft and receiving. 'These gentlemen were not only to perform all the functions confided to the judges at Westminster Hall,' remarked a Member, 'but to embody in their persons the powers both of petty and grand juries.' The controversial clause was rejected in a narrow division by the House of Lords.

One scarcely noticed result of the 1839 Act was to give the Bow Street Office an official status for the first time in its history. Henceforth it was incorporated into the system as an authorized Stipendiary Magistrates' Court, covering a district of its own like all the others.

Although the Police Magistrates had now been formally converted into a branch of the judiciary, this development had in no way affected the justices in the counties. But even they were undergoing their own metamorphosis. Beatrice and Sidney Webb, in their classic study of English Local Government, have stated: 'In 1815, the justices stood uncontrolled. By 1835, they had forfeited most of their administrative functions.' During this period, in fact, their powers of granting liquor licences had been modified; they had lost their control over the supervision of the Poor Law, the lighting and repairing of the highways, and the inspection of factories; and their direction of prisons, lunatic asylums, and the police had been subjected to the over-riding authority of the Home Office. There was growing tendency to transfer all administrative matters from the county justices to statutory boards, which culminated in the establishment of County Councils under the Local Government Act of 1888.

Coincident with the decline of the justice's executive role in county affairs, there was a general awakening of the fact that their considerable judicial powers were neither governed nor restricted by any rules of form and procedure. The position had been all the more apparent since 1792 when the magistrates' offices in the Metropolis had been transformed into virtual courts of law. An Act in 1828 directed that groups of justices in neighbouring parishes should amalgamate for their judicial work into divisions, and within a few years regular Divisional Sessions—later called Petty Sessions—held at weekly, fortnightly, or monthly intervals, had become almost universal throughout the country. What is more, the justices were beginning to conduct their judicial duties in places which were opened to the public.

When county justices were taking depositions before committing a case for trial, the prisoner was seldom present to hear the evidence against him. However, in 1839 it was enacted that he might be allowed to inspect the depositions before his trial, and ten years later, that he should actually be given a copy of them on his committal.

The judicial activities of the justices, outside their work at Quarter Sessions, were finally regularized by four Bills which passed through Parliament in 1848 and 1849. Amongst many other matters, this legislation empowered the counties to provide 'fitting places' in which justices could hold their Petty Sessions for, in the words of the Attorney General, it was 'highly inexpedient that they should be held at public houses, where witnesses and others must be exposed to great temptations'. Further, it was stated specifically that, 'the room or place in which justices shall sit to hear any complaint or information shall be deemed an open and public place to which the public generally may have access'.

And so, a century after De Veil had set up his office like a court-room, and Henry Fielding had started to employ there the practices and procedures of the higher courts, the system at Bow Street was finally accepted as the authorised model for the conduct of magisterial business in the whole of Britain.

Meanwhile the days of the old Bow Street Office were drawing to a close. In April 1860 the *Builder* commented upon the lack of ventilation and the inadequate sanitary arrangements in the court. The conditions, said the journal, were bad enough in winter; in summer they were 'perfectly abominable', and the premises required to be entirely reconstructed.

In 1867 it was decided that as soon as the existing lease expired in 1872, the court would be moved across to the other side of Bow Street and re-erected alongside the Police Station. This scheme, which would have entailed the demolition of several houses and stables, was abandoned in its infancy.

By the year 1873 a new location for the Bow Street Court had not yet been settled, so an extended lease on the old Office was taken out by the Commissioners of H.M. Works and Public Buildings, at an annual rent of £400. This tenancy

was to run for 12 months from Lady Day 1872, 'and thereafter from year to year unless remitted by notice'.

At the end of 1873 there was another plan, which never
materialized, to move the court to a site near Leicester Square.
Eventually, in 1876 an agreement was signed between the
Duke of Bedford and the Commissioners, leasing a site on the
East side of Bow Street for 99 years, from Christmas Day
1876, at a peppercorn rent for the first twelve months and
thereafter at a rental of £1,100 per annum. The Commissioners undertook to build the new court within three years,
and the work of construction was actually started in the
autumn of 1878.

Up to the last, the old Bow Street Office maintained its
fascination for the general public. Whenever a notable case
was being heard, it was invariably attended by people from
every walk of life. On one occasion during those final years
the small courtroom was described as being 'crowded to
suffocation', with ladies bringing in their own camp-stools and
distinguished personages being accommodated with seats on
the bench. Outside in the roadway, Percy Fitzgerald used to
watch what he called the 'strange and indecent' scene which
had been repeated daily since the beginning of the century.
'This was the arrival of the funereal-looking prison-van in
front of the straitened little office door. Clustered around it
could be seen patiently waiting, as strange a miscellany as
could be conceived.'

The new court, which was being erected at an approximate
cost of £40,000, was provided with an interior quadrangle so
that the prison-vans, in future, might pick up and set down
their prisoners in private. On the 11th October, 1880, a paragraph in *The Times* spoke about the 'spacious and imposing'
building nearing completion, and went on, 'The necessity for
replacing the dark, confined, shabby old court and offices has
long been felt.'

In general, the Press noticed without a great deal of interest
the eventual transfer of the court from one side of the road to
the other. Percy Fitzgerald, who was well aware of the historical significance of the occasion, has written:

April 2nd, 1881 was a day of mark in the Bow Street annals, for a
boy named McCarthy was charged at the old office with having

stolen some logs of wood with a view to cutting them up into firewood. This was on a Saturday, and after his case was heard, the old office closed for ever, and on Monday, April 4th, the business of the office was removed to the new and rather ambitious offices over the way.

Sir James Ingham, Chief Magistrate at the time, by an act of incredible thoughtlessness, permitted all the existing records and documents to be destroyed on the occasion of the transfer.

The old Bow Street Office was leased in 1881 to a theatrical costumier and wig-maker who remained as tenant for the next six years. In 1887 the Duke of Bedford decided that the building should be pulled down as part of a scheme for improving the area around the Covent Garden Market. Accordingly, in the autumn of that year the work of demolition commenced.

The houses at numbers 3 and 4 Bow Street were never re-erected. Most of the space on which they stood is now occupied by a sprawling vegetable warehouse. No trace of the Office remains; no stone, no plaque, and no relic. Its memory, like its origin, is shrouded in obscurity.

ACKNOWLEDGEMENTS

I HAVE received very valuable assistance in the preparation of this book from Mr. W. J. Smith, M.A., F.R.Hist.S., Deputy Head Archivist, and Miss P. S. King, B.A., Senior Assistant Archivist, of the Greater London Record Office (Middlesex Records). Also, from Mr. K. C. Harrison, M.B.E., F.L.A., City Librarian, and Miss Margaret Swarbrick, Archivist, of the City of Westminster Public Libraries.

I would like to thank the Bedford Office for their kindness in giving me permission to inspect, and to quote from their Records. Major T. Ingram, lately Archivist of the Bedford Estate Records, and his successor, Mrs. M. Draper, have been most co-operative and helpful. The formidable task of perusing so many ancient documents was considerably simplified by the help which I received from Miss E. D. Mercer, B.A., F.S.A., Head Archivist, Greater London Record Office, and Mr. John Greenacombe of the Survey of London.

From the moment he knew that I was writing a work on the Bow Street Office, Professor Hugh Amory of New Jersey, U.S.A., a student of the life and works of Henry Fielding, has made available to me the results and the sources of his own researches. I have constantly asked his advice, which he has always most generously given.

On the subject of research, I would like to mention the help I have received from my friend and neighbour, Mr. Reginald Colby, Miss C. Krysiak, Assistant Librarian of The Middle Temple Library, and the staffs of the London Library and the Reading Room at the British Museum.

Mr. Ronald Ryall and Mr. T. Peacock were kind enough to refer me to some interesting old newspaper reports which I have quoted in the course of the book.

BIBLIOGRAPHY

Bibliographical sources include:

ANON, *Memoirs of the Life and Times of Sir Thomas de Veil.* London, 1748.

ARMITAGE, Gilbert, *The History of the Bow Street Runners.* London, Wishart & Co., 1932.

BORER, Mary Cathcart, *Covent Garden.* London, Abelard-Schuman, 1967.

BOSWELL, James, *Life of Johnson.* London, 1791.
London Journey 1762–1763. London, William Heinemann, 1950.

BRYANT, Arthur, *The Age of Elegance.* London, Collins, 1950.

COLQUHOUN, Patrick, *A Treatise on the Police of the Metropolis.* London, 1797.

CROSS, Wilbur L., *The History of Henry Fielding* (3 Vols.) Yale University Press, 1918.

DE CASTRO, J. Paul, *The Gordon Riots.* London, Oxford University Press, 1926.

DE VEIL, Sir Thomas, *Observations on the Practice of a Justice of the Peace.* London, 1747.

DICKENS, Charles, *Oliver Twist. Sketches by Boz.* London, 1836.

DILNOT, George, *The Story of Scotland Yard.* London, Geoffrey Bles, 1926.

DOBSON, Austin, *Henry Fielding.* London, 1883.

DUDDEN, F. H., *Henry Fielding (His Life, Work and Times).* Oxford, Clarendon Press, 1952. (2 Vols.)

EVELYN, John, *John Evelyn's Diary,* London, The Folio Society, 1963.

FIELDING, Henry, *A Charge Delivered to the Grand Jury of Westminster,* 1749.
A True State of the Case of Bosavern Penlez, 1750.
An Enquiry into the Causes of the Late Increase of Robbers, etc., 1751.
A Clear State of the Case of Elizabeth Canning, 1753.
A Proposal for Making an Effectual Provision for the Poor, 1753.
The Journal of a Voyage to Lisbon, 1755.
Novels and Plays.

FIELDING, Sir John, *A Plan for Preventing Robberies within Twenty Miles of London,* 1755.
An Account of Henry Fielding's Police, 1758.
A Plan for Preserving Derelict Girls, 1758.
Extracts from the Penal Laws, 1761.
The Universal Mentor, 1763.

FITZGERALD, Percy, *Chronicles of Bow Street Police Office.* (2 Vols.) London, Chapman & Hall, 1888.

FULFORD, Roger, *George the Fourth.* London, Gerald Duckworth & Co., 1935.

GODDARD, Henry, *Memoirs of a Bow Street Runner.* (Ed. Patrick Pringle). London, Museum Press, 1956.

GODDEN, G. M., *Henry Fielding.* London, Sampson Low, Marston & Co., 1910.

GREENWOOD, James, *The Seven Curses of London.* London, 1869.

GRONOW, *Captain Gronow's Recollections and Anecdotes.* London, 1864.

HAWKINS, Laetitia Matilda, *Memoirs.* (2 Vols.) London, 1824.

HOLDSWORTH, W. S., *A History of English Law.* (Vols. 1 and 13) London, Methuen & Co., 1963.

JONES, B. M., *Henry Fielding, Novelist and Magistrate.* London, George Allen & Unwin, 1933.

KNIGHT, Charles (Ed.), *London.* Vol. IV. London, 1843.

LESLIE-MELVILLE, R., *The Life and Work of Sir John Fielding.* London, Lincoln Williams, 1934.

MAITLAND, F. W., *Justice and Police.* London, 1851.

MAYHEW, Henry, *London Labour and the London Poor.* Vol. I. London, 1851.
London Labour and the London Poor. (Those that will not work). London, 1862.

MELVILLE LEE, W. L., *A History of the Police in England.* London, Methuen & Co., 1901.

MOYLAN, J. F., *Scotland Yard and the Metropolitan Police.* London, G. P. Putnam's Sons, 1929.

MURPHY, A., *Essay on the Life and Genius of Henry Fielding.* London, 1775.

OSBORNE, Bertram, *Justices of the Peace, 1361–1848.* Shaftsbury, Sedgehill Press, 1960.

PRINGLE, Patrick, *Hue and Cry.* London, Museum Press, 1955.
The Thief-Takers. London, Museum Press, 1958.

RADZINOWICZ, Leon, *A History of English Criminal Law.* Vol. 3. London, Stevens, 1956.

REITH, Charles. *A New Study of Police History.* London, Oliver & Boyd, 1956.

SAYER, Edward, *Observations on the Police and Civil Government of Westminster.* London, 1784.

SMITH, John Thomas, *Nollekens and his Times.* (2 Vols.) London, 1829.

SOLMES, Alwyn, *The English Policeman, 1871–1935.* London, George Allen & Unwin, 1935.

SOMERVILLE, Thomas, *My Own Life and Times (1741–1830).* London, 1861.

STEPHEN, Sir James Fitzjames, *A History of the Criminal Law of England,* Vol. 1. London, Macmillan & Co., 1883.

SUMMERSON, John, *Georgian London.* London, Pleiades Books, 1945.

THOMAS, W. M. (Ed.), *Letters and Works of Lady Mary Wortley Montagu.* London, 1887.

TIMBS, John, *London and Westminster,* Vol. 2. London, 1868.

TREVELYAN, G. M., *English Social History.* London, Longmans, Green and Co., 1942.

TURBERVILLE, A. S. (Ed.), *Johnson's England.* (2 Vols.) Oxford, Clarendon Press, 1933.

WALPOLE, Horace, *Collected Letters* (Ed. Peter Cunningham). London, 1859.

WEBB, Beatrice and Sidney, *English Local Government. The Parish and the County.* Vol. 1. London, 1906.

WELCH, Saunders, *Observations on the Office of Constable,* 1754.
A Proposal to Remove the Nuisance of the Common Prostitute. 1758.

WILLCOCKS, M. P., *A True-Born Englishman.* London, George Allen & Unwin, 1947.

Also:

BEDFORD ESTATE RECORDS
Collecting Books of the Poor Rate for the Parish of St. Pauls, Covent Garden.
Hansard's Parliamentary Debates.
The Newgate Calendar.
The Records of the Middlesex Justices.
The Records of the Westminster Justices.
State Papers in the Public Record Office.

Journals and Newspapers

Modern Philosophy. (University of Chicago Press).
Vol. 51 (1954) Article by Archibald Bolling Shepperson.
Vol. 63 (1965/66) Article by W. B. Coley.
  Evening Advertiser.
  General Advertiser.
  Lloyd's Evening Post.
  Monthly Review.
  Morning Chronicle.
  Public Advertiser.
  The Builder.
  The Covent Garden Journal.
  The Daily Advertiser.
  The Gentleman's Magazine.
  The St. James's Evening Post.
  The Times.

INDEX